HITLER'S GAMES

HITLER'S GAMES

The 1936 Olympics

Duff Hart-Davis

CENTURY

LONDON MELBOURNE AUCKLAND JOHANNESBURG

First published in Great Britain in 1986
by Century Hutchinson Ltd,
Brookmount House, 62–65 Chandos Place, London WC2N 4NW

Century Hutchinson Publishing Group (Australia) Pty Ltd
16–22 Church Street, Hawthorn, Melbourne, Victoria 3122,
Australia

Century Hutchinson Group (NZ) Ltd
32–34 View Road, PO Box 40–086 Glenfield, Auckland 10

Century Hutchinson Group (SA) Pty Ltd
PO Box 337, Bergvlei 2012, South Africa

British Library Cataloguing in Publication Data
Hart-Davis, Duff
Hitler's games : the 1936 Olympics.
1. Olympic Games (*11th : 1936 : Berlin*)
I. Title
796.4′8′09043   GV722

ISBN 0–7126–1202–5

Typeset by Inforum Ltd, Portsmouth
Printed in Great Britain in 1986 by
St Edmundsbury Press, Bury St Edmunds, Suffolk
Bound by Butler & Tanner Ltd, Frome, Somerset

CONTENTS

ACKNOWLEDGEMENTS

I should like to thank the exceptionally helpful staffs of the Wiener Library, in London, and the Archive Centre at Churchill College, Cambridge, for their invaluable assistance. I am also most grateful to the staff of the British Olympic Association, who kindly allowed me free access to their records.

I have depended heavily on the memories of individuals, and I should particularly like to thank the following for their recollections, or for help of other kinds:
Sam Balter, George Berger, W.G.Booth, Edward Butcher, Lord Caccia, John Costello, Lord James Douglas-Hamilton, Major H.L.C. Fraser, Norman Gowers, Mrs. B.N. Grant, Geoff Grier, Leslie Jeffers, Frank Lubin, Tom McNab, Godfrey Rampling, Eric Rideal, Frank Rostron, Sir Stanley Rous, Ken Thomas, Roy Townsend, K.M. Treitel, Harold Whitlock and Ina Yates.

I am sad to record the death of Lady Vansittart, who, at the age of 95, remembered her visit to Berlin in August 1936, and her dinner as Hitler's principal guest, with astonishing precision.

LIST OF ILLUSTRATIONS

Between pages 128–129

1. Adolf Hitler at the time of his accession to power.
2. 5 October 1933. Hitler on the site of the Reich Sport Field with Dr Frick, Minister of the Interior.
3. Film-maker extraordinary: Leni Riefenstahl in full cry.
4. The great Olympic Bell, guarded by members of the Labour Service, on its ceremonial journey to Berlin.
5. The Olympic flame reaches the Lustgarten.
6. The girl who came in vain; banned American swimmer Eleanor Holm Jarrett.
7. Sir Robert Vansittart (left) with the British Ambassador in Berlin, Sir Eric Phipps.
8. 1 August 1936. Hitler leads the cavalcade through the Brandenburg Gate on his way to declare the Olympics open.
9. At the official opening, Hitler accepts a bouquet from five-year-old Gudrun Diem. On the left, Count Baillet-Latour, President of the International Olympic Committee; on the right, Dr Theodor Lewald, President of the Organising Committee.
10. Strength through joy: Karl Hein, German gold-medallist in the Hammer.

11. Jack Lovelock, in the black stripe of New Zealand, bides his time behind Ny of Sweden at the end of the second lap in the 1,500 Metres.

12. Helene Meyer gives the Nazi salute from the winners' dais after taking the silver medal in the Foil.

13. Jesse Owens with Leslie Jeffers, the British wrestler, in the Olympic village.

14. Dr Joseph Goebbels, Minister of Propaganda, weighs up some Olympic art.

15. Goering welcomes the guests at the Government banquet in the State Opera House.

16. Owens's triumphs are immortalised in stone on the pillar of the Marathon Gate.

INTRODUCTION

In staging the eleventh modern Olympiad in Berlin on a colossal scale, Adolf Hitler, Chancellor of the Third Reich, exploited a unique opportunity to the full. By acting as host to 52 foreign nations during the first two weeks of August, 1936, he was able to persuade the world that the New Germany, which he himself had raised from the ashes of the Weimar Republic, was a well organised, modern and above all civilised society. Visitors who went to the festival came away enormously impressed, not only by the Olympic preparations, which were on a scale never seen before, but also by the fact that Germany seemed a perfectly normal place, in which life went on as pleasantly as in any other European country. Many of them concluded that the tales they had heard about persecution of Jews, Catholics and political dissidents must have been grossly exaggerated, for as they moved around Berlin, or drove freely through the country, they saw no signs of harassment; besides, the ordinary people they met were hospitable and kind. They came home convinced that the Nazi regime was far less black than it had been painted, and not a few were converted to positive support of the new system.

With the advantage of 50 years' hindsight, the view of Berlin in 1936 looks rather different – and indeed it seems scarcely credible that the Nazis were able to stage the Games at all. The fact that they managed to carry them off was a triumph of bluff and propaganda, forced through in the first instance by the megalomaniac drive of the Führer himself,

9

but executed largely by the genius of his Minister for Propaganda, Joseph Goebbels.

Still more astonishing – and deplorable – is the fact that the various Olympic committees, at national and international level, insisted with such vehemence that the Games should go ahead in Berlin. The official attitude was exemplified by a single utterance from the President of the International Olympic Committee, the Belgian Count Henri de Baillet-Latour. During one of the recurrent crises brought on by attempts to organise a boycott of the Games, he announced to the press that nothing short of armed conflict would prevent the festival taking place as planned.

He knew, as well as anybody, that by 1936 Nazi Germany had become a police state, whose citizens were liable to disappear from their homes or from the street, arrested without warrant and imprisoned without trial. He and his committee knew that the Catholic Church had been forcibly suppressed. They knew that Jews had fled from Germany in tens of thousands, and that hundreds of their less fortunate brethren had been rounded up into concentration camps, where they were being humiliated and tortured in the most degrading circumstances imaginable. They knew that one of these camps, at Oranienburg, was flourishing in the northern suburbs of Berlin, scarcely half an hour's journey from the site in the Grunewald on which the Olympics were due to take place.

On the sporting front, they were fully aware that Nazi policy had made mockery of the Olympic code. Chauvinism and racial hatred, deliberately fostered by the State, had been carried into the realm of sport. Government spokesmen had declared that sporting competition between Germans and black people was impossible. Jews had been specifically excluded from all German sports clubs and associations; competition between them and Aryans had been forbidden. Official statements had declared that non-political sport could not exist in the Third Reich: there was no longer such a being as an individual athlete. Everybody in Germany belonged to the State. The amateur status of sportsmen – a keystone of the Olympic ideal – had been destroyed by order of the government.

Introduction

How, in such circumstances, did the International Olympic Committee allow the Games to go ahead? How did the national committees allow their countries' teams to take part? Why did no foreign government forbid its citizens to go to Berlin? Why did 52 countries, by their very participation, bolster the designs of a regime so manifestly dishonest and inhuman?

It is true that attempts were made to organise a boycott, but none of them came anywhere near success. 'Politics must not be brought into sport' was the constant cry – yet the introduction of politics into sport was precisely what the Nazis had perpetrated. For the first time in their history, the Olympic Games were deliberately exploited to make political capital.

The purpose of this book is to examine the circumstances, political, social and sporting, which led up to the Berlin Games, and to show how formidable German organisation, reinforced by extraordinary blindness in other countries, enabled the Nazis to get away with a monumental feat of deception.

1
THE NEW GERMANY

'The Chancellor is taking an enormous interest in the Olympic Games,' wrote Sir Eric Phipps, the British Ambassador in Berlin, in a despatch to London on 7 November, 1935. 'In fact he is beginning to regard political questions very much from the angle of their effect on the Games. . . . The German Government are simply terrified lest Jewish pressure may induce the United States Government to withdraw their team and so wreck the festival, the material and propagandist value of which, they think, can scarcely be exaggerated.'

In other words, Hitler knew full well that after nearly three years in power he had turned the New Germany into a country odious to many foreigners; and, if one is to grasp the magnitude of the bluff which he pulled off in staging the Eleventh Olympiad, it is essential to appreciate how unpleasant the Third Reich had become by the summer of 1936. Fifty years on, it is a common mistake to suppose that the persecution of the Jews did not properly begin until the Second World War. In fact it started almost as soon as the Nazis came to power in January, 1933, and the first concentration camps were opened within a few months of Hitler's accession. Their inmates, it is true, were not yet the victims of a mass-extermination programme, but they were being treated with a brutal inhumanity which should have made it unthinkable for the world's athletes to congregate in Berlin during August, 1936, and so express acceptance of a regime which had let loose a new barbarism in Europe.

Of all the Nazis' excesses, the most offensive to foreigners

13

was their racialism, which stemmed directly from the warped mind of their leader. It is difficult to doubt that Hitler genuinely feared and hated Jews. His whole existence was driven by an obsessive loathing of them, manifest on page after page of his autobiographical treatise *Mein Kampf*. In that leaden and humourless tome, which he wrote in Landsberg Prison during 1924 with the help of his secretary Rudolf Hess, he rambled from episodes of his own career to political theory and back, returning repeatedly to his belief that the Jews were a 'decomposing leaven' which destroyed the fabric of a nation, and that only by getting rid of them could Germany recover her former strength. 'The Jew is the exact opposite of the Aryan,' he wrote. 'He is guided by pure self-seeking . . . he is ever a parasite on the bodies of other nations . . . his innate, greedy brutality . . . If we review all the causes of the German collapse, the final and decisive one is seen to be the failure to recognise the racial problem, and more especially the Jewish menace.'

> There are numberless examples in history showing with terrible plainness how each time Aryan blood became mixed with that of inferior people the result has been the end of the culture-sustaining race . . . Blood-mixture, and the lowering of the racial level which accompanies it, are the only cause why old civilisations disappear.
>
> The trend of thought in Jewry is clear. It is to bolshevise Germany – i.e., to rot away German national intelligence, and so crush the forces of German labour under the yoke of Jewish world finance, as a preliminary to extending far and wide the Jewish plan of conquering the world.

For anyone who believed that, there was only one sensible course of action: to purge Germany of Jews. As *Mein Kampf* put it, 'the task of the National State will be to preserve the race', and the book's author was sufficiently deluded to believe that in fighting against the Jews he was on the side of the Almighty, 'doing the Lord's work'.

Mein Kampf was first published in 1924. English editions were brought out when Hitler came to power. It was therefore not difficult for foreigners to see what the new leader of Germany believed in. The obstacle to any practical response was the craziness of his ideas, which made it hard for outsiders to take them seriously. Hitler's ambitions seemed so far-fetched that very few people thought he could possibly put them into practice. Unfortunately, he could and did.

The first large anti-Jewish demonstration in Nazi Germany took place on 1 April, 1933, when gangs of Brown-Shirts enforced a two-day boycott of Jewish shops and offices. This was abandoned after a sharp reaction had flared up abroad, but less than a week later, on 7 April, the term *Nichtarier* ('non-Aryan') was adopted as legal currency. This facilitated the removal of Jews from the professions: lawyers, judges, public officials, artists, journalists and doctors were the first to go in an exodus that destroyed the structure of Jewish life in Germany. Completely assimilated though they were into German culture after many generations, Jews now found themselves branded as an alien race, automatically excluded from positions and privileges which they had always taken for granted. All over the country anti-Jewish signs were posted, most straightforwardly offensive, some soured with sick humour: 'Jews Not Wanted Here', 'No Jews or Dogs Here', 'Jews Enter This Place at their Own Risk', 'Jews are Uninvited Guests', 'Jews, Watch Out! The Road to Palestine does not Lead through this Place', and, on sharp road-bends, 'Take care! Danger! Jews, 75 miles per hour!'

The first concentration camps – not merely for Jews, but for all supposed enemies, including Communists, Catholics, Jehovah's Witnesses and Freemasons – came into being when the Nazi regime was only a few weeks old. An emergency decree of 28 February, 1933, gave legal sanction to arbitrary imprisonment by authorising the detention for an unlimited period of anyone suspected of hostility to the State. In an attempt to make the practice respectable, the new system was described as *Schutzhaft*, or 'protective custody', but in fact it merely offered the thugs of the *Sturmabteilung*, or SA, the chance to seize and beat up anyone who displeased them.

Within a few months of the Nazi takeover, Germany was gripped by a reign of terror. People disappeared from their homes and from the streets, often because some informer –

perhaps even a member of the family – alleged that they had made a single derogatory remark about the administration or one of its members. One German singer, for example, spent seven months in a concentration camp for referring to Hitler in private as 'that actor', and a British-born German called Walter Spielmann was sentenced to two and a half years' imprisonment after someone in a hairdressing saloon had heard him say that anybody who wanted to find out the truth about Germany had to read the English newspapers. Even foreign diplomats were not safe from arbitrary arrest: the embassies in Berlin spent many hours negotiating the release of members who had been seized and roughed up for failing to salute some squad of Brown-Shirts as they marched along the street.

By July, 1933, some 27,000 people had been interned in 50 improvised detention camps, of which the most notorious was Columbia Haus, the former military prison on the edge of Tempelhof Airport, in southern Berlin. After a storm of protest, most of these early camps were broken up, but Columbia Haus remained, as did Oranienburg, in the northern suburbs of the capital, half an hour's journey by rail from the site already designated for the Olympic games. With the eclipse of the SA in 1934, the camps passed into the control of the SS and its repulsive commanding officer, Heinrich Himmler, one of the most evil figures in the Third Reich. Under him, the detention centres steadily developed their techniques of brutality and sadism until the advent of the Second World War found them fully equipped to put into practice the regime's plans for the Final Solution of the Jewish Problem.

After the war Germans sought to defend themselves against charges of complicity or cowardice by maintaining that they did not know about the camps. Blanket censorship of press and radio meant that no word about them was published or broadcast in Germany, and anybody fortunate enough to escape from them was effectively silenced by fear of re-arrest. Nevertheless, rumours did circulate, and the child's prayer

Lieber Gott, mach mich fromm
Dass ich in den Himmel komm

(Dear God, make me good, so that I go to heaven) found an echo in a twisted new version:

Lieber Gott, mach mich fromm
Dass ich nicht in Dachau komm.

Persecution of the Roman Catholic Church started later than that of the Jews and was never so blatant, but to many people the direct assault upon religion was even more shocking. On 20 July, 1934, Hitler signed a concordat with the Vatican which guaranteed the freedom of the Catholic Church and its right to regulate its own affairs. Within days, however, the agreement was being broken all over the Reich by the arrest, on trumped-up charges of currency-smuggling or immorality, of Catholic priests, nuns and lay-readers. Protestants largely avoided conflict with the State until the summer of 1936; but then a memorandum addressed to Hitler by Pastor Niemöller of the Confessional Church Group, protesting against the regime's anti-religious stance, set off a ruthless purge of the Protestant Church as well.

That most Germans had little direct knowledge of what was happening is confirmed by the testimony of outsiders. One perceptive observer – the American journalist William Shirer, who lived and worked in Berlin from 1934 to 1941 – wrote about the racial laws in *The Rise and Fall of the Third Reich*:

A few Germans one met . . . were disgusted or even revolted by the persecution of the Jews, but though they helped to alleviate hardship in a number of cases, they did nothing to help stem the tide. What could they do? They would often put the question to you, and it was not an easy one to answer.

Nor, Shirer reported, did people worry much about the attack on religion:

Not many Germans lost much sleep over the arrest of a few thousand pastors and priests . . . and even fewer paused to reflect that . . . the Nazi regime intended eventually to destroy Christianity in Germany, if it could, and substitute the old paganism of the early tribal German gods.

17

Outside Germany, however, censorship did not prevail, and many accounts were published of the horrors that Hitler had set in train in his lunatic attempt to purify the Aryan race. It is important to emphasise that these accounts appeared in the early 1930s, long before the war: it was impossible for the people planning the 1936 Olympics at international level to be unaware of them, unless they deliberately chose not to read them.

One of the most horrifying exposures was *A Nation Terrorised*, a book by the leading Social Democrat politician Gerhart Seger, who described how he had spent six months in Oranienburg during 1933 before escaping into Czechoslovakia. In a brief Introduction, the author Heinrich Mann (brother of Thomas Mann, and himself an exile) wrote, 'You have escaped from one of the most evil places in the world,' and no one who read the book could disagree. The fact that the author had been a member of the Reichstag in four successive parliaments lent weight to his account, and the story itself was so graphic and shocking that the book sold 225,000 copies in Europe alone on its publication in 1934 (it came out in the United States a year later). When the Nazis found that Seger had got away, they retaliated by arresting his wife and 17-month-old child and putting them in the concentration camp at Rosslau. Seger, however, came to London and found a formidable ally in the shape of Lady Astor, who first arranged for him to give two lectures in the House of Commons, and then organised all the woman Members of Parliament to lobby Leopold von Hoesch, the German Ambassador in London. This they did to great effect: they gave Hoesch two weeks to secure Frau Seger's release, threatening that if he failed they would ask unpleasant questions in Parliament. One week later Frau Seger was released into house arrest, and she afterwards escaped from Germany altogether with the help of the Conservative Member of Parliament, Mavis C. Tate. After this episode, no British MP could honestly claim to be unaware of what was happening in Germany.

Another devastating indictment was *Fatherland*, a book by Karl Billinger published in New York in 1935. Arrested in 1934 for being a member of the Communist Party, the author became prisoner No. 880 in Columbia Haus, where he was flogged insensible with wet leather horsewhips and subjected to terrible humiliations. Repulsive details make his story unassailably authentic, not least in those sections which describe the perversions already practised by the SS guards. In this typical extract they have ordered one Jewish prisoner to attack a younger one, for their own amusement:

> The SS began to rain blows thick and fast over their heads and necks and backs, while like a maniac the officer kept yelling, 'Forward! Forward!' Hesitantly, appalled by what he was doing, then more rapidly to escape the onslaught of the guards, the older Jew struck the younger a blow – and another – until at length he was laying about him in a frenzy, his face racked with agony, his eyes glaring with madness. The younger man never so much as lifted his arms to ward off the blows about his head. Neither did he stir under the horsewhips. Erect and silent, he stood till he collapsed.

Forbidden to write or receive letters, not knowing what he was to be charged for, denied the most elementary rights, Billinger spent 28 days in Columbia Haus before being shifted to the concentration camp at Hubertshof. Afterwards, he painted an indelible picture of how the poison of Hitler's ideas had already infected the SS men who ran the camps, and who regarded Jews, Communists, pacifists and socialists as so much offal:

> The mere idea of feeding us, instead of exterminating us like the plague, was for them an insufferable form of kindness . . . Much as they would have liked to murder half the German people . . . their relations with other countries prevented them from achieving this ideal.

Fatherland was a cry from the heart for 'the catastrophe which had burst upon the German people'. In lamenting the 'awful cloud of darkness' that National Socialism had thrown over the country, the author drew up a powerful indictment, made all the more formidable by its eloquence and restraint:

> In Nazi Germany it has become a crime to believe that all men are equal in the sight of God. Woe to Catholics and Protestants alike,

19

but woe and woe again to those who dare raise their voice for the equality of man in the sight of men. Hitler's *Volksgemeinschaft* [people's community] will hunt them down and torture them, will slander and traduce them in a way that has never before been in the history of mankind.

History has demonstrated the truth of Billinger's impassioned outcry. Yet the paradox was that, as Shirer pointed out, so few Germans cared about the criminality of the new regime. What mattered to most of them was that Hitler had rescued the country from bankruptcy and chaos, and by his inspiring leadership had given people not only jobs and money but a new sense of purpose. As Shirer put it,

> The overwhelming majority of Germans did not seem to mind that their personal freedom had been taken away, and that so much of their culture had been destroyed and replaced by a mindless barbarism. . . . People did not seem to feel they were being cowed or held down by an unscrupulous dictatorship. On the contrary, they supported it with genuine enthusiasm.

Not even Hitler's most bitter enemies could deny that he had wrought economic wonders. From a high point of over six million in 1933, unemployment fell to fewer than one million in the year of the Olympics, and by the beginning of 1936 the semi-educated Austrian architectural student had become the subject of universal adulation. 'I am absolutely convinced that any man coming together with the Führer for just ten minutes a week is capable of ten times his normal output,' wrote Dr Fritz Todt, the engineer, in September 1933; and his extraordinary power was also witnessed – with very different emotions – by Shirer, who found himself shocked at the effect Hitler had on women during a party rally in Nuremberg:

> They reminded me of the crazed expressions I saw once in the back country of Louisiana on the faces of some Holy Rollers who were about to hit the trail. They looked up at him as if he were a Messiah, their faces transformed into something positively inhuman.

It was not the Führer's physical appearance which made such

an impact: contemporary accounts show that at the age of 47, which he was in 1936, he was physically unremarkable, even to an admirer as besotted as Diana Mitford, who described him in her book *A Life of Contrasts* as 'neither fat nor thin' and about 5ft 9in tall.

His eyes were dark blue, his skin fair and his brown hair exceptionally fine; it was neatly brushed; I never saw him with a lock of hair over his forehead. If he was out of doors in the sun and wind all day . . . he quickly got sunburnt, but it did not last, for his skin was pale. His hands were white and well-shaped. He was extremely neat and clean-looking, so much so that beside him nearly everyone looked coarse . . . He was extremely polite to women: he bowed and kissed hands as is the custom in Germany and France, and he never sat down until they did . . .

Few Germans fell more heavily for the new leader than Albert Speer, the young architect whom the Führer took up at the age of 28 to execute his long-term architectural plans. Driving through the Alps with Hitler, sitting in the jump-seat close behind him, Speer could never forget the 'surge of rejoicing, the ecstasy reflecting in so many faces', as he recorded in *Inside the Third Reich*:

Wherever Hitler went during those first years of his rule, wherever his car stopped for a short time, such scenes were repeated. The mass exultation was not called forth by rhetoric or suggestion, but solely by the effect of Hitler's presence.

Describing his own early infatuation, Speer recalled how, when he joined the Nazi Party, he felt he was not choosing a political party but becoming a follower of Hitler, 'whose magnetic force had reached out to me for the first time and had not thereafter released me':

His persuasiveness, the peculiar magic of his by no means pleasant voice, the oddity of his rather banal manner, the seductive simplicity with which he attacked the complexity of our problems – all that bewildered and fascinated me. I knew virtually nothing about his programme. He had taken hold of me before I grasped what was happening.

The same fate overtook millions of Speer's fellow country-men and women: they were mesmerised by the leader who had restored a sense of national pride, especially when they heard him hold forth from a platform. 'As a speaker Hitler exercises astonishing sway over a German audience,' said one contemporary Foreign Office report:

> His speeches are practically repetitions of a few simple main theses, in the course of which platitudes are uttered with such extraordinary emphasis that an unsophisticated audience mistakes them for newly-minted political aphorisms . . . None of his followers can approach him in demagogic talent. He alone can rouse the crowd to that state of political frenzy which makes all argument futile.

In the heady atmosphere of national rejuvenation, details of Hitler's ethical stance passed unnoticed in the face of the one central fact that he had given the country work, money, security and a reasonable amount of food. Nor did it worry people that a very high proportion of the new jobs were connected directly or indirectly with rearmament. Even the great project for building the new motor roads known as *Autobahnen* had strong military connotations.

The *Autobahn* construction programme, announced on 11 February, 1933, evoked enormous popular enthusiasm. Hitler himself ceremonially dug the first spadeful of earth outside Frankfurt early on the morning of 23 September, 1933; a 700-strong gang of workmen marched out to the site with bands playing, and the moment the Führer left there was a rush to snatch up a few grains of the soil he had shifted. Thus was launched a mighty project with three substantial advantages: first, it brought employment to a large number of men who had been out of work; second, it gave them a sense of achievement and helped restore their pride in their country; and third, it furnished Germany with a fast transit system which would become a great strategic advantage in time of war. By the summer of 1936 some 125,000 men were at work on the *Autobahnen*, and already the new roads extended for nearly 600 miles.

The concept of an unobstructed highway, on˙which one

hardly ever had to slow down, was then revolutionary, and the novelty of driving on an *Autobahn* was such that in 1936 the British Embassy in Berlin was moved to send the Foreign Office a report about it:

> The motor roads . . . are a fine engineering achievement. They make it possible for a large volume of traffic to flow both ways at a high speed with very considerable safety . . . The complete absence of the need to slacken speed, except at well-marked junctions, makes it possible for the cars in the faster of the two streams to travel almost continuously at any speed of which their engines are capable, up to 100 miles per hour . . . and the average speed at which distances are covered becomes identical with the cruising speed at which the driver decides to travel. The concrete surfaces of the roadways are uniformly excellent, and this, together with the distances between junctions, make a journey on the new roads seem to resemble an express railway journey rather than the usual type of road travel.

The report went on to stress the possible military implications, and to point out that, if the *Autobahnen* were used for troop movements, 'road capacity would cease to be a limiting feature'. For the moment, however, the most important feature of the roads was that they stood 'as a first-class advertisement for the practical side of National Socialism, of which every German is proud and which every foreigner must admire'.

A kindred project, in which Hitler also saw huge possibilities, was the production of a 'people's car', or *Volkswagen*. His proposal was that the vehicle should be produced by the combined German car industry, and that each factory should be required to manufacture a certain number. In 1935 he kept urging various firms to hurry into production; next year he put the experimental work into the hands of Dr Ferdinand Porsche of Stuttgart, who built three prototype four-seater limousines, with four-stroke, air-cooled engines at the rear, and proceeded to test them over 18,000 miles of roads.

With such imaginative schemes – by the people, for the people and of the people – did Hitler enslave his subjects. After him, in 1936, the next most powerful man in Germany

23

was Hermann Goering, the former fighter ace who, at the age of 43, had become Reich Air Minister, as well as Prime Minister of Prussia – a combination of offices that gave him enormous influence. Foreign observers found it hard to decide whether Goering was a shrewd politician or a buffoon. Ivone Kirkpatrick, a member of the British Embassy staff in Berlin, thought his 'uninhibited vulgarity . . . at once revolting and rather comic'. His great girth, his extravagance (in 1936 he had 43 official cars), his vast appetite and his fondness for Ruritanian uniforms gave many people the impression that he was no more than an overgrown schoolboy; others, however, detected behind his bombastic exterior a dangerous ambition and steeliness of purpose. In one important respect he was unique among the Nazi leaders: he had worked abroad – as a flying instructor in Denmark after the Great War – and so had some slight experience of the outside world. Even so, like Hitler, he spoke almost no English, and had no conception of how English minds functioned.

Nor, for that matter, had Joseph Goebbels, the small, dark and (ironically) Jewish-looking Rhinelander who became Hitler's Minister for Propaganda in 1934. Osteomyelitis caught in boyhood had left him with a twisted left foot, so that he did not fight in the Great War, but he was a fanatical supporter of Hitler as early as 1922, and in 1926 went to Berlin as editor of the Nazi evening paper *Der Angriff* ('The Attack'). One of his assets was a fine voice, which he used to great effect. In his early speeches he relied mainly on vituperation and abuse, but by 1936 many people considered him the best of the Nazi orators, sometimes exceeding even Hitler in his ability to whip up mass emotions. In private he was sardonically amusing, with a biting wit and ready repartee – the only one of the hierarchy with whom foreigners found conversation amusing. Diana Mitford, who frequently visited Germany with her sister Unity, thought him 'intelligent, witty and sarcastic', and reported that his wife Magda addressed him as *'Engel'*.

A lesser figure, but one who had a strong effect on outside opinion of Germany, was Joachim von Ribbentrop, the wine merchant whom Hitler appointed as his special roving ambassador in 1935. To the Führer, the great advantages of Ribbentrop were that, through his own success and his marriage into the Henkell champagne family, he was rich and well connected; he spoke good English, having been at school in London for a year, and had many friends in the English capital. What Hitler did not realise was that Ribbentrop was an ass, and the object of much derision in England. Nor did the Führer appreciate that the man had no moral courage, but flattered his leader obsequiously by telling him what he thought he wanted to hear. Nevertheless, Ribbentrop had considerable influence over Hitler's foreign policy.

Another second-ranker, but with a position that put him close to the Olympic preparations, was the Reich Youth Leader, Baldur von Schirach. Good-looking, with clean-cut features, he had the advantages of energy and youth (in 1936 he was still only 28), as well as a flair for organisation and the streak of brutality essential for advancement in Hitler's State. But behind his rather impressive façade there lurked a dire banality, and, according to William Shirer, who often met him, 'a dreadfully empty mind'.

A more sinister second-rank figure in the Reich hierarchy was Julius Streicher, the Gauleiter of Franconia, who harried the Jews with fanatical hatred and thus also had a powerful if indirect effect on public opinion in other countries. He is often referred to as a Jew-baiter, but the description is entirely inadequate, suggesting as it does that he teased his victims. He was a murderer, who took obscene relish in hounding Jews either out of the country or – if possible – to death.

Squat, shaven-headed, bull-necked, with low forehead, small, dark eyes, thick lips and a silly, artificial expression, Streicher could hardly have looked less Aryan, and his appearance made many people wonder whether some element of Jewishness in his own heredity might not partially explain his obsessive anti-semitism. His penchant for wearing riding-breeches, often white, and carrying a whip, did not render him any more attractive. Nor did his boasts about his sexual conquests, or his habit of blackmailing the husbands of the women he seduced.

Born in 1885, the son of a school-teacher, he began to agitate against the Jews as soon as he returned from the Great

War, and in 1923 he founded *Der Stürmer*, the anti-Jewish rag of which he remained editor for 15 years. In the early days, before Hitler's accession gave him protection, Streicher was repeatedly thrown into gaol for the violence of his racial outbursts, but once the Nazis were established in power his phobia, far from being curbed, was given ever-more outrageous expression. Final licence was granted him in September, 1935, by the passing of the Nuremberg Laws, which carried the State campaign against the Jews to new lengths, depriving them of citizenship and reducing them to the status of a subject people. Not only was marriage between Jews and Aryans forbidden: *Rassenschande*, or 'racial disgrace' – that is, sexual relations between Jews and Aryans – became a crime punishable by immediate imprisonment. By the time of the Olympics the standard lecture on race for units of the SS included the paragraph:

> The Jew is a parasite. Wherever he flourishes, people die . . .
> Elimination of the Jew from our community is to be regarded as
> an emergency defence measure.

Streicher's main platform was his fortnightly newspaper *Der Stürmer*, published in Berlin for which he claimed a circulation of 500,000. A large number of these copies were either distributed free or pinned up, with pages open, in reading-boxes specially erected at street-corners. To call the contents of the papers scurrilous would be to damn them with faint criticism. To any normal person they were disgusting – an unremitting barrage of the coarsest anti-Jewish insult and innuendo, much of it obscene and with pornographic overtones, the aim being to portray the Jews as a race of oversexed monsters from whose unbridled lechery no Aryan girl was safe.

Most pages of the paper carried at least one of Streicher's own aphorisms – specifically attributed to him – in large type, like a secondary headline: ALL JEWS ARE CRIMINALS. THERE ARE NO EXCEPTIONS AMONG THIS CORRUPT, STINKING RACE . . . HE WHO TAKES ON THE JEWS WRESTLES WITH THE DEVIL . . . WOMEN AND GIRLS – THE JEWS ARE YOUR RUIN . . . HE WHO KNOWS THE JEWS KNOWS THE DEVIL . . . WHOEVER RESPECTS

THE JEWS INSULTS THE GERMAN PEOPLE . . . ANYONE WHO
BUYS FROM A JEW IS A TRAITOR TO HIS COUNTRY . . . A typical
front-page cartoon – whose style was as coarse and exaggerated as that of the text – portrayed a Jewish butcher with
immense hooked nose and grotesquely thick lips, standing in
his shop with a wife as ugly as himself. All round the walls
hung Kosher-killed geese ready for his regular clients, but the
man himself was lowering a dead rat into the meat-grinder, to
make mince for his Christian customers. Another characteristic cartoon showed an equally hideous Jew handing over a
young white woman to a giant, simian Black, and the caption
explained that the ultimate aim of the Jewish people was to
engineer the destruction of the white race at the hands of the
black tribes of Africa.

Fortnight after fortnight, month after month, year after
year, this government-sponsored muck-spreader portrayed
the Jews as seducers of children, usurers, racketeers, spread-
ers of disease, the great danger to civilisation. There were no
depths to which *Der Stürmer* would not gladly sink. When the
employees of a department store in Magdeburg published a
memorial notice on the death of their employer, whom they
venerated, the paper ridiculed them by saying that, if they
wanted to meet her again, they would have to call at the
Jewish department of Heaven. When the infant son of
Charles Lindbergh, the American aviator, was kidnapped in
1932, *Der Stürmer* announced that the baby had of course
been stolen by Jews, who had used its blood to make ceremonial bread for their next *purim*. Every conviction of a Jew in
Germany – for whatever trumped-up offence – was hailed as a
triumph, every Jewish suicide an occasion for rejoicing.

The overseas impact of the paper was small. Copies
reached Paris, Rome and London, but few people took its
ravings seriously, because their extremity seemed to render
them harmless. When Streicher poured out hysterical pronouncements to the effect that the United States was ruled by
Jews and Jew-slaves, he seemed like a tiresome but innocuous
lunatic.

Within Germany, however, the campaign of which he was a
figurehead produced disastrous results. Life became impossible for Jews. Not only were they attacked verbally and

physically: they could not buy food, lost their jobs for no reason other than that of race, had their children thrown out of schools, were banned from clubs of all kinds. Usually no violence was needed to dislodge them; malice sufficed. By the end of 1935 the staff of the British Embassy in Berlin were struggling to help individuals who appealed to them, but found they could do nothing even for people who held British citizenship. The trouble – they soon discovered – was that they were fighting an enemy for whom the normal constraints of logic and decency had no meaning.

One typical incident took place in November, 1935, when a man called Walter Huttenbach sought the help of the Foreign Office over his father, a British subject born in Penang who was practising as a doctor in Munich. Until the passing of the Nuremberg Laws, he had never had any trouble with the authorities. Then suddenly, like all other Jews, he found himself banned from employing any female German servant under the age of 35. 'For the first time,' wrote his son,

> the German Government extends its race hatred to citizens of foreign countries, including a country whose world Empire is built upon the tolerance of rights and equality of many races.

The Foreign Office, in a tight corner, recommended the British Ambassador in Berlin to urge the Germans, 'without raising the legal issue, that the application to British Jews of the Laws is not likely to be conducive to the maintenance of harmonious relations between Germany and this country.'

In the six years that followed the Nazi takeover, more than 300,000 Jews fled the country, some 60,000 in 1933 alone, and the 'flight-tax' levied from them – theoretically a quarter of the value of their property – rose from one million Reichmarks in 1932-33 to 70 million in 1936-37. Not only did the exodus destroy the Jewish community in Germany: it also shattered the country's intellectual life, which before 1933 had been the most stimulating of any nation in Europe. Plays, films, books and above all music had been charged with vitality, but with the mass exodus of writers, artists and musicians there descended on the third Reich what one author graphically described as 'cultural night'.

'Empty theatres, bankrupt bookshops, starving authors, artists and composers are a constant reminder that the cultural life of Berlin is threatening to expire,' said a British Embassy report of 1936. Though professing to deride learning for learning's sake, Hitler keenly felt his Government's lack of prestige in intellectual circles, and was dismayed by the 'obstinate and taciturn opposition' of the intelligentsia, which he could see no way of disarming.

The Führer's attempt to purge his own country of extraneous elements was only one facet of a wider obsession: his fear and hatred of 'world-Jewish Bolshevism', which he conceived it his duty to combat. Since the centre of world-Jewish Bolshevism was Moscow, Hitler was not, in the middle 1930s, on speaking terms with Stalin, and there could be no question of the Soviet Union taking part in the Olympic Games.

Frequent denunciations of the Soviet Union, couched in violently offensive language, made Germany's enmity towards Moscow perfectly plain. In 1936, for instance, addressing 50,000 boys and girls of the Hitler Youth, the Führer described the Soviet Union in characteristically crude terms:

> There is another country full of cruelty, murder and arson, destruction and upheaval, filled not with life but with horror, despair, complaint and misery.

Goebbels, in the same year, spoke repeatedly of the fact that 'Jews and Bolsheviks cannot be distinguished from one another', and hammered out the message that the goal of Communist propaganda was the destruction of the world. 'Bolshevism,' he said at Nuremberg, 'is a pathological and criminal madness clearly originating from Jewish sources and led by Jews with the object of annihilating European civilisation.'

Less clearly articulated – and therefore less clearly perceived by foreign statesmen – were Hitler's plans for territorial aggrandisement; yet in fact these were closely connected with his vilification of the Soviet Union. His immediate, ostensible aim was to rescue Germany from what he regarded as the disgrace cast on her by the Treaty of Versailles – the agreement signed by the Allied Powers in June, 1919, which effectively dismembered the former German Empire and established the League of Nations. The Treaty, which Hitler denounced as vindictive and unfair, had shorn Germany of her overseas colonies and many outlying provinces: Alsace-Lorraine had gone to France, most of West Prussia and Posen to Poland, part of Upper Silesia to Czechoslovakia, and so on. It was these former possessions that Hitler first sought to recover. Yet he made no secret of the fact that his greater aim was to secure enough *Lebensraum*, or 'living-space', for the reconstituted German race. In a typical speech to the Reichstag he explained why the country was unable to feed itself:

There live here on a very limited and not universally fruitful territory 67 million persons. That is about 136 per square kilometre. These people are not less industrious than the other European peoples, but their requirements are also not less. They are not less intelligent, but also not less endowed with the will to live. . . The German man possesses per head of population eighteen times less territory than for example a Russian . . . What the German peasant has achieved in the last few years is unique and unparalleled. What the Nazi State has achieved in the cultivation of the last patch of heather and swamp in Germany cannot be exaggerated. Nevertheless there will never be enough on our own territory for our nourishment.

As Speer remarked, the great thing about Hitler was that he produced simple solutions to complex problems. The simple way of ending the lack of space was to expand the country, and this he proposed to do by pushing the frontiers of the Reich southwards and eastwards through the centre of Europe. It was at least partly to mask his own aggressive designs that he kept invoking the menace of Bolshevism and seeking to enlist the support of other European nations in tackling it . . . and yet might he himself not in the end be strong enough to invade Russia?

The political tragedy of 1935 and 1936 was the failure of foreign diplomats and statesmen to take Hitler's expansionist plans seriously. Just as they tended to see his harassment of the Jews as nothing worse than a bad joke, so they failed to appreciate the deadly earnest of his aim to extend the Reich. Even though he broke one promise after another, even though he kept going back on his word, even though each month that passed brought fresh proof of his mendacity, nobody took any firm step to check him. Foreign leaders – among them the British Prime Minister, Stanley Baldwin, like his successor Neville Chamberlain – were still stunned by the carnage of 1914-18, and simply could not bring themselves to believe that Hitler would risk another war.

Their last good chance of stopping him – the best that ever presented itself – came when, in bare-faced defiance of the Treaty of Versailles, he ordered the German Army to re-occupy the demilitarised zone of the Rhineland at dawn on 7 March, 1936. Had the French or British taken positive action then, they might have changed the course of history; as it was, they sought refuge in agitated diplomatic exchanges and threatened Hitler only with words, which had no effect at all.

2

THE OUTSIDERS' VIEW

How was it that for so long the outside world failed to see Hitler plain? One factor which undoubtedly contributed to the general lack of perception was the censorship of the press and radio exercised by the Ministry of Propaganda under Goebbels. The German people, wrapped in a cocoon of lies, distortion and suppression, could gain no accurate idea what was going on either in their country or outside, for the Nazis soon brought the flow of information under tight control. In 1933 and 1934 laws were passed to exclude Jews, Communists, socialists and other suspect classes from journalism and printing. By 1934 the Nazi Party directly controlled nearly 90 newspapers, and the principal party organ, the *Völkischer Beobachter*, had grown from an insignificant Munich daily into a national paper with a circulation of one and a half million. Like the other party rags, it was not worth reading, and the result was a tremendous demand for any foreign newspaper that people could lay their hands on. For a time the *Baseler Nachrichten*, a German-language paper printed in Switzerland, had a red-hot sale, but then that too was banned.

Control of the German press was essentially negative, and the secret daily orders given out by the Ministry of Propaganda to editors and journalists consisted mainly of prohibitions – as (to take a random example) on 23 November, 1935:

The dissolution of the Aero Club is to be reported in the technical press only.

The German press is not to be drawn by expressions of opinion abroad to the effect that Hitler is annoyed at the efficacy of the League [of Nations].
Forecasts regarding the outcome of the oil war may not be published.

Sometimes, however, Goebbels's minions struck a more positive note, as on 28 November:

The report of the Communist danger in British India has been given too little prominence and has not been sufficiently exploited.

Often, also, they were inadvertently ridiculous:

It is not desired that there should be any discussion of the question as to whether Mark Twain was a Jew, since it is impossible to obtain accurate information about his pedigree.

Altogether the briefings made, as William Shirer described it, 'rich reading, ordering daily suppression of this truth and substitution of that lie'. But for ordinary people the censorship and propaganda induced an atmosphere of stupefying tedium, well caught by one Englishman who visited Germany in 1935:

It is almost impossible to put on paper the scope of this today. There is no news but Government news, no view but the Government view, no voice but the Government voice . . . One of the most annoying things to foreigners, or at any rate to me, was the eternal prefix 'German'. This word is now synonymous with 'unequalled best'. It was only when I once complimented my friends on the wonderful German moon, and explained that we had nothing like it in England, that some sense of the absurdity of their attitude reached them.

The foreign correspondents based in Berlin were by no means exempt from the restrictions. On the contrary, they found their existence direly frustrating, for they knew that if their despatches came too near any unpalatable truth they ran the risk of being expelled. They also knew that any critical report published abroad would be ridiculed by the Nazi papers – and some of them in any case fell victim to the timidity or prejudice of their editors at home. In this respect none was more unfortunate than Norman Ebbutt, the Berlin correspondent of *The Times*, which in the mid-1930s became notorious in Britain for its policy of trying to appease Hitler. Its editor, Geoffrey Dawson, had never been outside England, and had no enthusiasm for any foreign news that did not concern the British Empire; he thus published as little about Germany as possible, and, since in those days his newspaper was still regarded as the voice of the Establishment, his short-sightedness became extremely damaging.

For Ebbutt, stuck in Berlin, it was exasperating, and he grew so discouraged that he constantly talked of resigning. Shirer has left a vivid glimpse of the *Stammtisch* or regular table reserved for the foreign correspondents in a corner of the Taverne, an Italian restaurant run by a mountainous German called Willi Lehmann. From ten at night until three in the morning the table would be full of journalists eating, drinking and gossiping in an effort to retain their sanity, presided over by Norman Ebbutt, 'sucking at an old pipe the night long, talking and arguing in a weak, high-pitched voice', and complaining that *The Times* would not print what he sent them. (He retaliated as best he could by passing stories on to other journalists, or to Sir Robert Vansittart, the Permanent Head of the Foreign Office in London.)

One correspondent not inconvenienced by the restrictions was the egregious George Ward Price, who worked for the *Daily Mail* and usually appeared, from the abysmally sycophantic tenor of his despatches, to be acting as public-relations officer for Hitler, Goering and Goebbels. Since the proprietor of his newspaper, Lord Rothermere, was a personal friend of the Nazi leaders, this worked very well, and Price was rewarded by numerous private audiences with the Führer and his colleagues. (In his book *I Knew These Dictators*, published in 1937, he excelled himself with grossly flattering portraits of Hitler and Mussolini.) The one British newspaper which maintained a persistently critical and objective view of Nazi policy was the *Manchester Guardian*; but, since it had no correspondent in Berlin, it had to rely on irregular freelance contributions and letters from its readers to inform the public of what was happening.

Another source of acute irritation for the foreign correspondents was that very few of their readers trusted their
reports, toned-down though they were. People in the United
States and Britain seemed hell-bent on believing that Germany was a fine country; they simply rejected any article that
challenged this view, and regarded the newspaper men in
Berlin as malicious cranks. This tendency so worried and
exasperated Shirer that during the Winter Olympics, in
February, 1936, he arranged a special lunch party to try to
spread some enlightenment. Seeing how visiting American
businessmen were being taken in by Nazi propaganda, he
invited them to meet Douglas Miller, the commercial attaché
at the American Embassy in Berlin, who was extremely well
informed on German affairs. 'He got nowhere,' Shirer reported:

> The genial tycoons told *him* what the situation in Nazi Germany
> was. They liked it, they said. The streets were clean and peaceful.
> Law and order. No strikes, no trouble-making unions. No agi-
> tators. No Commies. Miller, a patient man, could scarcely get a
> word in.

Even if the newspaper correspondents were muzzled and
frustrated, the foreign embassies in Berlin, with their own
lines of communication, were not, and it remains a source of
mystery and chagrin to this author that the Foreign Office in
London made so little use of the information, much of it
thoroughly alarming, which poured in from the German
capital. Had a tenth of the facts been leaked – for instance, to
the *Manchester Guardian* – the impact on public opinion
would have been enormous. But, then, the leaking of facts to
newspapers was a practice in which Whitehall would not have
dreamt of indulging.

Nobody had a more realistic view of the Nazi leaders than
the British Ambassador, Sir Eric Phipps, who provided
Whitehall with an unending flow of news, sometimes by
letter, sometimes by cypher telegram; and, although his
elegant English was almost always diplomatic in every sense
of the word, he occasionally resorted to basic expressions. In

a letter of 24 April, 1936, for instance, he wrote:

> The fact is that the Germans want to do that almost impossible thing (even with old English ladies and Bishops), viz., to deceive *everybody all the time*.

And on 11 February he said in a letter to Whitehall:

> I fancy one reason why Hitler gives Goering his head like he does, in regard to extravagance etc., is that he really fears him: he quite realises that Goering, like himself, is a gangster capable of any deed.

Phipps baffled the Germans. An experienced diplomat who had served in Paris, Rome, Constantinople, St Petersburg and Madrid, as well as on the peace delegation at Versailles in 1919, he was far more intelligent and cosmopolitan than any of the Nazi leaders. What was more, he did not look at all English, being short and dark, with a broad forehead and a neatly clipped moustache. His poker face and his habit of wearing a monocle – for he had lost one eye as a boy – made William Shirer think of him as a Hungarian dandy. Hitler could not stand him – no doubt because he sensed that the ambassador saw through him – and he used to mutter irritably to members of his staff, '*Man heisst nicht Phipps*' ('Nobody can be called Phipps'), a joke deriving from the well known German fictional character Fips der Afen (Fips the Ape): of course no human could be named Phipps, because Fips was a monkey.

Usually, when the ambassador called on Hitler for a formal audience, what began as a relatively normal conversation would turn into a one-sided harangue. After a difficult encounter on 13 December, 1935, for instance, Phipps reported: 'The Chancellor, who struck me as being in a not very amiable mood . . . painted the Russian picture blacker than ever and in ever louder and sharper tones . . . the Russians noxious microbes who should be politically isolated.'

Somehow a report of this conversation was leaked to foreign correspondents, and, as Phipps noted wryly in a letter to London on the last day of the year, 'my interview with the

Chancellor on Friday the 13th of December (unlucky day!) has given rise to more than the usual puffings-out of poison gas and lies'. In a cypher telegram to the Foreign Office on 13 January, 1936, he reported:

> I regret to say the Chancellor neither knows nor cares for danger of popular suspicion and misunderstandings created by official secrecy; nor does he appreciate our policy of making full public statements regarding programme of defence services. In any case he has not the slightest intention of following any such policy himself. Only last week in Berlin alone he had three unfortunate persons of no particular importance summarily executed for revealing State secrets.
>
> Whole machinery of this country is based on secrecy, any violation of which entails summary execution.

From the moment Phipps reached Berlin in May, 1933, he saw and described accurately the menace that Hitler represented to Europe. Nor did he mince words about the rest of the Nazi leaders, describing Goering, for instance, as a 'big, fat, spoilt child'. It was Phipps who made a celebrated jest at Goering's expense soon after the Night of the Long Knives (when some 80 opponents of the regime, including Captain Roehm, were murdered) in 1934: when the Reichsmarschall arrived late for a meeting and gave as his excuse the fact that he had been shooting, Phipps murmured, 'Animals, I hope.'

All through 1935 and the beginning of 1936 Phipps's despatches reflected the rapidly increasing danger implicit in Germany's surreptitious rearmament: in spite of repeated denials, Hitler was building his army, air force and navy beyond the limits agreed. Again and again Phipps said so. He also complained more than once that nothing was being done in London or Paris to check Hitler's progress. In April, 1935, for instance, he wrote that although Germany's foreign policy since his own arrival in Berlin had been 'a crescendo of violence', it had failed to evoke 'any stronger reaction on the part of the ex-Allies than some notes of Platonic protest'. By November, 1935, he was writing:

> The salient feature of German social, economic and political life is the reconstruction of the armed forces. It is difficult to drive

along any road in this country without seeing striking evidence of the truth of this statement. On every side giant military establishments are springing up. There are few towns of any importance where barracks or military schools are not being built. Enormous aerodromes, either finished or under construction, march, sometimes for miles, with the main road. The armed SS sentries at the gate of many factories and the high barbed wire fence surrounding them proclaim their military character.

Except that battles are not being fought, Germany may be said without exaggeration to be living in a state of war. Everything is subordinated to the needs of the defence forces . . .

The discussion of military matters is prohibited. It is high treason to impart information even of a nature not considered in the least confidential abroad. That military expansion will be followed by territorial expansion goes without saying. The question asked is *where* and not whether Germany should expand . . . It can safely be said that the rearmament of Germany on its present scale is not being carried out solely for self-defence. The youth of this country are not being trained from childhood to regard war as inevitable without good reason.

The message from Berlin could hardly have been clearer; and when on 7 March, 1936, Hitler's troops marched into the Rhineland, every warning that Phipps had sent was vindicated. Yet still the western powers took no decisive action. Anthony Eden, who had become British Foreign Secretary in December, found he had inherited a horribly difficult and perilous situation. In a paper entitled *The German Danger*, printed for the Cabinet in January, 1936, he brought together a collection of the Berlin Embassy's reports, from Hitler's accession to the present, and added a commentary of his own. His two main conclusions were that, in view of what was 'so openly proceeding in Germany', England must press ahead with her own rearmament as fast as she could, and that the government should consider whether it was 'still possible to come to some *modus vivendi* – to put it no higher – with Hitler's Germany'. In the meantime, he went on trying to humour the Führer and avoid giving him offence.

By then it was clear to Whitehall that Hitler's relationships with other countries were entirely governed by expediency. His closest ally was Italy, whose Fascist dictator Mussolini had beaten him to the draw in the matter of imperialist aggression, having invaded Abyssinia in October, 1935. Of France, his immediate neighbour in the west, Hitler was intensely suspicious. In *Mein Kampf* he had described the French as negroid and sub-human, and his apprehensions about their enmity were increased when their government signed a pact with the arch-enemy in Moscow. The United States, where President Roosevelt was pursuing a policy of isolation, seemed a still more distant and enigmatic proposition even than Britain.

Another man in Berlin perceived the menace of Hitlerism no less clearly than Phipps. This was William E. Dodd, the American Ambassador, who had been Professor of History at Chicago University, and before that had spent two years studying at the University of Leipzig. Having known Germany in earlier days, he both despised and hated the Nazis, and did not hesitate to say so in his despatches to Washington. There, however, the reaction to critical reports was much the same as in London. The State Department felt Dodd must be exaggerating, and that he should not be so derogatory about a friendly nation. He became increasingly disillusioned, and in the summer of 1936 offered to resign, although in the end he stayed on until the following year.

In London the most objective observer of Germany was Sir Robert Vansittart, also a diplomat of wide experience. By the beginning of 1936 he had become completely outspoken, both in his denunciation of Hitler's criminality and in his condemnation of the British Government for failing to take positive action. 'Hitler has never meant business in our sense of the word,' he wrote in a Foreign Office minute of May, 1936. 'The sooner the Cabinet realise that, the better for this long-misguided country.'

Vansittart's clear-sightedness by no means endeared him to the Führer, whose suspicions were exacerbated by the fact that he and Phipps were brothers-in-law, Frances Phipps being the sister of Vansittart's second wife, Sarita. To Hitler, as to many of his cronies, *Vansittartismus*, or malicious hostility towards the Reich, seemed the main obstacle in the way of establishing friendly relations with England.

There is little doubt that, during his early years in power, Hitler did genuinely want an association with Britain. He once told Phipps that, if Britain and Germany worked together, they could rule the world. Phipps replied bluntly that Britain did not *want* to rule the world . . . and went on to point out that violently anti-British propaganda was being taught in German schools, whereupon the Führer flew into a tantrum. Goering also made gushing overtures on this theme – as when he said to George Ward Price: 'With our two armies in agreement, the peace of Europe would be on unshakeable foundations. Who could stand against the British fleet and the German army?' It escaped the Nazi leaders that Britain was not bent on global aggression, as they were; so blinkered and insular were they that none of them could see that within three years the extremity of their own policies had rendered any close association with Britain out of the question.

Even so, many Anglo-German friendships were cultivated in both countries, by individuals and by societies. British support for 'our German cousins' began at the highest possible level with the Prince of Wales, who in 1933 was heard saying to Prince Louis Ferdinand of Prussia that it was 'no business of ours to interfere in Germany's internal affairs either *re* Jews or *re* anything else'. The fact that the prince had long discussions with Hoesch, the German Ambassador in London, increased suspicions about his pro-German stance, as did the speech which he made at the annual conference of the British Legion on 11 June, 1935. The legion, of which the prince was Patron, was about to set out on a goodwill tour of Germany; he gave the idea his blessing and said that nobody was more suitable for extending 'the hand of friendship to the Germans than we ex-service men, who fought them and have now forgotten all about it and the Great War'. This effusive utterance – seized on gleefully by the Nazi papers – earned the prince a reproof from his father, George V, who pointed out to him that his views ran counter to Foreign Office policy. The prince was not at all repentant, and continued to cultivate his German contacts so incautiously that, when he abdicated, many people imagined Baldwin had got rid of him because he was so soft on the Nazis.

His ideas were shared by a small but articulate group of upper and middle-class intellectuals, who found a ready platform for their views in the correspondence columns of

The Times. Lord Rothermere, with his own platform in the *Daily Mail*, was perhaps the most openly pro-Nazi of the German apologists – a fact which brought him many communications direct from the Führer, including this private letter of 3 May, 1935:

> All hope for the future is dead, so far as the human eye can see, unless it comes from England and Germany . . . An agreement between England and Germany would represent the weighty influence for peace and commonsense of 120 million of the most valuable people in the world. The historically unique colonial aptitude and the naval power of Britain would be combined with that of one of the finest military nations in the world.

Another ardent sympathiser was Lord Mount Temple, who, as Wilfrid Ashley, had been Minister of Transport from 1924 to 1929 and in 1935 became the first President of the Anglo-German Fellowship – an allegedly non-political body whose avowed purpose was to establish good relations between the two countries. In Germany the fellowship was mirrored by the Deutsch-Englische Gesellschaft, whose inaugural banquet in Berlin on 11 January, 1936, was attended by Hess, Ribbentrop and many other leading Nazis among the 160 guests. Afterwards, Mount Temple held forth with his customary effusiveness:

> The friendly feelings of the British people for their German cousins are deeper than you realise . . . [the British] are following with great admiration the bold and successful efforts of the German people to overthrow Bolshevism. Your strength and determination have liberated Europe from a real danger.

Much sympathy for Germany existed in the House of Commons – as was shown by an exchange on 22 July, 1936. On that day, less than a fortnight before the Olympics, a Mr Mander asked the Foreign Secretary, Anthony Eden, whether he would demand an assurance from the German Government that the Games would not be used for propaganda purposes. When Eden replied that he would not, but Mander persisted, another member, Lt. Col. Moore, jumped up to ask: 'Does the Right Honourable Gentleman not view with disfavour these impertinent pin-pricks to a friendly nation?' – and his intervention was greeted with cries of 'Hear! Hear!'

Fifty years on, the idea that anyone could be 'impertinent' to Nazi Germany seems ridiculous; and it is fascinating, if inconclusive, to speculate on the role that better international communications might have played in exposing the true nature of Hitler's regime. Even if censorship had remained effective within Germany, the ordeals of those who had escaped the system would surely have gone round the world in weeks or even days. If Karl Billinger had been able to describe on television how he had been beaten up in Columbia Haus, would he not have quickly cured many British people of woolly, Mount Temple-type idealism? And, if a full account of the Nazis' racial and political exploitation of sport had been broadcast in New York, Paris and London, would it not have shamed the International Olympic Committee into withdrawing the 1936 Games from Berlin?

3

PREPARING THE GROUND

Germany had missed her one earlier chance of staging the Games in modern times. At the fifth modern Olympiad, which took place in Stockholm during the summer of 1912, the next festival, due in 1916, had been awarded to Germany, and a handsome new stadium, designed by the architect Otto March, had been built in the Grunewald, beyond the western outskirts of the German capital. Financed entirely by private funds, it was dedicated by the Kaiser in 1913, and an Organising Committee, guided by its chairman, Dr Theodor Lewald, and its secretary, Carl Diem, began planning for the Games of 1916.

Both Lewald and Diem were already distinguished figures in the world of German sport. Lewald had helped organise his country's participation in two earlier Olympiads; he was a staunch admirer of Baron Pierre de Coubertin, the Frenchman who had restarted the Games in 1896, and he was well known in many countries for his philanthropic efforts to promote the Olympic ideal. Diem was still better known: himself a fine athlete, a scholar, an historian, an enthusiast for classical Greece, an expert on sport and sporting history the world over, he was the ideal man to organise an Olympiad. In 1912 he was 30 years old – short, stocky, fizzing with energy and ideas. In 1913 he became secretary of the Government Commission for Sport and Recreation – in effect, the Minister of Sport.

The sixth Olympiad, however, was still-born. Plans for it were killed at an early stage by the outbreak of the Great

43

War. Moreover, because of her role in the war, Germany was forbidden to take part in the Games of 1920 or 1924. All this represented a disaster for Lewald, Diem and their idealistic enthusiasm. Yet throughout the black period they worked away on their country's behalf, striving to get the nation readmitted to the international sporting fraternity. When Germany did again compete in the Olympics – at Amsterdam in 1928 – the performance of her team was surprisingly good: with a total of 31 medals, she came second only to the United States in the final tally.

But it was not until 1932 that the persuasive advocacy of Lewald and Diem was fully rewarded. That summer, at a meeting in Barcelona, the International Olympic Committee granted Germany the 1936 Games. There had been a suggestion that the Olympics should be held in Spain, for Barcelona had a brand-new stadium, but the Committee's decision was for Berlin, by 43 votes to 16. Thus Germany at last got a chance to restore her athletic and social reputation. It was also possible for Diem and Lewald to travel to Los Angeles and make a detailed study of the arrangements for the 1932 Olympics, and to bring back ideas about organisation.

Later, when international agitation for a boycott of the Nazi Olympics was mounting, the IOC sought to justify its refusal to abandon Berlin by pointing out that the Games had been awarded originally to a democracy – the Weimar Republic – rather than to a Fascist dictatorship. This was true, and in the early days before Hitler's takeover the organisers were handicapped by the shortage of money that bedevils amateur sporting activities all over the world.

The Organising Committee held its first meeting in the Council Chamber of the Berlin Town Hall on 24 January, 1933, six days before Hitler's accession to power. Lewald – now nearly 70 and dignified by the title of *Excellenz*, having been a secretary of state in the Ministry of the Interior – was president. Diem, now 51 and balding, was again the secretary, and the masterly organisation which characterised the Berlin Games stemmed largely from his own powerful drive and grasp of detail.

Scarcely had the committee started work before a political earthquake transformed the country: on 30 January the Nazis came to power – and all too soon the evil nature of the new regime was made manifest to the Olympic organisers. After a lifetime of service to German sport, Lewald suddenly found himself threatened with dismissal from the Organising Committee simply because one of his grandparents had been a Jew. He offered to resign but, after a sharp reaction from the International Olympic Committee, was reinstated, nominally at least. In fact, after that, most of the decisions were taken by Diem.

Quickly he and his colleagues decided that the 1913 stadium was too small, and that they must somehow increase its seating capacity; but they found themselves cramped by the strange legal status of the building. It stood in the middle of the Grunewald racecourse, on land leased from the Prussian Exchequer by the Berlin Racing Association, and one condition of its construction had been that no major changes in its shape or appearance might be made without the approval of the racing body. It had also been stipulated that no part of the stadium might extend over the racecourse or block the view. As a result, the only feasible method of increasing capacity was to sink the centre of the arena deeper into the ground.

This solution was adopted, and fund-raising began. Sports clubs all over the country were set to collect the 'Olympic penny', a contribution levied from spectators at sporting events. The Reich Post Ministry promised to issue commemorative stamps, slightly more expensive than normal ones. Schacht, the Minister of Economics, gave permission for a large-scale lottery to run for three years. Yet all these schemes, sound enough in themselves, got off to a slow start: such was the economic gloom prevailing in Germany that no one could raise much enthusiasm for financing an event more than three years in the future.

Then, on 16 March, 1933, Hitler received Lewald, together with the Mayor of Berlin, Dr Sahm. The visitors explained the significance of the Games, as they saw it, and told the Führer some of their difficulties. His attitude had changed a good deal in the past twelve months. In 1932, before his accession to power, he had denounced the Olympics as 'an invention of Jews and Freemasons' and 'a play inspired by

Judaism which cannot possibly be put on in a Reich ruled by National Socialists'. The virulence of his opposition may have been due to Lewald's partly-Jewish ancestry. In any case, Hitler now mastered his phobia sufficiently to promise that he would do all he could to help present the festival; the Games, he said, would contribute substantially to better understanding between the nations of the world. They would also promote the development of sport among German youth – something which he considered vitally important to the well-being of the nation.

From the brief account that remains, it sounds as if Hitler showed polite rather than enthusiastic interest at that first meeting. Beset as he was by the problems of the new-born Reich, he saw that Germany *should* hold the Games, but did not yet realise their enormous political potential. Afterwards, people said that the man who made him see the possibilities was Hans von Tschammer und Osten, the Reich Sport Leader. The newly appointed Minister for Propaganda, Dr Goebbels, must also have played some part in enthusing him. In any event, six months later, Hitler suddenly showed far greater keenness.

During the spring and summer of 1933, planning went ahead on a modest level. After a careful study of weather records, the dates for the Games were set as 1-16 August, 1936. The Ministry for Propaganda was brought into the picture, and ideas for publicity were submitted to Goebbels on 28 March. From Baron de Coubertin came the suggestion that the 'Ode to Joy' from Beethoven's Choral Symphony should be played during the opening ceremony. In general, the committee's aim was to keep expenditure as low as possible.

Then, on a single day in the autumn, everything changed. On 5 October, bringing with him the architect Werner March (son of Otto), and accompanied by Dr Frick (Minister of the Interior), Tschammer und Osten and Lewald, Hitler visited the Grunewald site. First he was shown models of the stadium before and after its proposed reconstruction. Then, wearing a belted-in fawn raincoat but no hat, he went to the arena itself and found workmen busy excavating the floor. Why were they doing that? he asked. Lewald explained that the agreement with the Berlin Racing Association bound them not to obstruct the view. The Führer's second question was no less direct. 'Is the racecourse necessary?' Lewald agreed that Berlin had two other racing centres, in Hoppegarten and Karlshorst, and that the Grunewald course had been running at a heavy loss in recent years.

Hitler at once came to a decision that had the most far-reaching consequences. The racecourse must go, he announced. If necessary, a new one could be made for the Berlin Racing Association somewhere else, but the Grunewald site must be given over entirely to a new athletics centre. The old stadium must be demolished, and one capable of seating 100,000 people erected in its place. 'The stadium must be built by the Reich,' Hitler declared. 'It will be the task of the nation. If Germany is to stand host to the entire world, her preparations must be complete and magnificent.' When the Führer said he wanted a large open-air theatre included in the complex, March took him to an ideal, bowl-shaped site close at hand in the Murellen Valley. Another requirement was that a large flat area – a parade or assembly ground – should flank the main arena. Work was to begin at once. March was to draw up plans.

Five days later, at a conference held in the Reich Chancellery on 10 October, Hitler elaborated on his ideas. In the presence of Goebbels, other ministers and members of the Organising Committee, he declared that in staging the Games Germany must show evidence of her 'cultural achievements and abilities'. Almost at once a crisis blew up when he took exception to the first plan drawn up by March for the new stadium. The design was for a concrete structure with glass partition walls, reminiscent of a stadium recently built in Vienna. According to Speer, who was present, Hitler took one look at it, threw a tantrum, and curtly ordered Hans Pfundtner, Secretary of State at the Ministry of the Interior, to cancel the Games. There was, the Chancellor declared, no option. An Olympic festival could be opened only by the head of the host state; and since he, Hitler, refused to enter a glass-and-concrete monstrosity such as March had proposed, the Games could not take place in Berlin. The outside of any new German stadium should be clad not with concrete, but with natural stone. 'When a nation has four million unemployed,' he said, 'it must seek ways and means of creating work for them.'

According to Speer, it was he himself who saved the situation – by overnight drawing a sketch to show how the steel skeleton could be clad in natural stone and enhanced by the addition of more massive cornices. The glass partitions were eliminated, and Hitler accepted the design. March could not but agree – and, whatever his feelings at the time, he must have been glad of the changes in the long run, for the stadium which finally emerged was hailed as a masterpiece, and the credit for its design went entirely to him. Speer was never sure whether Hitler would have carried out his threat to cancel the Games, or whether 'it was merely a flash of pique, which he often used to get his way'.

Already the Führer's conception of the Olympic installations was grandiose. When March suggested, from his preliminary calculations, that the stadium and assembly area would between them be able to hold some 130,000 people, Hitler declared this entirely inadequate. On a large-scale map he indicated the area immediately west of the stadium and asked how many people that piece of ground could accommodate. March said he thought half a million, and this was more acceptable. The architect added that he had already thought of leaving a large gap in the stands on the western end of the stadium so that there would be a view out to the assembly field and the open country beyond. This idea – of a visual connection between the stadium and the festival grounds – also found favour. At the same meeting Lewald brought up another idea already hatched by the committee: that they should organise the casting of a gigantic Olympic bell, which would toll the opening and closing of the Games, and would be hung in a tower outside the stadium, visible from many parts of Berlin.

Hitler's decisions left the prospect looking entirely different. Athletic and sporting organisations no longer faced the task of preparing for the Olympics alone. The Chancellor had accepted the entire responsibility on behalf of the nation. It was, as one member of the committee remarked, a 'stupendous change', especially for those who had been working on the project for several years. Further confirmation that the project was now a national one came from the Ministry of Defence, who handed over to the committee the barracks at Döberitz, nine miles west of the stadium, as the embryo of an Olympic village.

The site chosen for the new Olympic complex was the most favourable to be found in Berlin. It lay in what an official report described as 'undisturbed Brandenburg landscape', eight miles west of the city centre, at a mean height of 200 ft above sea level, twice as high as the main boulevard, Unter den Linden. Because the prevailing westerly winds carried off smoke and dust towards the east, it enjoyed clean air, and the area was then still quite rural, with open meadows and woods, and the roofs and towers of Berlin visible in the distance. The whole site extended to nearly 350 acres.

Galvanised by this fresh impetus, the planners made rapid progress. Now that expense was no longer a constraint, they could aim for the best of everything. Besides the new stadium, assembly area and open-air theatre, the Olympic facilities would include a swimming stadium with seats for 16,000 spectators, a hockey stadium with space for 20,000, a new Hall of German Sport – the Deutschland Halle – and a sleeping block with accommodation for 400 which would house the women competitors in the Games. The sailing events would take place at Kiel, on the Baltic, and the rowing at Grünau, in the east of Berlin, where new stands and boathouses would replace the old ones on the banks of the traditional regatta course.

An immense programme of construction was launched. The demolition of the old stadium – a huge job in itself – occupied most of 1934, and it was many months before the new one began to rise in its place. Gradually the labour force built up to a peak of 2,600 men, often with shifts working round the clock. Most of the men were unskilled, and most of them had been unemployed. At first as much as possible was done by hand, with the deliberate aim of employing the maximum number of people; but as unemployment eased during the period of building, labour became scarce, and more and more machines were brought into use. In accordance with Hitler's wishes, a large part of the stadium was

49

made of natural stone – limestone from Franconia, basalt from the Eifel, granite and marble from Silesia, travertine from Württemberg, tufaceous limestone from Schwabia, dolomite from Anröchte, porphyry from Saxony – 40,000 cubic yards of it in all.

The new stadium had space for 100,000 spectators in 71 tiers of seats, but its immense capacity was partially concealed from the outside by the fact that the amphitheatre descended more than 40ft below ground level and rose little more than 50ft into the air. The only features of the old stadium which survived were the tunnels; these were incorporated into the new design so that guests of honour could go straight to their boxes – or leave – without having to use the normal entrances and exits. Beneath the stands were 52 changing rooms, besides first-aid stations, telephone rooms and so on.

The construction of the stadium caused great excitement in Berlin, for the building was on an heroic scale, more massive than anything people had seen before. Of equally magnificent proportions was the assembly area laid out immediately to the west. This vast flat space, measuring 330 by 400 yards, was flanked by low tiers of stone seats capable of holding 40,000 people; but the open space itself, which soon became known as the May Field, could accommodate at least 250,000. On the western edge of the field was built a plain, slender tower, designed to house the Olympic Bell. For many people the jewel of the whole complex was the open-air theatre a short distance to the northwest of the stadium. Modelled on the theatres of ancient Greece, and named after the poet Dietrich Eckart, the natural amphitheatre was blessed with a setting of great beauty, a pine-covered hillside acting as a backdrop to the stage.

Another very large though less spectacular project was the construction of the Olympic village, to house male competitors, at Döberitz, nine miles west of the stadium. For many years Döberitz had been used as a training area by the German Army – Berlin's equivalent of Aldershot – and its pleasant landscape was made up of small hills and lakes with open pine, oak and birch forest. There, in a wooded valley above an old water-course, the German Army rapidly erected an assembly of 140 living-houses, each with ten or twelve double bedrooms, and several larger buildings for cooking, eating and meeting. Great care was taken to make the village and its surroundings as attractive as possible. The primaeval woodland to the northwest, known as the Enchanted Forest, was left undisturbed; the sleeping quarters, with their red-tiled roofs and cream-coloured walls, were fitted neatly into the contours, and looked well against the green background of the trees. The most vaunted feature of the whole place was the sauna bath – then a novelty outside Scandinavia – which was built to Finnish specifications and installed in a rustic hut at the corner of a lake. The area was already well populated by wild creatures – rabbits, squirrels, storks, ducks and swans – but the Germans, leaving nothing to chance, spattered the surrounding woods with bird-houses, feeding-troughs and baths. It was typical of their thoroughness that during the summer of 1935 they eradicated every mosquito within miles by spraying possible breeding places.

Not all the preparations were physical. The veteran composer Richard Strauss – the best known musician in Germany at that time – was asked to compose an Olympic hymn which would grace the opening ceremony. He agreed to produce one on condition that he was furnished with a suitable text. A competition was therefore launched to find the most stirring set of verses, with prizes of 700, 200 and 100 marks offered for the best trio. In due course seven authors submitted nine hymns, and the first prize was awarded to a man named Wilhelm von Scholz; but the judges belatedly decided that his poem, although suitable for an all-German occasion, was in-adequate for an international festival. Another competition was announced, this time with a first prize of 1,000 marks. Instead of nine entries, over 300 arrived. The judges selected the best four and sent them to the composer himself for final adjudication. He chose a poem of seven verses by a young elocutionist called Robert Lubahn, and set it to a rousing if rather obvious tune. Waiving payment – for the hymn was his contribution to the festival – he offered to conduct the work on opening day. The verses were nothing if not diplomatic.

Welcome as our guests, ye nations,
Through our open gates draw nigh . . .

went the refrain, and an official publication described how the chorus, 'rising above the stormy violin passages, hurls the invitation to the world'.

The prospect of staging the Olympics fanned Diem's enthusiasm for ancient Greece into a blazing fire, and he found a ready ally in the Führer, who already had a predilection for Doric architecture. Hitler had little trouble persuading himself that the modern Germans were directly descended from the Greeks of the classical age. The ancient Greeks, it was officially announced, had been fair-haired and blue-eyed, exactly like the modern Aryans, and it was only a weakening of the blood, brought on by marriage into other races, that had caused their latter-day descendants to become so swarthy. Now the Olympics would demonstrate this truth, and provide a perfect occasion for pointing out the kinship and cultural similarities between Periclean Athens and the Third Reich.

One obvious way of demonstrating the link would be to organise a torch run, to carry sacred Olympic fire, kindled in the original stadium at Olympia, all the way to Berlin. Preparations for the run were put in hand, and the giant steel firm of Krupp, which was then hard at work on rearmament projects, magnanimously agreed to present the Olympic Committee with 3,100 stainless-steel torches, one for each kilometre of the journey. Months of experiment perfected a brightly flaming magnesium torch, unaffected by rain, wind or heat, with a fuse on either side of its head so that it would constantly reignite.

Fortunately for the Führer's Hellenic fantasies, there already existed strong connections between Germany and classical Greece. It was the celebrated eighteenth-century scholar and traveller Joachim Winckelmann who had first suggested excavating the ancient sanctuary at Olympia, and had he not been killed by a robber in Trieste on his way back to Greece after a break at home, in 1768, he would doubtless have pursued the idea. As it was, the first excavations were not made until 1829; but thereafter much of the reclamation of the site was carried out by German archaelogists, notably Ernst Curtius, who began a large-scale dig in 1875. Even after great labours by successive German expeditions, the excavation of Olympia had been left incomplete, and now Hitler conceived the notion of asking the Greek government for permission to re-start it.

A man of greater sensitivity might have felt embarrassed by the weight of Greek sculpture already reposing in Berlin's museums, for Curtius and his contemporaries had carried off tremendous quantities of loot, both from Greece itself and from classical sites in Asia Minor. It is true that Heinrich Schliemann, the businessman-turned-archaeologist, had been forced to hand over to the Greek government the hoard of gold which he found at Mycenae, but he had managed to make away with the treasure which he had unearthed from the hill of Hissarlik, by the Dardanelles, and which became known as the Gold of Troy. In the 1930s this was exhibited in one of the Berlin museums on the island in the Spree, along with many colossal pieces of sculpture. The biggest single item, and one of the most impressive, was the Altar of Pergamon, which, with enormous labour and expense, had been cut away from its mountaintop in Turkey and transported piece-by-piece to Berlin.

The city itself was adorned by many neo-classical façades, like those of the Brandenburg Gate, the Reichstag (Parliament building) and the Opera House in Unter den Linden, all of which had columns supporting pediments; and, when Hitler's mind turned to the task of rebuilding his capital, it was natural that he should encourage his pet architect Speer to incorporate Greek influences in new buildings. As Speer remarked, the Führer 'appreciated the permanent qualities of the classical style all the more because he thought he had found certain points of relationship between the Dorians and his own Germanic world'. Speer himself, travelling in Greece for the first time, found himself 'overwhelmed by the reconstructed stadium of Athens'. Thus, when he designed a vast new stadium for Nuremberg, to be built in pink and white granite and to seat 400,000 people, he drew it like a horseshoe, with one end open, in the style of the ancient Greeks. Once, as he and Hitler stood before a model of this monster (which was never built), the Führer remarked, 'as if it were a matter settled beyond any possibility of discussion', that, although the 1940 Olympics were due to be held in Tokyo, 'thereafter they will take place in Germany, for all time to come, in this stadium'.

Hitler knew perfectly well that, as capital cities went, Berlin was not in the top league, even though it was spread over a large area and had four and a half million inhabitants. 'Look at Paris, the most beautiful city in the world,' he said to Speer, 'or even Vienna. Those are cities with grand style . . . We must surpass Paris and Vienna.' To this end, Berlin was to have a new central avenue 130 yards wide, and, on its north side, near the Reichstag, an immense new meeting hall, with a central dome 825ft across and room beneath it for over 150,000 people to assemble standing. There was also to be a triumphal arch which would make the Arc de Triomphe look like a model: a structure 400ft high, with the names of the 1,800,000 First World War dead chiselled in its granite.

These were projects for the future. Meanwhile, to get people's minds moving in the right direction, the monthly propaganda magazine *The Olympic Games* began to publish articles which pointed up the Greek connection. The second issue, appearing in July, 1935, opened with a quotation from Philostratos – 'Enter the stadium, become men, and learn how to fight' – which served well to endorse the Nazi enthusiasm for military sport, and went on with an article that sought to dignify the national obsession with physical exercise:

> The Greeks had a general appreciation for the perfect human figure, for the sinewy, nude body. Art and athletics were unified in upholding this ideal of unadorned beauty in physical perfection. The peak of national civilisation was contemporaneous with the flourishing age in physical culture, and athletic achievements spurred the artists on to new heights.

The message was driven home in Issue No. 5 by a long quotation from Ernst Curtius:

> The Greeks considered physical development and training an important and absolute dictate of the Gods. Health of body; beauty, perfection and strength of limb; endurance in competition and combat; a clear, courageous eye; that confidence which

comes only through facing danger: these were considered by the Greeks as being no less essential than mental development, shrewdness and artistic talent.

Professor Hege of Weimar was sent to Olympia to take a special series of photographs. A cast of the famous Athenian bronze Zeus the Spear-Thrower was commissioned, and an exhibition entitled 'Sport in Hellenic Times' was opened in Berlin to stress the links between ancient and modern Games. It was announced that the cultural festival accompanying the Olympics would open with Aeschylus' *Orestes*.

On every front the Organising Committee displayed formidable efficiency, not least in the planning of courses for the Marathon and the 50km walk. Not for Diem and his men the happy-go-lucky attitude of the British, who in 1908, to humour Princess Mary, had allowed the Marathon to start under the windows of the Royal Nursery at Windsor, and so had inadvertently extended its distance from 25 miles (40,234m) to 26 miles and 385 yards (42,195m). Rather than be a centimetre out, the German committee sent for the Reich Bureau of Topographical Photography and established a course of 42,195 metres exactly. Nor did they want to risk any repetition of the scandal that ruined the Marathon of 1904 at St Louis, when in a temperature of 100°F the American runner Fred Lorz took a lift for much of the way in a passing car, but then ran into the stadium as though he were the winner, thereby causing acrimony and confusion. For Berlin, the committee made elaborate arrangements to police the whole route, and produced a relief map of it, showing every slightest rise and fall in the ground.

Yet it was not only efficiency that Diem needed. As the months passed, and his preparations went ever further, his courage and nerve were severely tested. The excesses of the Nazi regime, particularly in the field of sport, produced increasingly hostile reactions abroad, and he must often have feared that the festival which he was planning so industriously might never take place. Much therefore depended on propaganda – and Goebbels did not let him down.

As the publicity machine got into its stride, the circulation of its monthly magazine built up to 60,000 copies, in German,

French, Spanish and English. The journal was well produced, lavishly illustrated, and literate enough in foreign languages to attract overseas advertisements. 'Ice-cold sparkling Coca Cola, around the corner from anywhere,' said one, which had a picture of two athletes going over a hurdle: 'Something that the Working Man can learn from the Athlete – the PAUSE THAT REFRESHES.' Outside Germany, 44 agencies were set up in foreign cities, and advertising was handled by the German Railways Bureau. Postcards by the thousand were published in four languages, and 35,000 booklets about Berlin were sent out free.

It was also the task of the public relations office to prevent or discourage unwelcome publicity, and all souvenirs bearing the five-ring Olympic design had to be approved by yet another body, the Committee for the Protection of the Olympic Symbols. Tschammer und Osten often lent his own weight to the public-relations drive – in December, 1935, for instance, when he, Diem and Lewald went on an official tour of European capitals, including Paris and London. In an age when air-travel was still uncommon, their means of transport struck a stylish note: a special aircraft provided for the occasion by the Lufthansa Corporation, decorated with Olympic rings and piloted by an outstanding German sportsman, Captain Gaim.

At home, one of the most effective means of spreading the word was the Olympic Caravan, a strange but ingenious travelling exhibition which toured the country for a year and was visited by more than a million people. The show was housed in four outsize diesel trucks and eight trailers, which were drawn up in a hollow square at every halt. Because transport regulations limited the width of vehicles on any main road, each trailer was built so that it could be split in half length-ways; at every stop the wagons were taken in two and expanded by the insertion of an extra section which almost doubled their breadth. Thus inflated, and connected by covered passageways, with a tent pitched between them, they made up into an enclosure big enough to seat 200 people. Altogether this curious assembly travelled more than 6,000 miles.

In the capital, an immense amount was done to improve

access to the Olympic area. A new station was built on the Underground, and the suburban railway station was refurbished so that it could handle 24 electric and six steam trains every hour – a theoretical maximum of 48,000 people. The main east-west axis of the city, from Alexander Platz in the east to the Reich Sport field in the west, was widened and improved in many places, and the entire eight-mile thoroughfare, which came to be known as the Via Triumphalis, was fitted with new, modern lighting. Householders along the route were amazed to find that they could get a subsidy of 20 per cent on any repairs they carried out before the summer of 1936.

Behind the scenes, the Prussian Criminal Police Office had already foreseen that professional crooks would try to take advantage of the huge gathering, and therefore took steps to deny criminals the chance of even crossing the border. In the summer of 1935 they communicated with numerous foreign police organisations, and collected so much information about known villains that they were able to put out a handbook containing more than 1,000 descriptions, with photographs, fingerprints and details of special identity marks.

As the months passed, facts and statistics poured forth from the publicity office in a torrent. The German Railways Bureau was offering a 60 per cent discount to all foreigners visiting the country for the Olympics. All 100,000 tickets for the opening ceremony had been sold, and could have been sold 25 times over. The Berlin student service was training 700 young men and 200 young women to act as guides. The city would be decorated with over 20 miles of garlands. A thousand flagstaffs would support 40,000 square yards of flags and bunting. Four hundred drivers were being recruited to maintain a continuous transport service between the Olympic village and the stadium. It was budgeted that the athletes would get through 72,000kg of meat and poultry, 110,000kg of fresh vegetables, 130,000 litres of milk and 280,000 eggs. King Boris of Bulgaria had asked permission to live in the Olympic Village. For the accommodation of other visitors, quarter of a million private bedrooms had been identified and inspected by a special team 80-strong. The stadium would be equipped with 60 broadcasting microphones. Besides the

Games proper, there was to be a 'Pedagogical Olympiad', in which various nations would demonstrate their particular systems of physical training.

For timing the races, a special camera, activated by the shot of the starting pistol and accurate to within one-thousandth of a second, had been developed by the Reich Physical-Technical Institute in conjunction with the Zeiss-Ikon and Agfa companies. In the stadium the Olympic flame would burn to a height of between 10 and 20 feet, and would be 6 feet wide. The take-off boards for the Long Jump would be made of ash, which had the requisite combination of hardness and flexibility (oak had been tried, but found to be *too* hard). The javelins and discuses would be made of Finnish birch, the cross-bars for the High Jump and Pole Vault of Oregon pine. The tape which the runners would break would in fact be a piece of yarn stretched through slots in the finishing posts, which were to be 1.73 metres above the ground . . .

So it went on. Without the continuous help of the army, the colossal task of preparation would never have been completed in time; and even with it the building of the stadium fell behind schedule. It should have been finished by February, 1936, but the formal handover to the Organising Committee had to be postponed until the end of April. Then at last Berliners got a chance to wander inside the vast grey arena – and a thrilling moment it was for anyone who did so, because the size and grandeur of the building made it seem certain that the approaching Olympics would be conducted on a scale fit for heroes.

4

NAZI SPORTSMEN

As Diem and his colleagues grappled with the physical problems of staging the Olympiad, the State began an unprecedented takeover of all sporting activities within the Reich. This started within a few weeks of the Nazis' accession to power, and steps to exclude non-Aryans from normal athletic competition swiftly followed. The first blow was struck on 1 April, 1933, when the German Boxing Federation forbade Jewish boxers or referees to take part or officiate in German championship contests; and from that moment ever-increasing pressure was maintained to make it impossible, either physically or psychologically, for Jews to train and compete at the highest level. It is worth emphasising that the discrimination was deliberate, relentless and frequently articulated in public by members of the Nazi administration – for, in the period leading up to the Olympics, foreigners who wanted the Games to go ahead repeatedly maintained that in the third Reich all athletes had an equal chance.

This was manifestly untrue, and became more so with every month that passed. On 12 April, 1933, Dr Danny Prenn, a leading member of Germany's Davis Cup tennis team, was dropped from the side because he was Jewish (he later moved to live in England), and in May Jews were expelled from all gymnastic clubs. The severity of this last deprivation probably went unnoticed by most outsiders, but in fact it had far-reaching consequences, for the *Turnvereine* (gymnastic associations) were extremely numerous – there were nearly 13,000 associations, with one and a half million members –

59

and their aims were social and patriotic as well as purely physical. They dated back to Friedrich Jahn, the nineteenth-century patriot and founder of German athletics, who by their creation had sought to fortify his countrymen during the Napoleonic occupation; they were thus woven into the fabric of German society.

On 2 June, 1933, Dr Bernhard Rust, the Minister of Education (no less), gave instructions that Jews were to be excluded also from youth and welfare organisations, and that the facilities of such bodies were to be closed to them. It was on that same day that Lewald was threatened with expulsion from the Organising Committee.

Such was the background against which the International Olympic Committee began a meeting in Vienna on 7 June. Their position was difficult, to say the least. The Olympic Games were still more than three years off. The new regime in Germany was less than six months old: it had made an ominous start . . . but perhaps a vigorous protest might bring the Nazis to their senses.

A protest was duly made, mainly at the instigation of the three American members of the committee – General Charles Sherrill, Colonel William May Garland and Commodore Ernest Lee Jahncke. Under their pressure, the IOC threatened to withdraw the Games from Berlin unless Germany guaranteed both that Lewald would be allowed to retain his office and that the regime would cease to discriminate against Jewish citizens in the field of sport. In private Sherrill let fall the remark that he did not see how the Germans could possibly meet these conditions; yet the immediate crisis was averted when Lewald was authorised to declare that all Olympic rules would be obeyed, and that German Jews would not be excluded from the national team.

There is no doubt that at this stage Sherrill did his best to secure fair play. On 12 June, as he travelled home, he wrote to Rabbi Stephen Wise from Paris:

It was a trying fight . . . The Germans yielded slowly, very slowly. First they conceded that other nations could bring Jews. Then, after that fight was over, telephones came from Berlin that no publication [sic] should be given to their Government's back-down on Jews, but only the vague statement that they agreed to follow our rules . . . Then I went at them hard, insisting that as they had expressly excluded Jews, now they must expressly declare the Jews not even be excluded from German teams . . . Finally they yielded because they found that I had lined up the necessary votes.

Lewald retained his position, but in only a token role, and to his own great shame found himself forced to act as a frontman, passing on Nazi assurances that were designed to allay foreign apprehensions but which he knew were worthless and false. From now on the pretence was maintained that Jews would be allowed to train and qualify for the German Olympic team – yet it was only a pretence, and no honest foreign observers were taken in by it. 'It is not impossible that, in order to put up a screen, a few Jews may be allowed to train and figure on teams,' wrote George S. Messersmith, the United States Consul General in Berlin, in a report to the State Department in Washington on 28 November, 1933:

> But I think that it should be understood that this will be merely a screen for the real discrimination which is taking place, and will be action on the part of the authorities similar to that which they took in permitting Dr von Lewald to remain on the Olympic Committee . . .
>
> Personalities such as Dr von Lewald in the world of sport, Dr Sauerbruch [a celebrated surgeon] in the field of medicine, and others in various fields, are being used to endeavor to give the outside world improper or incomplete pictures of the situation here. This form of propaganda is a definite and favoured instrument of the Ministry of Propaganda.

Scarcely a month passed without some incident that revealed the true nature of the regime's attitude to sport. One such was the death of Fritz Rosenfelder, a Jew of Cannstadt, near Württemberg, who committed suicide after being expelled from the local sports club which he had run for many years. On 1 August *Der Stürmer* exulted at this Aryan triumph:

> It is evident why Rosenfelder was expelled from the sports club. We need waste no words here. Jews are Jews, and there is

no place for them in German sport. Germany is the fatherland of Germans and not Jews. Germans have the right to do what they wish in their own country.

On 7 August the municipality of Oberndorf, near Nuremberg, banned Jews from using its swimming pools, and so started a fashion which spread rapidly all over the Reich. In July the town of Breslau barred Jews from acting as lifesavers. By the autumn of 1933 it was established that Jews might train and compete only with other Jews, using only their separate facilities. Soon the police began to harass the Jewish clubs and sports grounds, so that many Jews had in effect nowhere to train, and could not even compete among themselves without molestation. By 1934 there were only two Jewish sports associations left in the whole of Germany – the Maccabi and the Organisation of Jewish War Veterans. More and more German sports facilities – among them the ice stadium at Garmisch-Partenkirchen, where the Winter Olympics were due to be held – had signs saying *Juden Unerwünscht* (not wanted) posted over their entrances.

This racial discrimination – so obvious and deliberate – was more than some foreign sports organisations could stomach. As a contemporary American pamphlet put it,

> Germany's introduction of race is not an expression of the kind of prejudice against Jews which unfortunately exists in this and other countries, and which manifests itself principally in private, social relations. It is, on the contrary, the expression of a fundamental principle of Nazi ideology, of German political theory and law. The principle is the dogma of racial inequality, the superiority of the Aryans not only to the Jews, but to all people whom the Germans do not regard as members of their own race.

Apart from being offensive to normal human beings, the Nazi attitude was also diametrically opposed to the principle of free competition on which the Olympics were supposed to be based. Agitation for action against it mounted most quickly in the United States, and especially in New York, where there were more than two million Jews in the city. Americans pointed out that, although the fanatical racialism of Hitler's

Germany was of most immediate and deadly peril to the Jews, it was also a potential threat and danger to all races and all nations. As the summer of 1933 wore on, Congress was besieged by demands that the United States should do something to help the Jews in Germany.

On the sporting front, the first countermeasure came in November, when, at its annual convention in Pittsburgh, the Amateur Athletic Union, under its outspoken President, Judge Jeremiah Mahoney, passed a resolution calling on the International Olympic Committee to inform Germany that, unless Jewish athletes were allowed to prepare for and participate in the Olympic games, American athletes would not take part. The President of the American Olympic Committee, Avery Brundage, seems at that stage also to have opposed participation, for on 22 November a similar message emanated from the AOC, who, at a meeting in Washington, adopted a resolution expressing the hope that Germany would lift all restrictions on Jewish athletes.

Resolutions passed 3,000 miles away, however well meant, had absolutely no effect on Nazi policy over sport, which moved rapidly further away from the Olympic ideal. The introduction of racialism was only one element in Germany's surrender to athletic barbarity. Still more alarming was the politicisation of sport and the investing of all athletic activity with military overtones.

Unmistakable evidence of these developments emerged in 1934, with the publication of a book by Bruno Malitz, Sport Leader of the Berlin Storm Troops. A copy of *The Spirit of Sport in the National Socialist Ideology* was sent to every sports club in Germany, and Goebbels had it placed on a list of books that all Nazis should read. Although nobody could have claimed that the work was well written, its message was brutally clear. Sport, wrote the author, is supposed to be a link between nations,

> but all the sport in the world cannot cancel those shameful paragraphs in the Versailles Treaty relating to war guilt. Frenchmen, Belgians, Polaks and Jew-Niggers run on German tracks and swim in German pools. Good money is thrown away, and nobody can truthfully say that international relationships be-

tween Germany and its enemies have been bettered. . .

There is no room in our German land for Jewish sports leaders
and their friends infested with the Talmud, for pacifists, political
Catholics, pan-Europeans and the rest. They are worse than
cholera and syphilis, much worse than famine, drought and
poison gas. Do we then want to have the Olympic Games in
Germany? Yes, we must have them! We think they are important
for international reasons. There could not be better propaganda
for Germany. The difference with us will be that no private clubs
or associations will name the teams in the name of Germany and
put Germany to shame. The State will name the team.

Sport, in other words, was to be the Third Reich's means of
gaining revenge on all those enemies who had benefited from
Germany's defeat in the First World War, and the Olympics
the particular occasion on which that revenge would be
exacted. How, in the face of such a nakedly aggressive stance,
could members of the foreign Olympic organisations still
press for the Games to be held in Berlin? Only, from that
point, by evasion and deliberate refusal to accept what was
happening.

By early 1934 feeling in New York had run so high that, on
8 March, 20,000 people flocked to a mock trial held in
Madison Square Gardens. In an event unparalleled in American history, 22 witnesses gave evidence against Hitler and his
government on the charge of committing crimes against
civilisation. Among those who testified were the former
Governor of New York, Alfred E. Smith, and the half-
Italian, half-Jewish Mayor of New York, Figuerola La Guardia. The police turned out in strength, expecting trouble, but
the feelings of everybody present were so much the same that
practically no dissent was voiced. Smith said that Hitler had
returned Germany 'to the law of the caveman', and La
Guardia that Hitler was showing the very conceit, arrogance
and ruthlessness which had precipitated the Great War.
Nobody defended the Nazi Government, and an empty chair
pointedly marked the absence of its intended occupant, Dr
Hans Luther, the German Ambassador to the United States,
who had been invited to represent his country but had not
dared to turn out. All he had done was appeal to the State
Department, asking them to ban the meeting on the grounds

that it would be an insult to a friendly nation; but the State Department had declined to intervene, because no government ministers or officials were due to take part in the trial.

That summer, Avery Brundage found himself forced by pressure of public opinion to make a fact-finding tour of Germany. By now a fervent advocate of participation, he it was, more than any other individual, who made sure in the end that the Americans went to the Games. Half a century later, his motive – and indeed his character – remains puzzling. Born in Detroit in 1887, he was orphaned at the age of 11 and brought up by his uncle and aunt. At the University of Illinois he proved himself an outstanding scholar and athlete, taking a first-class degree in engineering and becoming intercollegiate discus champion. In 1912 he competed at the Stockholm Olympics, and came sixth in the decathlon. From that moment he was a fanatical – and quite illogical – upholder of the principle of amateurism. Himself an amateur *par excellence* – he was three times voted Amateur All-Round Champion of America – he conceived an obsessive admiration for Baron de Coubertin, and joined forces with him to promote the Olympic ideal. In many ways he was practical and realistic: in 1915 he formed his own construction company, which flourished and earned him a fortune; but in others he was blinkered and bigoted to an extraordinary degree. Though he devoted much of his life to philanthropic sports administration – first in his spare time, later *all* the time – he made a great many enemies.

When he visited Germany in 1934, the Nazis had just announced that 21 German Jewish athletes had been nominated for Olympic training. By then, however, the anti-semitic campaign was so obvious that Brundage was driven to the expedient of saying that participation in the Olympics would not necessarily signify support for the Nazi regime. During his tour, which lasted less than a week, he did indeed meet some Jews, although only in the presence of German officials; he afterwards reported to the American Olympic Committee that the Reich Sport Leader, Tschammer und Osten, had promised for the third time that no Jewish athlete would be excluded. It was Brundage's superficial assessment which swung the American Olympic Committee round and persuaded them to vote, after long hesitation, for participation in Berlin.

Only a very short time passed before the outside world discovered that Tschammer und Osten's promises were as worthless as those of his colleagues. Later it became known that, only 12 days after Brundage was safely out of the way, seven of the Jewish athletes nominated for Olympic trials had received formal letters from their district sports leaders saying that, because their performance was not at a high enough level, they had been struck from the list of eligibles.

It is no longer possible to establish whether Tschammer und Osten supported the Party line on sport out of conviction or from necessity. Some foreign observers dismissed him as a Party hack, but others saw qualities in him. A small, dark, good-looking man, he had perfect manners and, unlike most of his colleagues in government, spoke excellent English. Phipps considered him 'a pleasant personality', and sympathy for him seems to have been increased by the fact that, while an infantryman during the Great War, he had been badly wounded in the right wrist, so that his arm was withered. At least once he made an effort to warn British friends about the true state of affairs in Germany. When he visited England during December, 1935, he spent a night at Burghley House, the palatial home of the Marquess of Exeter; there he urgently confided to his host that Hitler was planning a major war in Europe, and begged him to do anything he could to alert the British government to the danger. To have said any such thing in public would have cost him his life.

Whatever his true beliefs, he seems to have been curiously naïve. After the IOC meeting in Vienna, for instance, he told German press reporters: 'You are probably astonished by the decision [to allow Jews to take part in the German team] . . . but we had to consider the political situation. It was my duty to foster relations with foreign countries.' It does not seem to have occurred to him that such remarks would inevitably be reported abroad, thus undermining any confidence in his own integrity that he might have established.

In any case, Tschammer und Osten's position obliged him to lead the way in spreading Nazi sporting gospel, and compelled him to make many odious pronouncements. In

November, 1934, he issued an order to all German athletic associations forbidding them to have any contact with non-Aryans, and during 1935 almost every issue of *Der Dietwart*, his official publication, contained virulent abuse of Jews. The issue for July that year was typical:

> Anyone who sets himself up as a defender of Jewry no longer has any place in our associations. Every personal contact with Jews is to be avoided. There is absolutely nothing for any Jew in German men's associations. Let us take as our example the heroic struggle that Julius Streicher, the Gauleiter of Franconia, has been waging for many years against the Jews. We too, with our societies, must help him on to final victory. It is the obvious duty of our associations to give the defence movement against Jewry our energetic support.

The August number of the magazine brought a further elucidation of the principle:

> We cannot afford to keep any Jews as members because (a) we see ourselves being viciously attacked from within, and (b) they are organised as an international movement and put their racial interests above national ones. It is for this reason that we keep the Jews at a distance from our own organisations.

Less immediately offensive than the racialism, but in the long term almost equally sinister, was the obsession with physical training which gripped the Nazi leaders, and its close corollary, the overtly militaristic nature of much sporting activity. Under the direction of Tschammer und Osten, all sport in Germany became *gleichgeschaltet*, or 'coordinated'.

All boys and girls were compelled to play games at school, and on 1 October, 1935, sport became compulsory for university students. As part of their obligation to acquit themselves as all-round sportsmen, students were required to learn how to handle a light rifle. Soon a professor at Bonn University was complaining – to his own considerable risk, one would imagine – that his pupils were not doing enough academic work because they were forced to devote so many hours to playing-field and running-track. The *Kölnische Zeitung* reported a remarkable dearth of high-quality students and apprentices in the Ruhr and Rhineland; young men had taken to spending so much of their time on sports fields and parade grounds that local firms were having trouble finding suitable candidates for junior positions.

Among the workers a drive to foster sport was made by means of the *Kraft durch Freude* ('Strength through Joy') movement, which opened 48 sports offices, each with a number of branches. These organised sports and games in 350 towns and villages, employing a full-time staff of more than 1,000 instructors. All over the country workmen were encouraged to compete for the Reich sport badge; in the mountains they were taught to ski and skate. Advocates of sport freely admitted that one of its great advantages was that it made men *wehrhaftig*, or good material for the army.

For boys, membership of the Hitler Youth, though not yet compulsory, was almost inevitable. Apart from the fact that most boys anyway wanted to conform, they and their families knew quite well that they probably would not get far in life if they had not belonged to the country's leading youth organisation. Besides, pressure was put on their parents to make them enrol. In 1935 Dr Wilhelm Frick, the Minister of the Interior, issued a decree to the effect that civil servants were expected to show their devotion to the Third Reich by putting their sons into the Hitler Youth, and in January, 1936, an order from the War Minister stated that he expected all members of the defence forces to 'facilitate the entry of their children into the Hitler Youth, and so support the work of the Führer'.

The foreword to a 'Proficiency Book for German Youth' outlined the Nazi doctrine which was leading the regime to take such a grip on sport:

Physical training is not the private concern of the individual. The National Socialist movement orders every German to place his whole self at its service. Your body belongs to your country, since it is to your country that you owe your existence. You are responsible to your country for your body. Fulfil the demands of this manual, and you will fulfil your duty to the German people.

Far from being bored or embarrassed by such high-flown

ideas, most German boys found them tremendously exciting. Kurt Treitel, who was 14 in 1936, vividly remembered a mass gymnastic parade in the Berlin Post Stadium on Midsummer Eve – a day of heroic memory in Nordic tradition. In his green-and-white school colours, along with thousands of other boys and girls, he performed in the display and then stood rigidly to hear a speech from the Reich Sport Leader. At the end Tschammer und Osten made a surprise announcement: the Reich Youth Leader, Baldur von Schirach, had come especially to address the parade. This news sent a great wave of excitement sweeping through the stadium, and when Schirach began, '*Jungels und Mädels von gross Berlin, ich komme direkt vom Führer* . . .' a terrific roar of delight and enthusiasm erupted. A message straight from Hitler! After every phrase – 'You are the future, not only of Germany, but of the world' – there was a fresh explosion of excitement. Nobody had rehearsed or orchestrated these outbursts: they were spontaneous and heartfelt.

To boys in whom such patriotic fervour had been ignited, there was nothing sinister about the fact that their curriculum included *Wehrsport*, or 'military sport'. On two afternoons a week they would go off to a nearby stadium and train on the assault course maintained there as part of the normal facilities, throwing wooden grenades, scaling walls and nets, crossing imaginary chasms on ropes – all great fun.

Outsiders, however, found it unnatural and alarming that the State should seek to mould the bodies and minds of its young people with such overpowering attention to detail. Even the Hitler Youth cubs' test, for boys under 12, contained political elements: besides being versed in haversack-packing, and taking part in a journey of one and a half days' duration, aspirants were required to show knowledge of the Young Folk slogans, the Horst Wessel Song and the Hitler Youth Flag Song. To gain their first proficiency badge, they had to pass a test on the Führer's life, Germanism abroad, National Holidays of the German people, five Solemn Promises and six Hitler Youth songs.

As boys grew up, fresh levels of attainment were demanded of them annually. Some were purely physical – running, jumping, shot-putting – but others contained strong military overtones. At 15, for example, Section Two of the proficiency test was devoted to 'Target and March Practices', and included shooting, marching and an aggressive form of discus-throwing: each boy, wearing Hitler Youth service dress but without a pack, had to throw a discus into a target ring from varying distances, the pass standard being three hits out of five. Section Three of the same test comprised *Geländesport* – literally 'country sport', but more often translated as 'manoeuvre sport', and closely akin to the *Wehrsport* taught in schools. Map-reading, knowledge of country, orientation, sharpness of vision and estimation of distance all came into this section, as did use of camouflage and ways of taking cover. Boys also had to carry in their heads messages 'composed by a messenger about observation of the enemy'.

Regulations laid down that boys would be examined in their 11th, 16th and 18th years 'for weight, type of build (slight, muscular or rotund), physical condition . . . size, physical defects and general condition . . . Further, the boy will be examined for biological heredity, and his aptitude for his profession will be established.'

By such means, which reached deep into the lives of every subject, the Nazi regime sought to produce and shape a stream of potential recruits, who could be converted into full-scale soldiers with the minimum of time and training.

All through 1935 the authorities maintained steady pressure to make sport more political. Far from seeking to conceal what they were doing, they took every opportunity of forcing their ideas upon the population, and the most naked expression of them ever published appeared in a handbook compiled by Kurt Münch, the head of a new organisation called the Reichdiet. This, it was officially explained, was an institution 'for the promotion of national characteristics', and the book was a manual, in question-and-answer form, designed to furnish German athletes with a basic course in Nazi ideology.

The central point of the treatise was that 'non-political, so-called neutral sportsmen are unthinkable in Hitler's State'. Amateurs, individuals even, were a thing of the past.

National Socialism cannot permit even a single phase of life to remain outside the general organisation of the nation . . . Every athlete and sportsman in the third Reich must serve the State and contribute to the production of a standard National Socialist human body . . . All athletic associations must receive instructions in politics and philosophy from the Political Organisation or from the Labour Front . . . Athletics and sport are the preparatory school of political driving power in the service of the State.

Having established this fundamental principle, the booklet went on to vilify the supposed enemies of the Third Reich, among them Jews, Roman Catholics and Freemasons. Jews were described as 'a devilish power in the life of the peoples', and damned in the sporting sphere with a remark which later caused the Germans much embarrassment:

Among the inferior races the Jews have done nothing in the athletic sphere. They are surpassed even by the lowest of the negro tribes.

The religious content of this allegedly sporting book was no less repulsive. The author rejected the basic Christian belief that all men are equal in the sight of God as 'contrary to all natural law, life-experience and historical teaching'. He condemned the idea of the equality of mankind as a notion both false and immoral. He described the Roman Catholic Church as 'inimical to the people', and said that the aim of the Pope was the subjugation of the world by force. Far more important than religious fantasies, he claimed, was the principle of race:

Race is blood and spirit. The blood which predominates in the people gives it leadership and direction. In the German people Nordic blood predominates. The individual has value, significance, justification and a future only as a member of his race.

With the Olympic Games in prospect, it was convenient for Münch to be able to recall the well known truth that the rise and fall of nations is due to

the increase or decrease of light Nordic blood in that of the darker race. To take an example – the Hellenes were blond

71

Aryans of Nordic extraction. The descendants of those exponents of the marvels of Greek civilisation are now dark Levantines. What civilisation they still possess is due to later additions of German stock.

The most dangerous feature of the book was its insistence that all young sportsmen must read, learn and inwardly digest the poisonous rubbish which it purveyed as fact. Nowhere were the author's own malice and confusion more evident than in his conclusion, which laid down that sport 'is a protest against the tyranny of liberalism and similar philosophies over the living man'. To ram his message home, he repeated finally:

> German athletics are in the complete sense of the word political. It is impossible for individual or private clubs to indulge in physical exercises and games. These are the business of the State.

The publication of this one outrageous textbook should have finished Germany's chances of acting as Olympic host. Yet it did not. Fifty years later, it is hard to see why Münch's State-sponsored ravings provoked so little reaction among the sporting organisations of other countries. The only possible explanation seems to be that still, in spite of the atrocities already committed, few foreigners took Nazi posturings seriously. Although parts of Münch's text were reprinted in overseas newspapers, the attitude of the reports was one of faint amusement, rather than of alarm or condemnation. People outside Germany still tended to treat Hitler and his henchmen as comical rather than dangerous.

Within the Reich, however, it was immediately obvious that theory was being put into practice. In the summer of 1935 the Blue-and-White tennis team from Dresden won the Middle German Championship, but were deprived of their victory because, on being interrogated about political matters by a local Party official, they were found to have an insufficient grasp of Nazi ideology. (It was said that, when one boy was asked the importance of Leipzig in German history, he replied, 'How the hell should I know? I come from Chemnitz.') From that point, adequate political knowledge became a prerequisite of victory in any sporting contest.

Another absurd but potentially dangerous result of Nazi sports policy was that no individual or newspaper was allowed to criticise the selection or performance of any German team. The reason given was that criticism might undermine the confidence of a team chosen to carry out a task of political importance – and as a result no sports commentator dared make any but the mildest suggestions.

Few athletes found themselves as cruelly victimised by the new ideas as poor Jim Wango, a 38-year-old black wrestler who had won a following at the Herkules Velodrome in Nuremberg. At the beginning of March, 1935, under contract to a German impresario named Zurth, he appeared in an international professional wrestling contest and beat one white wrestler after another. His fame grew rapidly until, on 8 March, his career was brought to a sudden end by the appearance in the hall of Julius Streicher, whose home town Nuremberg was.

Making an abrupt and unexpected appearance, Streicher stopped the wrestling and launched into an impassioned harangue, which was duly reported by his sycophantic official newspaper, the *Frankische Tageszeitung*. 'We are in favour of sporting contests, including wrestling, in the compass of sports involving strength,' Streicher began:

> What we oppose is the linking of sport with dirty business interests and sales gimmicks. It is a sales gimmick, an appeal to inferior people, to subhumans, to put a negro on view and let him compete with white people. It is not in the spirit of the inhabitants of Nuremberg to let white men be subdued by a black man. Anyone who applauds when a black man throws a white man of our blood to the ground is no Nuremberger. No woman married to a negro can expect anything from Nuremberg.

According to the newspaper, this speech let loose a torrent of feeling. Roars of approval greeted Streicher's words, and 'there was no end to the jubilation' when the Gauleiter let it be known that, because the Black's wrestling had generated such dangerous excitement among the public, the Chief of Police had banned him from taking further part in the tournament. Descending to new depths of hypocrisy, the newspaper then reported:

It was interesting to observe how the wrestlers reacted when freed from the burden of the negro's participation. There were no more bad performances. Racially valuable and beautiful people turned in wonderful, good, sporting, aesthetically perfect bouts.

Wango himself never recovered from the shock. He found himself not only banned from the ring but boycotted in the town. The people of Nuremberg would not even sell him food. Then he fell ill. A Nazi doctor who was called refused to put him in hospital, even though his condition was obviously serious; and Zurth, seeing that he would get no proper treatment in Nuremberg, hastily moved him to Berlin. By the time Wango reached a hospital in the capital, he had a temperature of 39.6°C, (103.3°F) and doctors diagnosed a severe kidney ailment. He had reached help too late: a few hours after being admitted to hospital, he died.

In a report to the Ministry of Foreign Affairs in Paris, the French Ambassador in Berlin pointed out that, although Wango's death was not directly attributable to the intervention by Streicher, it certainly followed from it, and from the fact that the wrestler found himself *'en butte aux vexations d'une population excitée contre lui'*. The message added:

> The French Ambassador would very much like to know how, in general terms, the German Government intends to treat coloured people . . . and in particular, at the time of the Olympic Games, whether countries which send delegations including coloured athletes can expect to be exposed to incidents as painful as the one in Nuremberg, and to risk having some of their competitors banned from certain events.

It was a good question, and one which at last began to cause serious concern in the United States, where many of the finest sprinters were Blacks. In New York anti-Nazi feeling erupted again in July, when a mob of 1,000 people, many of them Communists, rushed the German liner *Bremen* just before she sailed and managed to rip down her Swastika flag. In hand-to-hand fighting between demonstrators and police, many people were injured – and when, a month later, a Jewish judge, Louis Bronsky, acquitted five men who had been apprehended, German papers complained vociferously that he was venting 'his race's vain hatred against the rising National Socialist German people'. The German Ambassador delivered a strong protest to the Secretary of State, Cordell Hull, and in due course the United States Govenment made a formal apology.

Such was the uneasy relationship between Germany and the United States in the summer of 1935. By August, Olympic debate was raging all over America. The American Federation of Labour asked athletes not to go to Berlin. Many leading sports writers urged that the United States have nothing to do with the Nazi Olympics, and they were supported by numerous distinguished athletes, not least Jim Bausch, gold-medal winner in the Decathlon of 1932. Civic, religious and sporting organisations all urged the Amateur Athletic Union to secure a transfer of the Games to some other city, or to withdraw the American team.

Anxieties were increased by the promulgation on 15 September of the infamous Nuremberg Laws, which effectively reduced anyone in Germany of even partially Jewish descent to the status of second-class citizen. When, a month later, the Berlin correspondent of the *New York Times* interviewed Lewald and the official Press spokesman for Tschammer und Osten, Herr Gärtner, his despatch concluded that neither of the Germans had been able 'to assert that Jewish athletes were receiving the same amount of opportunity for competition with good athletes as non-Jewish athletes'.

The whole situation had by then become a nightmare for Lewald: hamstrung by his own part-Jewish ancestry, he knew that his kinsmen were being treated abominably but could admit only a fraction of the truth. His distress was compounded by a letter from Judge Mahoney, President of the AAU, saying that he hoped all Americans would join him in striving to have the Games moved from Berlin:

> The present Government has injected race, religion and politics into sport in general and into the Olympic Games in particular, and has destroyed their free and independent character; and . . . if Germany today has no Jews of Olympic calibre, it is because

she has denied them adequate facilities for training and has forced them into exile or suicide.

Lewald knew that every word of this was true. His state of mind was revealed in a long and damning report addressed to the American Secretary of State by George S. Messersmith, on 15 November, 1935. 'I have known Dr von Lewald well and held him in very high regard,' wrote Messersmith. But

> when I asked him what reply he had made to the [earlier inquiries of the] American Committee, he told me, with tears in his eyes, that he had replied that there was no discrimination. When, as a friend, I reproached him . . . he replied that I must know what the consequences would be to him if he had made any other reply.

Messersmith went on to show, with exceptional precision, why the Nazi regime was setting such store on holding the Games:

> The main support of the Party from the outset has been principally among the youth, and today its actual power base is practically confined to them. This . . . explains the really enormous interest which the Party has in the Olympic Games being held in Berlin. The youth of Germany believe that National Socialist ideology is being rapidly accepted in other countries. The Party, through its controlled press and other propaganda means, has definitely instilled this idea into the minds of the young people of Germany. To the Party and to the youth of Germany, the holding of the Olympic Games in Berlin in 1936 has become the symbol of the conquest of the world by National Socialist doctrine. Should the Games not be held in Berlin, it would be one of the most serious blows which National Socialist prestige could suffer.

Messersmith estimated that out of a nation of 65 million people some four or five Jewish athletes were being allowed to train for the Olympics and were being 'presented to the world as proof that there is no discrimination'. It was perfectly obvious, he went on, that the Nazis were using the Olympic Games for political purposes, and that it was 'exactly this situation' which was being ignored by the American Committee:

In view of this situation, it is inconceivable that the American Olympic Committee should continue its stand that sport in Germany is non-political, that there is no discrimination, and that therefore American athletes should compete in Berlin in 1936. In face of all the information which is available, and which is so notoriously clear, the American Committee could not, without seriously stultifying itself and without betraying its obligations towards American athletic organisations and American youth, maintain its present attitude.

History does not relate how the State Department handled this powerful broadside, which suggested that the Americans should withdraw from the Games and speculated that, if they did, many other countries would follow them. But one man on whom the document had minimal effect – and on whom the facts of Nazi life seemed to make no impression at all – was Count Henri de Baillet-Latour, the President of the International Olympic Committee.

A Belgian aristocrat, whose 60th birthday fell in the Olympic year, with a background of some diplomatic service during which he had once been briefly attached to the Prince of Wales, he gave his recreations as racing and hunting. His brother-in-law, Prince Clary, described him tersely as a man of very strong opinions. His opinion about the 1936 Olympics was that they should take place in Berlin come what might, and the obstinacy with which he ignored the evils of Nazi ideology is enough to take away the breath of later generations.

In response to American pressure, he did travel to Berlin at the end of October, 1935, to see for himself what the fuss was about. He stayed for two days, had a meeting with Hitler, and before he left gave an interview to a representative of the *New York Times*. This in itself was an astonishing performance. There were, said the Count, no grounds for trying to remove the Games from Germany. Everything was in order. Even as he said this, he refused to discuss at any length the specific charges against Nazi policy which had been levelled in the United States. When asked about the treatment of Roman Catholic and Protestant athletes, he replied that the IOC did not interfere with the internal policies of other countries, which were purely domestic questions. When told that the

Lake Shore Swimming Club of Chicago, before a recent
match against the provisional German Olympic team in Berlin, had found the entrances to the municipal baths plastered
with slogans saying 'Jews Not Wanted Here', he replied that
he was interested in the situation during the Olympics, and
not in past history. Finally, when questioned about the fact
that in Germany only those who had accepted Nazi ideology
were any longer allowed to win athletic contests, he replied,
'The IOC does not go into such details.'

Back at the IOC's headquarters in Lausanne – brilliantly
named 'Mon Repos' – he issued a statement saying that the
campaign of opposition to the Games was political, and based
on false assertions, 'whose falsity it has been easy for me to
unmask'.

In the face of such bland evasions, it is tempting to write
him off as a buffoon. Yet one remark which he happened to
let fall during the Games themselves suggests that in fact he
knew perfectly well what was going on. At a dinner party
given by Hitler as part of the Olympic festivities, Baillet-
Latour sat next to Henriette, the wife of Baldur von Schirach,
and shocked her by countering one of her innocent conversa-
tional sallies with an emphatic denial. When she said how
happy she was to see the great festival of youth, peace and
reconciliation going so well, he listened carefully and replied:
'May God preserve you from your illusions, Madame! If you
ask me, we shall have war in three years.'

Why then did he play so cravenly into Hitler's hands and
insist that the Games remain in Berlin? The most charitable
explanation is that he believed in the efficacy of the Olympic
movement and thought that to let Germany stage the festival
might somehow reduce Hitler's aggression; the least generous, that he simply wanted his own party to go ahead. Either
way, he cuts a sorry figure, round whom the Nazis ran easy
Olympic rings.

The IOC found no grounds for action because, in the words
of one commentator, it looked for none, having deliberately
shut its eyes to Germany's violation of her pledges in the
Olympic code. Baillet-Latour and his colleagues must certainly have seen a booklet entitled *Preserve the Olympic
Ideal*, published in New York by a body styling itself 'The

Committee on Fair Play in Sports', which put together an impressive case for boycotting Berlin. 'The question whether or not America should participate is now being debated through the length and breadth of this country,' said the Introduction. 'In the last analysis the question will have to be decided by Americans themselves. If we know them correctly, they will not permit it to be decided for them, either by the International Olympic Committee or by the American Olympic Committee.'

The AOC, through its failure to take an anti-Nazi stand, had by then become extremely unpopular among some sections of the American sporting community; a wide split had opened up between it and the Amateur Athletic Union. Under its fiery President, Judge Mahoney, the AAU had the backing of several universities, including Harvard, Boston, Columbia, Fordham and City College of New York. Also behind it were many leading public figures, not least J. W. Gerard, the former American Ambassador in Berlin, and Governor James Curley of Massachusetts. The AAU was on strong moral ground, for it had already twice refused to hold its own championships in southern cities because of the racial prejudice there. Because it controlled all athletics outside the universities, the union could, in theory, prevent any non-university athlete going to Berlin. Ranged against it were all those who had a direct interest in the Olympics, and the very large number of people who felt that it would be bad luck on the athletes if they were dragged into a political battle not of their own making.

Soon the whole issue was being made murky by smear campaigns. 'To their everlasting shame,' said the booklet,

> some members of the American Olympic Committee have gone so far as to threaten the Jews of America with retaliatory anti-Semitic measures if the opposition [to the Games] should be successful. By trying to make the opposition appear as an attempt by the Communists to destroy the Olympic Games themselves, they seek to appeal to prejudice against Communism.

Even though the American Olympic Committee, under Avery Brundage's guidance, refused to change its position, external pressure did force the Nazis to make one token concession. In the autumn of 1935 General Sherrill again visited Germany, and at the close of his stay Tschammer und Osten announced that two leading German Jewish athletes, who were already in exile, were being invited to return and join the German Olympic team. One was Gretel Bergmann, an outstanding high-jumper from Stuttgart who had settled in England (where she won the English championships in 1934). The other was Helene Meyer, who had won the gold medal in the foil at the 1928 Olympics at the age of 17, had competed again at Los Angeles, and after the Games there had settled in California, where she studied international law. Only her father had been Jewish; her mother was Christian, and she herself looked like an advertisement for the Aryan race, being tall, fair and handsome, and known to her fans at home a '*Die blonde He*'. In 1933 she was amazed to hear that she had been expelled, *in absentia*, from her original fencing club in Offenbach. By 1935 she had become a language teacher, and was living in Oakland, California. She must have realised that, according to the new Nuremberg Laws, she was now classed as a *Mischling* – someone tainted with Jewish blood – and so would never be accepted as a German citizen. Even so, for reasons that are no longer clear, she accepted the Nazis' invitation to take part. So, too, did Gretel Bergmann; and by this one gesture – so calculating, so cynical, so empty of real intent – the Nazis probably saved their Olympics, for the move let much of the steam out of the protest organisations.

Afterwards General Sherrill claimed it had taken him two years of hard bargaining to secure Helene Meyer's reinstatement. Even if it had, as he returned to the United States he was met by a blast of scorn from Judge Mahoney, and handed a formal request from the AAU that the United States withdraw from the Games. Although Sherrill appeared to think he had won a vital concession, he was bitterly attacked for having changed his stance and branded as a Fascist sympathiser. His colleague Commodore Jahncke, who did *not* change his mind, was later quietly dropped from the International Olympic Committee.

The issue came to a head at the beginning of December, when the AAU held its annual convention. By then the union had received more than 100,000 individual protests, and the meeting that followed was the stormiest in its history. The argument, full of violent exchanges, raged for three days until it ended in great bitterness and a narrow majority in favour of taking part. The resolution included a ritual declaration that the decision to go to Berlin should not be construed as indicating approval of the Nazi regime, but real resistance was at an end. As soon as the vote had been taken, Judge Mahoney, who had led the union for six years and directed the fight against Nazism, announced that he would not stand for re-election. Avery Brundage, already President of the American Olympic Committee, was unanimously chosen to take his place.

And so, in spite of severe doubts, the United States decided to play ball with the Nazis. The division of opinion was reflected by a nation-wide poll of sports editors conducted in November: 13 per cent voted against going to Berlin, 51 per cent said they did not care what happened, and 35 per cent were firmly for participation. As one of this last category remarked, 'the best protest against the Nazis is to go over there and clean up the Games against them'.

5

TEST CASE

In comparison with the Americans, the British were slow to mobilise protests against Nazi sports practice, and their conduct was characterised by a reticence and decency markedly lacking in the rulers of the Third Reich. Having made such enquiries as they could in Germany during 1934, having received repeated assurances that the Olympic Code would be observed, and having accepted the invitation to take part in the Games, the British felt it would be unethical to send spies over on further research missions. All the same, athletics bodies in Britain had a good idea of what was going on in Germany, for they maintained regular contact with their opposite numbers in the United States, and by the autumn of 1935 disquiet had taken firm root on the eastern seaboard of the Atlantic as well.

If any foreign protest were to be effective, it would have to be made by Britain or the United States, for, as the *Manchester Guardian* remarked, the two nations had more influence in athletic matters 'than any other ten', the United States because of her athletic prowess, and Britain 'because she is still regarded as the mother of sport and the final arbiter of sportsmanship'.

As 1935 drew towards its close, the final arbiter found herself faced with a tricky decision. An international football match between England and Germany had been planned to take place in London during December, but the Olympic controversy had alerted so many people to the state of sport in Hitler's Reich that opposition to the game began to surface as

early as September. On the 15th of that month over 3,000
people packed into the Free Trade Hall in Manchester for a
demonstration against Nazi persecution, and a collection
organised by the British Anti-Nazi council raised £75 for
victims of repression. On 28 October, at an even larger
demonstration in Hyde Park, a resolution was passed calling
for the football match to be abandoned; the Socialist leader,
Mr C. R. Attlee, claimed in his speech that developments in
Germany were dangerous to civilisation and 'would lead the
world to war and destruction'.

For many people, the most worrying factor about the
match was a report that 10,000 German supporters were
planning to come over on a special outing, and that they
would march through North London to the ground at Tottenham where the game was to be played. On 20 October Mr
H. S. Barnett, Assistant Secretary of the Wood Green branch
of the National Union of Railwaymen, wrote to the Foreign
Secretary:

> I understand that the German team propose to march through
> the districts of Stoke Newington and Stamford Hill with their
> thousands of supporters. These districts are Jewish residential
> areas, and such a demonstration can only lead to serious
> trouble . . . I am instructed to emphatically protest against
> thousands of Fascists being allowed to use this match for political
> propaganda, and demand that the match be banned.

Apprehension was heightened by newspaper reports about a
fatality which had recently occurred during a football match
at Breslau in Upper Silesia, where the German team of
Patibor had been playing a Polish club, Rybnik. Accounts of
what had happened varied. The man who had died was
Edmund Baumgartner, a 21-year-old Jew, and local indigna-
tion was increased by the fact that the young man's father had
been killed fighting for the German Army during the Great
War. According to a local newspaper, Baumgartner had been
a member of the 50,000-strong crowd, and it was after the
game, as everyone streamed away from the ground, that
Nazis jumped on him and battered him to death. The paper
sought to exculpate the murderers by saying that Baumgartner had been attacked because he had gone to the match in

defiance of an order banning Jews from the event.

The New York *Daily Mirror*, however, told a quite different story, passed on from Warsaw by the local correspondent of the weekly magazine *American Hebrew*. According to this report, Baumgartner was the Polish team's leading player, and had been attacked on the field when his side started winning. Spectators invaded the pitch, made a concerted rush for him, and beat him to a pulp with sticks and stones. By the time the police rescued him, he was moribund, and died in hospital.

The American story, though bearing signs of exaggeration, clearly reported a most unpleasant occurrence. In London, members of the German Embassy were called to the Foreign Office to discuss the incident, and Prince Bismarck, the Chargé d'Affaires, unconvincingly described the whole report as an invention. Setting up a counter-attack, he formally requested that the British Government should take steps to call off a poster campaign with which anti-Nazi organisations were proposing to decry the international game scheduled for 4 December.

This led to a flurry of bureaucratic buck-passing. The Foreign Office consulted the Home Office. The Home Office said that they thought little could be achieved by trying to dismantle the poster campaign, since the removal of notices might lead to breaches of the peace. This was more than Sir Robert Vansittart could stand. 'I think this is an intolerable attitude to take,' he minuted furiously. 'We do not want incidents, and yet no one will do anything to stop it . . . We must not take refuge behind red tape.' Another Foreign Office minute added:

> What is objectionable is not so much the match but the fact that 10,000 Nazis are coming over to attend it. Such an exodus from Germany could never take place except by the granting of special financial facilities by the German Government; for, as we know, it is practically impossible for any German to go abroad because he cannot obtain the necessary foreign currency.

This writer touched on the truth of the whole matter, which escaped almost everyone else in Britain: that the Reich sports authorities had spotted an opportunity of pulling off a gigantic propaganda trick. The sending of the 10,000 was indeed an exceptional undertaking, and would never have been contemplated if it had not promised to yield some rich dividend. Ostensibly, the German Government's aim in allowing the horde to travel was to support the country's football team. The further motive, however, was to show Britain that Nazi sport and Nazi sports fans were perfectly normal. If that could be demonstrated by the despatch of 10,000 well drilled subjects, a great blow would be struck in the struggle to persuade Britain to take part in the Olympic Games, and to make her ignore the Jew-inspired chorus of protest reaching her from across the Atlantic.

Potential victims though they were of a huge political trick, the British authorities clung like limpets to the rock of no-politics-in-sport. Like the Americans, they were incapable of realising that the Nazis had bulldozed politics into sport in a way never before attempted. 'The Home Office are very anxious to get this match put off altogether,' said a Foreign Office note of 25 October. 'It is a Home Office affair . . . we have agreed not to intervene.' Soon afterwards, the Secretary of the Football Association, Stanley Rous, wrote inviting the Foreign Office to be represented at the match and at the banquet afterwards; after some deliberation, Whitehall decided to accept for two members of the department to attend the match, but declined the dinner. 'This is the match at which . . . ugly scenes are anticipated,' said another minute:

> We have already advised the Prince of Wales to keep away . . .
> After all, there is no particular reason why the FO *should* be represented. The German Embassy naturally enough go to the match; but official Governmental or FO representation on an occasion of this sort, which has been privately arranged without our knowledge, is not entirely necessary . . . It is undesirable that the FO should be associated [too closely] with international football.

In spite of the prodigious output of memoranda and minutes, a muddle had already been created. The Prince of Wales had *not* been officially instructed to steer clear of the game, and he had told Hoesch, the German Ambassador, that he would go.

'This will of course have to be called off,' wrote Vansittart in yet another internal note. 'But how did it happen?' In the midst of the confusion a message arrived from Phipps in Berlin to warn the Foreign Secretary that Tschammer und Osten, the Reich Sport Leader, would be making an official visit to London between 2 and 6 December, accompanied by Dr Lewald, the President of the Committee organising the Olympics, and by Dr Diem, the Secretary. The immediate object of the Germans' visit, Phipps wrote, was to attend the football match, but they would also probably take the opportunity of 'discussing questions relating to English participation in the Olympic games'. Tschammer und Osten, Phipps added, 'is a quiet, unassuming man of pleasant appearance, who is likely to make a good impression in English sporting circles'.

That same day – 18 November – Sir Walter Citrine, General Secretary of the Trades Union Council, was composing a tough letter to the Home Secretary, Sir John Simon, calling for the match to be banned:

> The dissolution of the Trade Union and Labour Movement in Germany has produced bitter feelings among wide sections of our people, added to which the general brutal intolerance displayed by the Nazi Government has called forth world-wide condemnation.
>
> Great Britain is giving shelter to many of the victims of that system who have been obliged to flee from the terror. With these living examples of persecution among us, with the knowledge of inhuman cruelties still being perpetrated in prisons and concentration camps, great public indignation would almost certainly be manifested, leading possibly to grave disturbances of the peace.
>
> I appeal to you to prohibit the projected football match and the visit to London of this large contingent of Nazis . . . Their presence in London would undoubtedly be interpreted by many people as a gesture of sympathy from the British Government to a movement whose aims and methods have evoked the strongest condemnation from every section of public opinion in the country, including the Prime Minister and members of the Cabinet.

The attempt at intervention by the TUC excited the London *Evening News* to a state of great fury. Under the heading test

'TUC HUMBUG' the paper claimed that 'the TUC and politicians hate Nazism and all that concerns it with a vicious and abiding hatred . . . not because it has abolished free speech and other undemocratic things, but because it threw Communism out of Germany'.

The Home Secretary by then was in severe doubt as to what action he should take. A Home Office note to Vansittart described 'Sir John Simon's grave anxiety as to the consequences that are likely to follow from this encounter', but also stressed that 'it seems to him that a decision not to intervene will need to be defended primarily on grounds of internal policy'. Vansittart remained in favour of letting events take their own course. 'After all,' he wrote on 26 November, 'the match is a private affair arranged by private individuals, and it is not clear why the Government should interfere in an affair of this kind any more than in other contracts between private individuals.'

Perhaps it was Vansittart who most influenced the Home Secretary; in any event, Simon finally decided not to intervene, and on 29 November he wrote in answer to Sir Walter Citrine:

> Government approval was neither sought nor required, and the introduction of political feeling into what should be purely a sporting contest is, as I am sure your council will agree, most undesirable . . .
>
> Wednesday's match has no political significance whatever, and does not imply any view of either Government as to the policy or institutions of the other. It is a game of football, which nobody need attend unless he wishes, and I hope all who take an interest in it from any side will do their utmost to discourage the idea that a sporting fixture in this country has any political implication.

There lay the great divergence. In Britain sport still *was* entirely non-political, but in Germany it had been entirely taken over by the State. Had Hitler seen Simon's letter to Citrine, he would surely have been delighted, for it was as if the British had rolled the ball gently to him in front of an undefended goal. When he was offered a last-minute chance to cancel the match and the departure of the supporting army, he returned it with perfect diplomacy. A 'Very Urgent' message flashed from the Embassy in Berlin on 2 December reported that the German Chancellor had personally considered the matter 'and did not want to cause any difficulties for His Majesty's Government'.

> He therefore left it entirely to HMG to decide whether, in view of the threatened difficulties, they thought it desirable that the match should be cancelled.

The match went ahead, but the proposed march did not, and, although the game led to none of the disturbances forecast, it proved a memorable occasion. Specially chartered ships brought the 10,000 German fans to England overnight. Some 1,800 came on the *Columbus* to Southampton, whence trains took them to Waterloo; but the main contingent of nearly 8,000 travelled *via* Dover. All had been encouraged to make the journey by the absurdly low fare – 60 marks, or about £3 at the official rate of exchange, for the round trip.

In London, Leicester Square was closed to ordinary traffic and made into a base for the travellers. Restaurants in the area served lunch in relays. It was widely remarked that the Germans were all smartly dressed; a great many of them had cameras or binoculars, and there was a surprisingly high turn-out of wives. After lunch and some time for shopping – though not much, because the visitors had been allowed to bring only 10 marks apiece – a fleet of coaches began lifting them to Tottenham, where hundreds of police had been posted along the approaches to the ground two hours before play was due to begin. Inside the stadium more police were positioned all round the field at ten-yard intervals, but apart from one or two scuffles as the law took possession of anti-Nazi pamphlets, there was no trouble of any kind.

On the contrary, the atmosphere was full of goodwill, the crowd genial, generous and always ready with a joke (the German captain, Szepan, instantly became known as 'Greta' because of his platinum-blond hair). The Union Jack and the Swastika banner flew alongside each other, and the fact that Germany lost 3-0 seemed in no way to diminish the success of the afternoon.

That night the Football Association entertained the team

and its officials to dinner at the Victoria Hotel. Herr Erbach, in his speech on behalf of the guests, referred to the game as a 'grand match', and said that the Germans had come 'as apprentices to the masters who had taught them'. Tschammer und Osten referred lyrically to the blue sky of friendship and fellowship that illuminated the sporting relationship between the two countries, and altogether the atmosphere was extremely cordial.

So it was the next evening, when the Hotel Victoria was again the scene of an international gathering. The first dinner of the Anglo-German Fellowship was held in honour of Tschammer und Osten and attended by many dignitaries, among them several British Members of Parliament and the Duke of Saxe-Coburg Gotha. Dr Lewald, referring to the Olympic Games next August, said that the village for the competitors was already well advanced. Several of the other guests felt slightly nervous when Tschammer und Osten himself replied to suggestions that sport in Germany had taken a military turn by remarking that all good Englishmen must surely be of the opinion that if a rifle had got to be fired, it must be in the hands of someone strong enough to fire it properly. Yet it was left to Lord Mount Temple, that archapostle of friendship with Germany, to make the gaffe of the evening.

Having declared that the international football match had been a turning-point in the good feeling between the two countries, he denounced the TUC for its 'stupid' attempt to sow discord between the nations. The Home Secretary, he said, had handled the protestors in far too gentle a manner.

I would have told them to mind their own damned business . . . The Germans always have been our good friends. They always fought fair in the war, and I hope we did the same. If another war comes . . . well, I must not say what I was going to say. I hope the partners will be changed.

This blundering sally brought cheers from the people at the dinner, and the evening ended with everyone in high good humour. Next day, when the team flew home from Croydon, the German manager said they did not mind losing, for the

English were still the acknowledged masters of the game, and as a result of the match the Germans had received invitations from the Scottish and Irish football associations.

As *The Times* reported, Germany was determined to 'read as much as possible in the way of political and psychological rapprochement into this occasion':

> It is hardly a secret . . . that a resumption of closer contact with Great Britain is earnestly desired. Things are approaching a pass at which any straw may be eagerly clutched at. The exaggerated importance and the exceptionally friendly turn given to the Anglo-German football match by the untimely manifestation of political misgivings must have come as a godsend to some quarters.

This report aroused the wrath of the Berlin *Börsen Zeitung*, which, excelling even its own high standards of mendacity, declared that no country had declined to connect sport with politics more categorically than the new Germany. *Der Angriff* – more brazen – did not resort to any such attempt at a smokescreen, but openly professed its delight that the British Trades Union 'provocation' had been a failure. The paper saw the Tottenham crowd's exemplary behaviour as a reaction against the attempt by 'political intriguers' to cripple the match through hostile propaganda, and concluded that for Germany the game had been 'an unrestricted political, psychological and also sporting success'.

A week later Phipps sent the Foreign Office a long memorandum on the way in which the Nazis were 'slowly but surely tightening their hold on German sport'. To illustrate his theme he included many quotations from the handbook by Bruno Malitz, which he described as the '400-page political bible of the German sportsman', and illustrated some of its 'grossest distortions'. From a section on the First World War, for instance, he quoted a passage claiming that the peace-time strength of the armies opposing Germany had amounted to 3,355 million men, and pointed out that even if there had been 50 enemies, they would have had to have armies of 70 million each. He showed how the book dealt with political problems by question and answer – 'How did the Nordic race originate?

Why must gymnasts and sportsmen fight against Jewry?' –
and quoted passages about the pride of German sportsmen 'in
being allowed to fight under the Swastika'. At the end of his
report he drily concluded: 'The Trade Union leaders, had
they been in possession of this book . . . would have had a
stronger case.'

In fact the TUC was by no means abashed, and Citrine soon
brought out a pamphlet vigorously defending the attempt to
have the match put off. Beneath the headline UNDER THE
HEEL OF HITLER: THE DICTATORSHIP OVER SPORT IN GERMANY,
he pointed out that the President of the German Football
League, Herr Lindemann, held his position at the discretion
of a government official:

> Would the English Football Association tolerate the interference
> of a Home Office official in the election of officers? That's what
> happens in Germany, not only in football but in every branch of
> sport. British sportsmen would laugh to scorn the notion that a
> man's political views should determine his right to take part in
> any organised game. They would resent the exclusion of a player
> from any club or contest because his grandfather was a Jew. They
> would ridicule the imposition of racial or political tests in any
> kind of athletic competition, where physical fitness and skill can
> alone decide prominence.

The truth of this must have been evident to all but the most
blinkered of British readers. But still they were extraordinarily blind. A football match against Germany had just gone
off perfectly. A huge crowd of supporters had behaved in a
thoroughly sportsmanlike fashion. What then was there to
worry about?

The fact was that a complete ideological separation had
grown up between the regimes of Britain and Germany, in
sport as much as in politics. Both on the athletics field and in
government Britain was still behaving in a traditionally
sportsmanlike manner. Her ultimate opponent in Germany
was a gangster without morals, the least sportsmanlike man in
the world, to whom concern over fair play was a laughable
anachronism and a manifestation of weakness. The great
disaster was that, with the exception of a few men like
Vansittart, Phipps and Citrine, nobody in Britain realised

that Hitler was completely treacherous whenever it suited him to be so, whether in sporting or in more serious matters. However much lip-service he might pay to the glory of Olympic sport, his words meant nothing at all.

6

THE WINTER GAMES

If any of the Nazi leaders still believed in divine retribution, they must have thought it was being visited on them at the beginning of February, 1936, for after years of preparation for the Winter Olympics in the little town of Garmisch-Partenkirchen, they found the Bavarian Alps laid bare by an unprecedented shortage of snow. An immense amount of money and effort had been put into the task of elevating Garmisch from its status as a homely mountain resort to a place capable of entertaining top-class skiers and skaters from all over the world . . . and now there was no snow.

A giant Olympic ski-jump, with a tower 142 ft high, had been completed in the winter of 1934. Around its base, where the jumpers would land after travelling up to 300ft through the air, was a stadium with space for 150,000 people. The Riessersee bob-run had been remodelled and rebuilt, with curves sharper and more steeply banked. To check the angles and the gradients, a car had been driven down the run during the summer months, and now, in the winter, it had been lined with blocks of ice cut from the Riesser lake. On the valley floor a new ice stadium, with an artificially cooled rink 100ft by 200ft, had been built: the wooden stands surrounding it could accommodate 12,000 spectators, and they included a post office and press headquarters, with 10 soundproof booths for broadcasting – facilities which seemed ultra-modern in the context of winter sports. The whole complex had been tested, and found satisfactory, during the German championships of 1935 – and, even should snow be short in the valley, there were reserve courses on the north-facing slopes at Klais and Elmau, where good skiing conditions were always assured. Until the last moment, it looked as though the fall-back facilities were going to be needed, and the organisers had some sleepless nights. The snow famine throughout the Alps was the worst for 25 years. The bob run was unusable, and several teams decamped to St. Moritz, to practise there. In Garmisch emergency plans were drawn up to ferry competitors and spectators up to the Kreuzeck mountain hotel. But the capacity of the cable car was only 20 people every 20 minutes . . . Chaos threatened.

It is true that, compared with the Olympic Games themselves, the Winter Games were of minor importance in purely sporting terms; nevertheless, they were the first chance that the Third Reich had had to show off its organisational and athletic prowess to visitors from abroad. As Phipps wrote to Eden, the Foreign Secretary, from Berlin on 13 February,

> The German Government attach enormous importance to the Olympic Games from the point of view of propaganda, and hope to be able to take the opportunity of impressing foreign countries with the capacity and solidity of the Nazi regime.

Hitler and his colleagues were therefore determined that everything should pass off well, and their sensitivity had already been demonstrated by a row which had broken out at the Ministry of Propaganda in Berlin. The American journalist William Shirer had written an article saying that in Garmisch the Nazis had removed all the anti-semitic propaganda – this was true – so that Olympic visitors would be spared any signs 'of the kind of treatment meted out to Jews in this country'. He had also remarked that Nazi officials had taken all the good hotels for themselves and put the journalists up in inconvenient *pensions*. This also was true – but the report touched off a tirade from Wilfred Bade, the member of the Propaganda Ministry temporarily in charge of the foreign press, who bellowed at Shirer in his office and had him denounced violently in the Nazi press.

Insolent foreign correspondents could at least be abused, and if necessary sent packing. Snow, on the other hand, could not be brought down out of a clear sky by threats of violence. But, as so often seemed to happen, luck came to Hitler's aid. At almost the last possible minute the weather changed and began to behave as if it were under the control of the organising committee. Six inches of powder snow fell on 5 February, and when the Führer arrived to open the Games next morning the blizzard was still raging.

The official opening was easily the most spectacular event that Garmisch had ever seen. The little mountain resort – an old-fashioned place, its wide-eaved houses painted with scenes of peasant life – was already packed, with people sleeping in hotel corridors and bars, but on the morning of the 6th thousands more poured in by train from Munich, and a crowd estimated at 60,000 gathered in the ski stadium. To the thud of military bands muffled by the new snow blanket, and the surge of party songs, regiments of Hitler Youth, Nazi Labour Battalions and detachments from sports organisations processed through the streets. So too did 28 national teams, who marched to the saluting base, where Hitler, beaming with health and goodwill, but hatless in the blizzard, was given a tumultuous reception. The British team, who had no official uniform, were dressed in various colours, but all wore black crêpe arm-bands as tokens of mourning for King George V, who had died on 21 January. One fashion-conscious observer noticed that 'the blue zip-fastener wind jacket and ski trousers of contrasting shades favoured by Edward, when he visited Kitzbühel as Prince of Wales' were in evidence everywhere.

In the stadium most teams elicited roars of applause when they raised their hands to the Führer in what appeared to be Nazi salutes. In fact they were supposed to be Olympic salutes, with hand and arm outstretched, but the crowd took them for straightforward tributes to their leader. The Americans, by contrast, gave only an eyes-right, and, on being greeted by no more than a ripple of applause, at once took offence, believing themselves to have been snubbed. Nevertheless the show went on. With one simple sentence Hitler declared the Winter Games open. From a stainless-steel bowl set high on a latticework tower the Olympic flame flared up. Across on the opposite side of the ski-run the five-ring

Olympic flag floated free. A cannon boomed and the bells of the village rang out. The stadium roared with a great eruption of '*Heils*', then fell silent as the German skier Willi Bogner mounted a small rostrum clad with fir boughs to recite the Olympic Oath, as the flags of the competing nations were dipped in formation around him. By then Hitler's toothbrush moustache was plastered with snow, and it may have been this that made many people fancy they saw him smirk and glance lovingly over the mountains to the south when the Austrian team was cheered loudly out of the arena.

Although outwardly all was set for a sporting festival, political tensions were fizzing just beneath the surface. Hitler had not come to the opening alone: he had brought with him the strongest possible turn-out of Nazi leaders – Goering, Goebbels, Streicher, Frick, Blomberg and many others. Anti-Jewish propaganda signs had been removed from the town, and it was common knowledge that instructions had been discreetly circulated to all German participants and visitors that anti-Jewish feeling and comment should be suppressed until the Olympics were over. The correspondent of the London *Daily Telegraph* reported that special care had been taken 'to protect the Spanish team from any unpleasantness owing to their non-Nordic features', and everyone was talking about the fact that Rudi Ball, a Jew and one of Germany's leading ice-hockey players, had been recalled from Spain, where he was living in voluntary exile, to play for the German team.

Behind the scenes the hosts were extremely nervous that some untoward incident would wreck the cordial atmosphere. The German authorities had been unsettled by the intensity of the Olympic debate in the United States, and they were therefore greatly relieved when the American team actually arrived in Garmisch; but at once they found themselves in new difficulties, when the Americans were miffed by the tepidity of their reception. Worse followed, when the American press corps complained that too few seats had been allotted to them. The Germans reacted by going out of their way to humour the transatlantic visitors: at some inconvenience to themselves, they handed over more press seats, and sent post-haste to Berlin for a special envoy from the Ministry of Foreign Affairs, whose sole task it became to cosset the United States contingent.

'The Press has not been allowed to breathe a hint of this sporting team in a teacup,' Phipps told Whitehall; and it was typical of the obsessive secrecy which beset the Nazi regime that, although the opening ceremony received extensive newspaper coverage both in Germany and overseas, another extraordinary incident which took place the same day went entirely unreported in the German press. As Hitler was declaring the Games open, a horrifying air-crash devastated part of Neuhauser Strasse, the main shopping street of Munich, not 50 miles from Garmisch. Two new training aircraft from the military flying school at Schleisheim collided over the city. One crashed into the centre of Munich, bouncing off the roof of the old Academy University building, cutting electricity and telephone cables and exploding in the street, where it killed four people and severely burned several more. The other fell outside the Schwabinger hospital, two miles away.

On this – one of the worst disasters so far suffered by the Luftwaffe – the police ordered an immediate clamp-down. Flying squads of SS men sealed off the areas in which the planes had crashed and ordered everyone in the vicinity not to give information about what had happened, on pain of immediate imprisonment. Thus, once again, news of an incident which reflected no credit on the regime was suppressed, and hidden from almost everyone in Germany.

Another incident which went unreported was the interview which Baillet-Latour had with Hitler. As he drove towards Garmisch the President of the IOC was amazed and horrified – he said – to see anti-semitic signs posted along the roads, so he demanded an audience with, and an explanation from, the Führer. A sharp argument is said to have taken place, Baillet-Latour threatening to call off both Winter and Summer Olympics, and Hitler claiming that he could not change 'a question of the highest importance within Germany . . . for a small point of Olympic protocol'. After some tense exchanges, the Führer gave ground and agreed to have the signs removed. When Baillet-Latour drove home after the Games, he saw – or said he had seen – nothing, and seems to have been naïve enough to believe he had won a great victory.

The polar weather which had saved the Olympics from fiasco moved in to grip the whole of Europe. At Garmisch fresh blizzards frequently renewed the snow which swarms of spectators kept trampling into ice and slush on the lower slopes. During the ice-hockey match between Germany and the United States it snowed so hard that the rink had to be swept 10 times. In Britain people died from cold in the streets, violent snow-storms buried Dartmoor, and at Shoeburyness the sea froze. On 12 February huge storms wrecked the Golden Horn bridge over the Bosphorus. On the 13th, at Dalwhinnie in the Scottish Highlands, the temperature fell to 2° F.

The Winter Olympics were dominated – as expected – by the Scandinavians. The most spectacular event – the ski-jumping – was won by the diminutive Birger Ruud of Norway, who was only 5ft 5in tall and baby-faced, but magnificently muscled. The other great Norwegian, Ivar Ballangrud, won gold medals in three of the skating races (500m, 5,000m and 10,000m), and in the fourth, the 1,500m, came in only one second behind his compatriot Charles Matthisen. Altogether the Norwegians carried off seven gold, five silver and three bronze medals from a total of 17 events. The long-distance ski-races also all went to the men from the north: Finland won the 4 × 10km relay, Erik August Larsson of Sweden the 18km cross-country, Oddbjörn Hagen of Norway the combination cross-country and jumping, and Elis Viklund of Sweden the 50km endurance.

Only in the pairs figure-skating and the downhill skiing, both men's and women's, did the host nation excel. For the first time in the Winter Olympics, an element of slalom was included in the downhill races. As *Time Magazine* explained, 'Slalom – Norwegian dialect word meaning zig-zag – is the latest craze of Alpine skiers', and at Garmisch it was combined with a downhill race for one trophy. The women's Gold Medal was won by the dashing Christel Cranz, and the men's by Franz Pfnür.

One event which Germany would have greatly liked to win was the extra item added to the curriculum at her own instigation – the unofficial Military Patrol Race, in which teams of four soldiers equipped with rifle and full kit covered a 25km course on skis, stopping halfway to snap-shoot three balloon targets. The race was won by Italy, but Austria took the sharp-shooting prize when her team, though out of breath, destroyed their target balloons with their first three shots.

British skiers did not distinguish themselves, but nobody was much surprised for, according to Arnold Lunn, manager of the British team, his entire training budget had amounted to less than £400. With this paltry sum, made up of voluntary contributions, he had tried to bring 22 people to match-fitness. The German team, in contrast, had been treated like 'gladiators maintained at their country's expense for no other purpose except skiing' since the beginning of 1935, and the girl who represented Germany in the women's figure skating had spent the whole summer training at public expense in the ballet school of the Munich Opera. It gave impoverished foreign competitors no small satisfaction to observe that in spite of this star treatment she was not placed in the first six – and for the British there was a delightful surprise in the performance of their schoolgirl prodigy, 15-year-old Cecilia Colledge, who, but for one fall which left her with the Silver Medal, might have beaten the famous Sonja Henie of Norway, who won the Gold Medal for the third time in succession.

By far the greatest surprise, however, was the performance of the British ice-hockey team, who against all expectations became the new Olympic champions. The success of the underdogs, though immensely popular with the crowd, was not achieved without a number of scorching rows, most of them instigated by the Canadians. The first broke out before play had begun, when two of the British players – Alec Archer and the goalkeeper Jimmy Foster – were suspended at the last minute after an objection from the Canadians that they were not true amateurs. The complaint was rejected, and the players reinstated, by a meeting of the International Ice Hockey Committee – and when on 11 February Great Britain beat Canada 2-1, the crowd was openly partisan. It was reckoned that some 15,000 spectators had crammed themselves into the stadium's 12,000 seats, and, when Britain scored the winning goal 90 seconds from the end, the whole lot went wild. According to the *Daily Telegraph*,

The game finished in a roar of cheers and *Heils*, and as the British team skated off the ice the strong military guard could not keep their cordon intact. Thousands rushed forward to mob their heroes . . . the journey back from the stadium to the hotel was a triumphal procession.

Next day Britain played another thrilling match, this time against Germany, which ended drawn after three periods of extra time. Unfortunately the Führer was not there to see it: political expediency had drawn him to Schwerin and the funeral of Wilhelm Gustloff, the Nazi official assassinated by a Jew in Switzerland. The fact that representatives of 28 foreign countries were gathered in Bavaria did not inhibit him from launching an hysterical attack on Jews in a speech that was broadcast all over Germany. Having announced that the Nazi movement had been responsible for no bloodshed, he screamed out:

> There marches before our eyes an endless line of murdered National Socialists, assassinated in dastardly fashion . . . Behind every murder is the same power which is responsible for this crime, the hate-inspired influence of our Jewish foes . . . We have done nothing to harm the enemy. Yet he tries to place the German people beneath his yoke and make them his slaves.

Next day Hitler was back in Garmisch, along with Goering and Tschammer und Osten, to watch Britain trounce Hungary 5-1. Again the enthusiasm of the crowd was immense. After the game the Führer sent his congratulations to the British dressing-room and agreed to autograph every player's card. On the same afternoon feeling ran so high during the match between Germany and Canada – one of the roughest in living memory – that officials repeatedly broadcast appeals for the crowd to stay calm and for the players to chase the puck rather than each other. With a riot still threatening, first Goering and then Goebbels took the microphone, begging the spectators to observe the Olympic spirit and remember that the Canadians were Germany's guests. When the game-cum-battle eventually came to an end, the score was Canada 6, Germany 2.

On Friday, 14 February, Great Britain scored yet another·

100

triumph in beating Czechoslovakia 5-0; but now the Canadians, seeing that the British stood a good chance of winning the whole competition, launched a formal complaint against the decision of the Olympic Ice Hockey Association to award the Olympic Championship to the team with the highest number of points. When their attempted intervention was rejected, the Canadians were so angry that they threatened to cancel all their post-Olympic engagements, including a match against England in London. Their pique availed them nothing, and the British, duly winning the Gold Medal, became the heroes of the tournament. For hours crowds stood in the cold outside their hotel, cheering and begging for autographs, particularly from Jimmy Foster, who by then was regarded as the finest goal-minder in the world, having stopped 219 shots and conceded only three goals in the course of all his matches.

Neither Great Britain's victory nor the Winter Olympics as a whole did anything to retard Germany's descent into racial infamy. On the day that Britain was beating Czechoslovakia, the Weimar labour court endorsed the new legal principle that the will of the people had superseded the letter of the law, and rejected the appeal of a Jew who had been dismissed from his job because of his race. Having decided that the views of the Nazi Party were finding an ever-greater appeal among the German people, the court laid down that in the economic life of the country a cleavage must be established between Jews and non-Jews.

Such incidents by no means inhibited the Nazi leaders from using the occasion of the Winter Olympics to entertain distinguished foreign visitors who might, if suitably impressed, sing the praises of the New Germany abroad. One such couple was Lord and Lady Londonderry, who passed through Berlin at the end of January on their way to Garmisch. Although their visit was said to be private, they were lavishly entertained in the capital by both Goering and Hitler.

On 30 January they dined with Goering, who announced that, in view of the late King George V's death, the party would be a small and intimate one. There were thus only 35 people present, and the host distinguished himself by loudly proclaiming that the villains of the present political situation were the French, with whom it was impossible to come to any understanding. The Londonderrys also dined with Hitler, and were formally received by him in the Chancellery, before travelling on to Garmisch as Goering's guests.

Afterwards Ivone Kirkpatrick, a member of the British Embassy staff in Berlin, wrote to a friend in the Foreign Office saying that Londonderry himself had appeared 'thoroughly frightened by all he had seen', and 'did not at all give the impression of having been "nobbled" by Goering, despite the latter's efforts'. This, it seems, was an optimistic assessment, for towards the end of February, in a speech at Durham, Londonderry praised the Germans effusively, saying that their aircraft factories could turn out new products far more quickly than English ones and that, if we found ourselves on a different side from Germany in another war, it would be the result of 'a lack of statesmanship'. The last thing the Germans wanted, he said, was 'an alignment of nations for warlike purposes, and to find themselves opposed to Britain and France'.

These remarks drew a stinging rebuke from the *Manchester Guardian*, which said that people would be 'more than ever grateful to Mr Baldwin' for having pushed Londonderry out of the National Government. His wife also drew heavy fire, for she too had succumbed to Hitler's magnetism. 'I saw him drive to the opening of the Olympic Games in Garmisch,' she later wrote in a newspaper article:

> He went in an open car, he stood, an easy target. More than 100,000 people were there to greet him. They were in a frenzy to acclaim him. He gave a dinner for me and my husband at his house in Berlin. I sat next to him. I beheld a man of arresting personality, a man with wonderful, far-seeing eyes. I felt I was in the presence of one truly great. He is simple, dignified, humble. He is a leader of men. And I was greatly impressed.
>
> I am convinced Germany wants friendship with France. The last thing that Germany wants is another war.

Whatever was in his mind, the object of Lady Londonderry's adulation returned to Garmisch to close the Games officially on 16 February. The final ceremony, carried out before the biggest crowd ever seen in the Alps, was dignified, impressive and strongly militaristic. One side of the ski stadium was lined by a crack army regiment in field-grey overcoats and steel helmets. Opposite them were ranks of Labour Service youth, and even the Reich Navy had been called upon to furnish midshipmen, who ran flags up and down the victory flagstaffs in the centre of the arena. Almost all the Olympic medals were presented by a civilian, Dr Ritter von Halt, and, as he handed over each award, artillery boomed out a salute that echoed away among the mountains. (The prizes for the unofficial Military Patrol Race were given by Blomberg, the War Minister.) After dark, as the Olympic flame was extinguished, 10 big anti-aircraft searchlights wove their beams into fantastic patterns across the sky and cast ghostly illumination on the surrounding snow faces. While fireworks flared and smoked, the Olympic flag was lowered and borne into the valley, undulating gently as six skiers carried it off in a horizontal attitude.

With the possible exception of the Canadians, everyone afterwards voted the Winter Games a great success. The organisation had been first-class, the weather almost perfect, and there had been no unseemly racial or social incidents. The New Germany both gained and gave confidence, which bolstered her resolve to put on a world-winning show at the much bigger festival later in the year.

Few of the spectators at Garmisch attracted more attention than Leni Riefenstahl, the actress-turned-film-director, of striking looks and achievement, who had been taken up so enthusiastically by Hitler that many people imagined she was having an affair with him. In fact his admiration was as much for her work as for her person; and she, although quoted as saying that she believed the Führer to be the greatest man alive, claimed that she was never an intimate friend of his.

Born in 1904, the daughter of a Berlin plumber, she trained with the Russian Ballet and made her first professional appearance as a dancer. At the age of 18 she was taken up by the film director Dr Arnold Fanck, and her success was so rapid that soon, besides starring in films, she was writing and directing them as well. Mountains were her milieu: *The White Hell of Pitz Palu*, *Avalanche* and *The Blue Light* (filmed in the Dolomites) all featured stunning mountain scenery, and in all of them Leni Riefenstahl was physically to the fore. A powerful skier, she caused many a sensation by taking to the slopes in a bathing suit, and once excited feverish gossip by spending six weeks in a cabin on Mont Blanc with eight male members of her cast. To make *SOS Greenland* she went to the far north, flew hazardous missions with Ernst Udet, the air ace, skied, climbed, filmed on icebergs, hunted and ate seals. Her combination of strong, angular good looks, physical prowess, powerful intellect and, above all, style fascinated contemporaries; one man who met her in 1934 described her as 'a vigorous outdoor type' who reminded him of a tennis champion but was much better looking.

Her admiration of the Führer was quite uncritical. 'Her adoration of Hitler was pathetic,' wrote one contemporary. 'Her voice breathed reverence whenever she uttered the sacred name.' Later, when defending herself against charges of Nazism, she claimed that she had never subscribed to Hitler's theories about race, had never been a member of the Party, had refused Party medals and honours. Nevertheless, she admitted that she was infatuated with the Führer himself, and it was his admiration for her – the embodiment, as he thought, of all the virtues desirable in an Aryan woman – that had led him to give her the job of filming the Party rallies at Nuremberg.

This great task, of which she made a spectacular success, began in 1933; but in June, 1934, when the film was half-finished, she suffered the unfortunate experience of having some of her leading actors shot – in cold blood rather than on celluloid – during the Roehm purge, so that many scenes had to be taken again, in the autumn of 1934. Even so, *Triumph of the Will* turned out a propaganda epic, enshrining as it did the quintessential Nazi obsession with militaristic pageants held on a colossal scale; and it was after this success that Hitler awarded her the prize task of making the official film of the Olympic Games.

At Garmisch – where she went to pick up ideas for the summer – it was too cold for skiing in the buff. Instead, she indulged her weakness for appearing against mountain backdrops by sporting a full-length white fur coat and looking anything but the *Ölige Ziege* (Oily Goat) which one German film critic had disobligingly christened her.

7
ENGLAND EXPECTS

The Nazis' move in inviting Helene Meyer and Gretel Bergmann to represent Germany struck Sir Eric Phipps as 'a
remarkable decision to take at the present moment'; and it
turned out to be the beginning of a surreptitious easing of
pressure by the German Government, a relaxation which in
due course became known as the Olympic Pause. For most of
1936 Hitler was less strident than in previous years, both at
home and abroad, and supporters of the decision to let the
Games go ahead in Berlin could claim with some justification
that the Festival had led to a form of truce, exactly as in
ancient times. Opponents of the Games could claim with
equal conviction that the Pause was pernicious, since it lulled
the suspicions of foreign governments and gave Hitler a
breathing space in which to press ahead with rearmament. In
January, 1936, British newspapers reported that Germany
seemed to be sailing into a period of calm, even if the calm
preceded a major storm.

In London it does not seem to have occurred to anyone in
the Foreign Office to make capital out of Hitler's fears that his
racist policies might destroy the Games. Even though
Whitehall knew from the reports of the Berlin Embassy how
much store the Nazis had set on making a success of the
Olympics, it took no initiative in using the Games as a lever to
obtain political concessions; and, with inertia prevailing on
the official front, it was left to private individuals to carry on
the debate. Few were more articulate than K. R. Welbore
Ker, who wrote from Malvern to the *Manchester Guardian* in
January:

Is it too late to rouse the nation to take this unique opportunity of expressing our dislike not of the German people, for whom great numbers of us have the sincerest affection, but of the methods of their present rulers, which are in direct contrast to the spirit of the Games? I hope that a strenuous effort may still be made to prevent our sharing in this fantastic and hypocritical farce.

The short answer to Mr Welbore Ker's question was, Yes: it *was* too late to rouse the nation, not least because appeals like his bounced off the British Olympic officials like peas off pachyderms. A glance at the hierarchy of the British Olympic Association shows how aristocratic the direction of athletics in Britain was at that date. The President was Lord Portal, a businessman and landowner. The Chairman of the Council was Lord Burghley, the great hurdler and most famous of British athletes, who had won a Gold Medal in the 400m Hurdles at Amsterdam in 1928 and a Silver Medal in the 4 × 400m Relay at Los Angeles in 1932. The three British representatives on the International Olympic Committee were Lord Burghley, Lord Aberdare and Sir Noel Curtis-Bennett. All these worthies defended the indefensible with unswerving devotion.

On 13 January, 1936, at a lunch given by the British Ice Hockey Association for the American Olympic ice-hockey team, which was passing through London on its way to Garmisch, Curtis-Bennett held forth with characteristic bombast. 'There are a lot of well-meaning busybodies who are trying to mix sport with politics,' he announced during his speech. 'All I have to say to them is, "Hands off sport, politicians." ' As one cynical newspaper reader pointed out, he should have tried saying that in Berlin.

On the academic front, a dogged debate broke out as to whether Oxford and Cambridge should send representatives to the 550th-anniversary celebrations at Heidelberg University. After much argument Oxford decided to send not a representative but an address extolling the greatness of German learning in the past. This by no means pleased the Rector of Heidelberg, Professor Wilhelm Groh, who cancelled Oxford's invitation; but, since he himself had already been party to the dismissal from his university of 44 professors and lecturers for political reasons, his complaint that a British academic institution had 'confused politics' with anniversary celebrations commanded minimal respect. 'It is perhaps not yet generally known in England,' wrote one correspondent acidly, 'that only Nazis are unconditionally allowed to "confuse politics" with learning, art and sport.'

Glimpses of life in Berlin came out with travellers who returned to Britain and were free to describe things as they found them. One such was Eric Dunstan, who visited the German capital in January. Walking the streets with a soldier friend, he reported, was a curious experience, because the man was required to salute not only officers but all other soldiers and indeed anyone in uniform, including policemen. In consequence he was constantly whipping his right arm up and down like a frenzied puppet.

Another friend told Dunstan that for the past few months he had been leaving his flat every night at 1am and returning at 8am, because police raids took place at four or five in the morning. Though his conscience was clear, he had no means of knowing who might have informed against him, or for what.

In February the Winter Olympics at Garmisch temporarily diverted the attention of sporting organisations, but soon the British Olympic Council was under fire again. The Oxford University undergraduate magazine *Isis* came out against the Games, saying that they would take place 'in a hate-poisoned, crazy atmosphere'. Instantly Lord Aberdare struck back with a letter to the *Oxford Magazine*. 'It does not seem generally known,' he wrote, 'that these Games are entirely in the hands of the International Olympic Committee.'

The Committee were seriously alarmed at the time of the ill-treatment of the Jews, but decided that they could not be drawn into political and other controversies. To safeguard Olympic sport, they got guarantees from the German authorities that German Jews should not be debarred from representing Germany, that Jews of all nations will be welcome, that there would be no demonstration against any Jewish competitor at the Games.

Germany will be represented by more Jews than has ever been

the case before, and there are today German Jews training and competing for places. The difficulty for Jews to get training in Germany has been grossly exaggerated, to which the Jewish organisations in Germany will testify.

The myopic complacency of this statement exactly typified the attitude of the British Olympic Council. In fairness it must be said that their position was extremely difficult; at the same time, it is hard to see how they could ignore the truth and close their eyes so firmly to the fact that the persecution of Jews and Catholics was by then highly organised and vindictive. What did Aberdare mean by writing that his Committee had been seriously alarmed 'at the time of the ill-treatment of the Jews'? Did he believe that the ill-treatment had ceased?

Whatever he thought, there were many people in England who supported his general view. When a correspondent styling himself 'Aryan' protested to *The Times* about the military nature of sport in Germany, another reader, Mr T. D. Richardson, stuck up for the Reich and its methods:

> Has 'Aryan' forgotten that for generations we have been told with snobbish satisfaction that the battle of Waterloo was won on the playing fields of Eton? Can one therefore blame Germany for taking a leaf out of our book? The fact that Germany is taking the trouble to organise sport thoroughly, to bring it within the grasp of all, whether rich or poor, instead of leaving it to organise itself in our own haphazard way, is in accordance with national character and is merely another proof of the wonderful new spirit that animates all, from old to young, in that country today.
>
> Sport in Germany . . . is producing in the young a sense of duty, a respect for discipline, a realisation of their obligations to their country. . . . Were this spirit, be it military or not, inculcated into our athletes . . . nothing but good would come of it.

The various British athletic bodies were determined that the Games should go ahead, come what might. Dr George Gretton, an Englishman who happened to be working in Germany early in 1936, got hold of a directive sent round by the central authorities to all Nazi-controlled offices, ordering them to give three months' leave, with full pay, to every candidate for the Olympic team, so that he or she could go into full-time training. Gretton sent the notice to a friend on the committee of the Amateur Athletics Association in London, pointing out that the order made all the German competitors professionals. According to the rules of the day, any amateur who competed with a professional *ipso facto* lost his own amateur status. Therefore, Gretton suggested, the British team should withdraw from the Games. He heard later that his motion was debated at a special meeting, but was defeated by the casting vote of the Chairman, on the ground that sport should be kept out of politics.

Nor would the British Olympic Council associate itself with an appeal to Hitler secretly submitted by Dr William Temple, the Archbishop of York. Reminding the Führer that the ancient Games had always brought a truce, Temple wrote:

> We appeal to your Excellency to show yourself no less generous than the Greeks, and to issue a general act of amnesty for the benefit of all those who are suffering imprisonment for religious or racial reasons.

When the BOC refused to have anything to do with the appeal, it was sent privately to a leading official in the German sports world – perhaps Carl Diem – but seems never to have reached its intended recipient.

Hitler's sudden reoccupation of the Rhineland on 7 March – the most blatant act of promise-breaking which he had so far dared commit – naturally fanned the Olympic controversy into a still more active fire. In Paris M Jules Rimet, President of the French National Sports Committee, said that there could no longer be any question of France taking part in the Games, and the newspaper *Paris Soir* suggested that a boycott would prove a very effective form of economic sanction against Germany. Its article estimated that Germany would benefit from the Games to the extent of £14 million in foreign currency, and that refusal by other nations to participate would mean a severe loss of money as well as prestige. In Geneva it was suggested unofficially at the League of Nations that teams of member-countries should organise a mass abstention from the Olympics. In London *The Daily Telegraph* floated rumours that the entire Olympiad would be abandoned, but these were immediately discounted by a member of the British Olympic Committee, who assured the paper that no move to organise a boycott had been heard of by either the British or the French authorities. From Honolulu, through which he happened to be passing, Count Baillet-Latour lent authority to the denials with one of his inimitable pronouncements. Only an armed conflict, he told a press conference, would prevent the holding of the Olympic Games in Berlin. Otherwise, no change in the arrangements was acceptable.

The upheaval evidently left the British authorities feeling apprehensive, for on 17 March the heavy guns of the British Olympic Council all signed a letter to *The Times* in which they made a plea for adequate representation at the Games:

> The British Olympic Council are convinced that in sending a team to Berlin they are acting in the best interests of sport. The Olympic Games have always stood for the ideal of harmony and reconciliation between nations, and it would have been nothing short of a calamity if, at this very critical stage in world affairs, this country, to whom the world so often looks for a lead, were not fully represented at a gathering which will include athletes from almost every other nation.

In explaining the need for money – and the fact that the British team would have to rely on the support of the public – the Council appealed to 'generosity and patriotism, to help us maintain not only Great Britain's reputation in games and sportsmanship, but the influential place the country has always occupied in world affairs'. The authors did not seem to notice that in their letter they endorsed the very idea which until then they had so strenuously sought to deny: that the Games would inevitably have political overtones, and did involve matters of national prestige.

Doubt, by then, had seeped into the bones of even the most strongly committed organisations. On 22 March, at the annual general meeting of the Amateur Athletic Association, a motion was put forward by a representative of the National Workers' Sports Association that Britain should not go to Berlin. The proposal excited keen debate, and one person present reported a sharp change of attitude from a few months earlier. Before, no one had given much thought to what was going on in Germany; now almost every speaker deplored the state of the country. But there were two considerations which, above all others, made the majority uneasy about pulling out. One was the idea that it would be inconsistent for the British, having taken part at Garmisch, not to take part in Berlin; the other, that people felt that this was 'a moment for behaving with particular tact towards Germany, and not increasing the bitterness which she at present feels for her neighbours'. (This idea exactly matched that of the Foreign Secretary, who thought that the most dangerous thing to do to Hitler would be to annoy him.)

One of the most influential speakers who supported participation was Harold Abrahams, himself Jewish, an outstanding sprinter, and Gold Medallist in the 100m at Paris in 1924. The isolation of Germany, he thought, would not be good for world peace. 'If the British team goes to Berlin, it will be an influence for the good.' No vote was taken, and the NWSA representative was persuaded to withdraw his motion on the understanding that the AAA would call a special meeting later if his organisation insisted. This was the nearest the British ever came to backing out of the Games, and over the next few weeks many people evidently swung back in favour of participation: when the NWSA did insist on having its motion debated, and an extraordinary general meeting of the AAA was called in May, the proposal for abstention was defeated by an overwhelming majority of 200 votes to 8.

On 23 March the matter was raised in the House of Commons, when Commander Oliver Locker-Lampson, the Conservative Member of Parliament for Handsworth, asked the Chancellor of the Exchequer if he was aware that the Olympic Games would benefit German finance by several million pounds, and that such currency was now being used to subsidise rearmament; and if he would prohibit the use of British money for this purpose. Replying for the government, Mr Morrison, the Financial Secretary, said that Mr Chamberlain had no power to prevent persons in Britain from spending money in Germany if they wanted to.

Anglo-German relations, already tense, became still more difficult with the sudden death of Hoesch, the German

111

Ambassador in London, who expired at the Embassy in Carlton House Terrace on 10 April with a suddenness that set tongues wagging. Two other German envoys had died unexpectedly in recent months – in Paris and Brussels – and, because Hoesch had been notoriously anti-Nazi, rumour immediately flew that he had been poisoned. 'The latest addition to the story,' recorded one Foreign Office minute, 'is that Princess Bismarck was seen coming down the Embassy steps with an empty bottle of poison in her hands.' Her husband, the German Chargé d'Affaires, denied the rumours emphatically and said that the cause of death had been heart-failure. Nevertheless, on 26 May a Mr H. A. Gray of Barnes wrote a private and confidential letter to Vansittart, saying:

> Information has reached me from an unimpeachable source that the sudden death of the late German Ambassador . . . was not due to natural causes but to potassium cyanide self-administered.

By then the minds of many British Members of Parliament were exercised about the fate of Ernst Thälmann, the former head of the German Communist Party, who had been in gaol, without trial, for three years. One hundred and eight of them had signed a memorandum to the German Government demanding that Thälmann should either be released immediately or given an early trial. Getting no reply, the group deputed two of their number, S. O. Davies and Ellis Smith, to go to Berlin and press for an answer. The little delegation set out on 15 April, but – it need hardly be said – was unable to obtain any definite assurance.

Throughout the Olympic controversy the Foreign Office was at pains to remain aloof. Thus in March, when Lord Burghley invited the Prime Minister to attend the official British Olympic dinner on 19 May, a Foreign Office minute recorded:

> It is, I understand, the habit of HMG to make clear that they have no connection with, and no responsibility for, the British Olympic Committee and its works.

A decision about whether or not the Prime Minister should

accept the invitation was delayed as long as possible, but in the end it was agreed that he ought to decline.

More direct pressure came on the Foreign Office in April, when Señor Condé of the Spanish Embassy in London wrote asking if the British athletic associations were going to take part in the Olympic games, and, if they were, whether the entry of the British teams would be 'of a purely private nature', or whether they would 'receive assistance of any kind from the Government'.

This inquiry produced a large scatter of hand-written minutes. 'HMG studiously avoid any official connexion with the British Olympic Games Committee,' said one:

> When we receive invitations officially from Foreign Governments to take part in the Games, we usually return a non-committal reply, to the effect that British participation is left entirely in the hands of the British National Committee, but that should any members of the fighting services be selected to participate or compete, facilities will be given for them to do so.

The official answer sent to the Spanish Embassy was singularly unhelpful. The Foreign Office affected not to know – though one telephone call or a glance at the newspapers would have told them – whether a British team would go to Berlin or not:

> The question of British participation . . . is left entirely in the hands of the above Association, a private organisation with whom His Majesty's Government have no connexion, and there is no question of any official patronage or assistance (financial or otherwise) being given to the British team.

The truly amateur status of the British team was emphasised by the scale of the fund-raising which supported it. In a testy note the British Olympic Council remarked that 'few, if any, of the competitors subscribe to the Appeal fund, and some have no idea how the money which takes them to the Games is obtained. Perhaps if they realised how difficult it is to obtain, and how limited the amount, the complaints received would be considerably lessened.'

British society was then solidly stratified into upper, middle and working classes. (A glance at the Personal advertisement columns of *The Times* gives an immediate idea of the rigidity that prevailed, vacancies in 'The Household' being sub-divided into Cooks, Cook-Generals, Housemaids, Kitchen Maids, Housekeepers, Parlourmaids, House Parlourmaids, Companions and Helps, Au Pair, Nurses and General Servants.) The committee found it necessary to emphasise that the team would be 'drawn from all classes of the community . . . without any regard whatsoever to the origin, religious belief or political creed of competitors'. The council's general appeal repeated several of the points made in the letter to *The Times* and struck an unctuous note in proclaiming:

> This is the first time that the International Olympic Committee have held the Games in Germany, and the Germans are deeply conscious of the obligations into which they have entered.

The target for the appeal was between £10,000 and £15,000, but, perhaps because of the uncertain political climate, the response was disappointing. The total amount collected was only £9,034 10s.2d., and of this nearly a third came from two munificent benefactors – Lord Portal, who gave £2,000, and Lord Nuffield, who gave £1,000. Other donors included Portals (the firm), which gave £500, *The News of the World* (£250) and *The Daily Telegraph* (£50). Lord Louis Mountbatten, Watford Grammar School and James Purdey & Sons, the gunmakers, each contributed £5.

In the event, the modest sum raised proved more than enough. The entire cost of the Berlin expedition came to just over £4,000, and that of the trip to the Winter Olympics only £259. Office expenses for the year amounted to £831, leaving the association with a surplus for 1936 of nearly £4,000.

As fund-raising proceeded, some private protestors, misguidedly putting their faith in Whitehall, wrote to the Foreign Office rather than to the newspapers. Among them was Dr A. G. Yahuda, a professor of Hebrew literature who had lived in Germany for more than 20 years before moving to the safety of England. Like the French, he claimed that a successful boycott of the Olympics would deal a crippling blow to the status of the Nazi leaders. There was nothing to which they, and especially Goebbels, attached such importance as the success of the Games, he wrote.

> Nothing would so much weaken the position of the Nazis and shatter their prestige as the failure of the Olympiad. . . . It would finish Goebbels' career and further deepen against him the hatred of the people everywhere.

Dr Yahuda professed himself outraged by the tolerant view of Hitler taken in Britain. 'Everyone who comes from Germany speaks with amazement of the lenient British policy towards Germany,' he wrote. He demanded that the British people should be enlightened about 'the real purpose of the Olympiad' – the glorification of the Nazi regime – and that

> all possible means should be employed to frustrate the hopes laid by Nazi propagandists upon the success of the Games. The lessons of the past three years of continuous breaches of treaties and campaigns of lies should at least convince everyone of the futility of dealing with such people, and of the great danger it involves.

Hitler, he presciently observed, 'is the new Mahdi who is going mad with his success, and is driving Germany and the whole world into an abyss of despair and annihilation'.

There is no evidence that the Foreign Office paid any heed to this stirring appeal, or that its author received anything but a formal acknowledgement. This is not to suggest that people in the Foreign Office regarded Hitler with equanimity. Far from it. They were extremely apprehensive, and in the summer of 1936 they got the British Embassy in Berlin to prepare a digest of the central ideas in *Mein Kampf*, which they printed and circulated to many foreign governments, as well as to the League of Nations. They also commissioned E. L. Woodward, Professor of History at All Souls, to write a long memorandum on the mentality of Hitler and the militant German State. After an extensive historical survey, he came to a stark but clear conclusion:

> The facts of history are there; the philosophy is there. The machine is working again at full steam. It would be absurd not to

face the situation. Facing the situation means realising that you cannot trust any promise these people make. Of course they are trying to beguile us – why not? . . . I think myself that I should go for calling spades what they are. I should be quite open and say that we cannot trust the present regime, and will come to no agreement with them. If agreements are worthless, why make them? . . . We know that about 300 people a month are still being done in by the Nazi police, but we shall hurrah all right at the Olympic Games.

In the margin alongside these paragraphs Anthony Eden, the Foreign Secretary, scrawled in his soft, loopy writing, in red ink as usual: 'This is so interesting that I feel tempted to circulate it to my colleagues, or to some of them.' In due course the paper was circulated. Mountains of memoranda were circulated. But nobody did anything to check Hitler, because nobody had the first idea how to tackle him.

8

COUNTDOWN IN BERLIN

While the British belatedly argued, preparations in Germany were grinding inexorably forward. The first great event of 1936 – a triumph of publicity in itself – was the transport of the mighty Olympic bell from Bochum to Berlin. The bell itself weighed 9,635kg (9½ tons) and, according to the official description, was 'pitched in E of the minor octave; the first overtone, lying in the interval of the minor third of the main tone, was pitched in G, so that the total effect was a minor one'. Round the rim of this monster, in Gothic script, ran the legend, *'Ich rufe die Jugend der Welt'* – 'I call the youth of the world'. The clapper alone weighed 791kg (15½ cwt), and the wooden yoke on which the bell was to be hung another 3,415kg (3½ tons).

To move the assembly to Berlin, a special vehicle was needed, and luckily one already existed – a flat truck which had been built for the transport of an immense block of granite to the Hindenburg Memorial at Tannenberg, and which was now graciously given to the Olympic Committee by the German Railways.

On 16 January, travelling at a stately 12mph, the vehicle set off from Bochum on what turned out to be a triumphal procession. The bell progressed slowly enough for word to run ahead of it, so that immense enthusiasm built up along its route. On the first day it passed through Dortmund, Unna and Werl to Herm, where it was greeted by bands, marching troops and speeches. Then it went on to Bielefeld, where it was escorted into the town by runners and a squadron of the

117

Nazi Motor Corps. On the stretches between Bielefeld and Oeynhausen ice reduced its progress to a crawl, and it took 10 hours to cover less than 20 miles, with the result that a day of rest planned for Hanover had to be eliminated. In Brunswick it was greeted by factory sirens, church bells, the band of the Luftwaffe and the inevitable address of welcome; as it ground on towards Magdeburg, schoolchildren, stormtroopers, special bodyguards and countless onlookers formed escorts for it in every village, constantly interrupting its advance. In Magdeburg itself the entire population turned out to salute it: torch-bearers, spotlights and flags surrounded it while a chorus of children gave a rendering of the Olympic Hymn.

The journey to Potsdam brought special difficulties. Near Eiche a long detour had been planned to avoid a low railway bridge, but at the last minute it was discovered that a wooden bridge on the alternative route was too weak to bear the bell, and the structure had to be reinforced by pioneers. In Potsdam – the final stop before Berlin itself – the police had installed floodlights in the town square. Thousands of people thronged the streets, and the mayor made a speech of welcome.

In Berlin at last, the bell processed through the city by way of Kurfürstendamm and Charlottenburgerchaussee to the Brandenburg Gate, then along Unter den Linden, and finally to Kaiser Franz Josef Platz, where, in an elaborate ceremony, it was presented to the Olympic Committee. During the next few weeks it was exhibited in four other main squares before being taken to the May Field. The date and time of its elevation into the Bell Tower were kept secret, so as to avoid attracting crowds, and there were only about 100 people present when lifting began at 7am on Monday, 11 May. The difficult feat was quickly accomplished: by 7.55am the bell had reached its position at the top of the 220ft tower, and an announcement to this effect was made at 9am. The first ringing trial took place on 20 May. Altogether, the saga of the bell captured the imagination of the German people, and focused their attention on the approaching Festival, with a success unexpected even by Goebbels. Only one error marred the campaign – the juxtaposition, in some publicity material, of the slogan 'I Call the Youth of the World' and a photograph of the Führer. Goebbels was realistic enough to know that the idea of Hitler himself summoning the youth of the world would be both offensive and ludicrous to many foreigners, so as quickly as possible the photograph was dropped.

All the time the propaganda machine continued to pour out information, both at home and abroad. Foreign capitals from London to Buenos Aires were flooded with posters. In London, during the Oxford and Cambridge boat-race, in March, 40 sandwich-men were hired by the German Railways bureau to carry placards along the banks of the Thames and through the streets of the city. Above Chicago the stunt flyer Gerd Achgelis performed aerobatics in a machine painted with the five-ring Olympic symbol.

On 15 April the politicisation of German sport was carried still further by an announcement in Berlin from Dr Frick, Minister for the Interior, and Dr Rust, Minister for Education, who proclaimed the foundation of a new Reich Academy of Athletics. The main function of this body would be to train instructors for 'the physical development of German youth'; but it was also frankly admitted that the academy's aim would be to impart 'political German athletic education', and that to pass out of its courses students would have to furnish proof of their capability as political instructors. Once the Olympic Games were over, the academy would set up its headquarters in the new buildings of the Reich Sport Field, and the dormitory to be used by the women competitors in the Games would accommodate 500 students.

This development further increased British doubts about the propriety of taking part in the Festival, with the result that the annual dinner of the British Olympic Association, held at the Dorchester Hotel on 19 May, took place in an uneasy atmosphere. By then even the Olympic officials could not help being aware of the strong current of public feeling against the Games, and tension at the dinner was increased by the presence of Sir Thomas Inskip, Minister for the Coordination of Defence, and Prince von Bismarck, from the German Embassy. Portal, proposing the health of the guests, gamely described Germany as a 'wonderful country, guaranteeing everyone fair treatment', and Inskip, replying, resorted to elephantine jocularity. He hoped, he said, that one result of the Games would be to make his own post a sinecure.

Among those lobbying for the Games, however, Aberdare was by now in a class of his own, having established a position almost of self-parody. In the issue of the magazine *World Sports* for May, 1936, he claimed that Hitler had not 'attempted to influence the organisation and control over the Games in any way, his only concern being that the guests of Germany shall be happy and go away satisfied and convinced that he and his colleagues hold the welfare of international sport very dear'. Aberdare also insisted that in Germany every facility had been given to non-Aryans 'of the necessary standard to take part in the Games and train for them'. He also claimed that although he had investigated complaints about injustice to individual Jewish athletes, neither he nor his colleagues 'had yet heard of a genuine case of an Olympic athlete being boycotted or impeded because of his non-Aryan origin'. His most fatuous remark of all concerned the International Olympic Committee. This organisation, he said,

> is more closely in touch with the affairs of world sport than any other body. The public may rest assured that if that body suspected for an instant that its object would be assailed or its charter violated, there would be no Olympic Games in Berlin this year.

Aberdare laid the blame for the general unease about Berlin squarely on the newspapers:

> The Press seems to me to fail lamentably in its duty of giving the true state of affairs to the public. It chooses to link its political aversion and hatred of international sport, instead of spreading the true doctrine that sport should be non-political.

As spring gave way to summer the French – who felt more immediately threatened than any other nation by Hitler's expansionist policies – dithered desperately over the question of whether a boycott of the Games would do good or bad. In a telegram to the Foreign Office marked 'Very Confidential' and sent on 16 May, Phipps remarked:

Left parties in France are putting pressure on French Government to refuse to send French candidates to Olympic Games. French Ambassador is doing his utmost to oppose any such decision. He points out to his Government that it would mean the end of any hope of agreement between France and Germany, and that unless France could persuade several other countries to boycott Olympic Games, it would be futile. His Excellency feels sure Soviets are behind this as they have of course not been invited to the Games.

This despatch attracted a characteristic Foreign Office minute:

This sort of thing leads one to believe that HMG are right to have no official connection whatever with the Olympic Games. They lend themselves to every possible kind of propaganda.

While the French struggled towards a decision – which was, eventually, that their team should take part – a discreet attempt was being made to effect a meeting between Hitler and Stanley Baldwin, the British Prime Minister. The intermediary was Tom Jones, a retired civil servant who held no official position but enjoyed the confidence of Baldwin and other senior politicians. Having lunched alone with Ribbentrop in London during April, Jones found himself invited to Berlin on an unofficial visit in May, and stayed with Ribbentrop at his house in Dahlem. There he learnt that the Führer had expressed a strong desire to meet Baldwin. Hitler, Ribbentrop assured him, was exactly *like* Mr Baldwin: 'He lives the life of an artist and is devoted to music and pictures . . . The fundamental idea of National Socialism is not to conquer and dominate others, but to be ourselves.'

Falling for Ribbentrop's smooth overtures, Jones went along with the plan. After a visit to the new Olympic installations, he flew to Munich and met Hitler in his official flat at 16 Prinzregenstrasse. The Führer did not harangue his visitor, and made no attempt to 'impress or aggress' him, but urged upon him the importance of forging an alliance with Britain and his own great desire to meet Baldwin. When Jones pointed out that Baldwin was 'a shy and modest statesman who had never entirely got over his astonishment at

finding himself Prime Minister', Hitler smiled and inter-
jected, 'And I also.'

Returning to London, Jones at once wrote Baldwin a
memorandum: 'If it is our policy to get alongside Germany,
then the sooner Phipps is transferred elsewhere, the better.
He should be replaced by a man . . . able . . . to enter with
sympathetic interest into Hitler's aspirations.' He urged
Baldwin to aim for a secret meeting as soon as possible, and
set about trying to arrange one. The difficulties, however,
proved formidable. That Hitler should set foot in Britain was
out of the question. Baldwin might conceivably go to Germany, but he had never flown and hated the sea. Ribbentrop
proposed a compromise: the statesmen should meet on board
a vessel 'quite close to our coast, two or three miles off Dover
or Folkestone'. Before this improbable rendezvous could be
set up, Baldwin became exhausted and was sent off by his
doctors on two months' holiday, thereby effectively knocking
the plan on the head.

In Europe memories of the Great War were still far too
vivid for most people to feel easy about German intentions.
Already there had taken place in France the annual *désobus-
age* or de-shelling of the Western Front, during which, even in
the 18th year after the Armistice, the former battlefields
yielded unexploded shells by the thousand; and in July King
Edward VIII travelled to the Vimy Ridge to unveil a memorial to the Canadians who had died there. Together with his
official party, the royal visitor toured part of the trench-
system, which had been preserved in concrete as a permanent
and terrible warning to future generations.

Any hopes that the Nazi attitude to sport might become less
chauvinistic at the last minute were dispelled by the unexpected victory of the heavyweight boxer Max Schmeling over
the American Black Joe Louis on 19 June. Already a popular
sporting figure in Germany, and a friend of Goebbels,
Schmeling became a national hero overnight when, as a 10-1
outsider, he knocked out Louis in the 12th round of a
non-title fight in New York. Returning home in the Zeppelin
Hindenburg, he found himself fêted and invited to meet the
Führer. As the huge airship arrived at Frankfurt on 29 June,
after battling against a gale, Schmeling was allowed to dis-

embark as soon as she was moored to the tower, although all the other passengers had to wait till she was in the hangar. On the ground he found his wife, the dashing filmstar Annie Ondra, and his mother, both of whom had been flown to meet him in a special plane arranged by Goebbels. There was also a Nazi band, and a posse of sports officials. After a reception, Schmeling was driven through streets lined by cheering crowds to the Town Hall, where he was welcomed by the mayor and appeared on the balcony before a vast throng – after which he hastened to Berlin for tea with the Führer. It was left to *Die Schwarze Korps* – the official organ of the SS – to explain with its customary refinement what the victory meant:

> It was more than a boxing match. Here black and white confronted each other, and all the foes of Nazi Germany, whatever their colour, reckoned on the brutal overthrow of the German. It was not only Joe Louis that was defeated. The sporting spirit of the great masses of population felt instinctively that our comrade saved the reputation of the white race.
>
> Schmeling's victory was not only sport. It was a question of prestige for our race. With his hard fists he has won the respect of the world for the German nation – from which we shall conclude that we have only ourselves to rely upon, and that nobody presents us with anything for which we have not fought.

Stirred up by this Aryan triumph, the German newspapers began to demand that a world-heavyweight-title fight between Schmeling and the holder, James Braddock, should be staged in Germany, perhaps in the Olympic Stadium, after the Games. (Later, when Louis knocked out Schmeling in their return match, *Der Arbeitsmann*, the organ of the Nazi Labour Corps, explained that the American was 'a wild monster of the jungle, who knows how to beat white men by a barrage of cheating blows to the liver'.)

In spite of the torrent of soothing propaganda from Berlin, protests continued to splutter in other countries. On 20 June it was reported in Paris that France would not take part in the Games officially, even if individual French sports federations still wanted to send teams; and on 23 June there came from Barcelona an announcement that threw Goebbels into a great rage. The Spanish Government had organised a meeting of sporting representatives from 20 countries to plan a rival Olympic Festival at the end of July. The aim was to express opposition to Nazi exploitation of sport, the official object 'to counter the Berlin Games with a popular sports festival which does not hope for record feats, but intends to preserve the true Olympic spirit of peace and cooperation between nations'. Already Canada, the United States, Poland, Palestine, Denmark, Norway, Sweden, Holland and Russia had promised to take part, and the British National Workers' Sports Association hoped to send a team of 40. Altogether some 10,000 visitors were expected, the only condition for entry being possession of 'the true sporting spirit and an honest will against Fascism'.

Soon the rot spread to Austria. On 5 July Judith Deutsch, the leading woman swimmer in her country, a Jew, and the holder of 12 national records, announced that she would not go to Berlin. When nominated for the team by the Austrian Olympic Committee, she said, 'I refuse to enter a contest in a land which so shamefully persecutes my people.' The Austrian Swimming Association immediately banned her for two years, but she received more than 100 telegrams from all over Europe congratulating her on taking such a courageous stand. Soon she was joined by two fellow-swimmers, also Jewish – Ruth Langer and Lucy Goldman – both of whom were also banned. Not surprisingly, the Austrian women's swimming team did not distinguish itself in Berlin.

As athletes agonised in other countries, a combination of brute force and silvicultural wizardry had transformed the appearance of the Olympic complex. As the construction work ran down, more than 1,000 mature trees were dug up and transported to the Reich Sport Field with their roots still embedded in great lumps of earth. Replanted, heavily watered, and if necessary shaded by vertically slung banners of canvas, oaks, birches and pines grew as if they had always stood there, so that many visitors to the Games imagined they were strolling through old-established parkland. Some 30,000 hedge-birches were also installed, and, because it had recently been discovered that soil bacteria were sensitive to light, the planting was all done at night, so as to disturb the microbes as little as possible. The trick seemed to work, for the hedges also flourished, and scarcely a single bush failed.

The Olympic city itself was given a face-lift by the labours of engineer, mason, architect and house-painter. The Tiergarten railway station, at which most visitors arrived, was rebuilt to look light and gay. Even the backs of houses facing the main railway terminals were painted white or cream. Dingy corner sites were patched up, and empty shops let at artificially low rents to give an air of prosperity and bustle. Unter den Linden had been changed almost out of recognition by the removal of the ancient lime avenues and the fitting of new lights. Such drastic surgery made many Berliners uneasy: a popular song reminded them that, as long as the trees remained in Unter den Linden, *'Berlin bleibt doch Berlin'* – Berlin will always be Berlin. Now that the trees had gone, might not something terrible happen? For the moment, however, all was hectic progress. Friedrichstrasse, whose shabbiness had, in the eyes of one visitor, given it a 'peculiar and slightly sinister' charm, had been done up with dazzling white stone 'and rather massive vitreous smartness' at its junction with Unter den Linden. New paint gleamed everywhere, and every shop-front was emblazoned with the five Olympic rings. Householders had been exhorted to plant their window-boxes with summer flowers rather than with vegetables.

Out in the country, a similar drive was being pushed through. On 23 May a circular had gone out from Walther Darré, the Minister of Food and Agriculture, to all branches of the government's Food Control Board, with instructions on how the rural population was to conduct itself. 'Hundreds of thousands of foreigners will arrive for the Olympic Games,' said the notice, 'so we must make it our duty to display the German countryside and the German village to their very best advantage.' All rubbish was to be cleared from villages and arterial roads. Streets and footpaths were to be cleaned. Houses on main roads were to be whitewashed or painted, fences and signposts renovated. In the period 1 July to 15 September gangs of farm labourers, hay-mowers and others working in the fields were forbidden to spend their breakfast or lunch intervals, 'or intervals of any kind', on the edges of the roads, where passing tourists might see them idling.

> In districts where convict labourers are working on the land, these labourers must not be employed near the roads. If this is impossible, their labour must be suspended altogether for the period in question. Political prisoners and inmates of concentration camps are in no circumstances to work on the land from 1 July to 1 September.

Darré found it necessary to make special mention of the fact that among the tourists there might be Jews. 'Possible Jews must therefore be treated just as politely as Aryan guests,' he wrote, and he gave orders that everybody was to 'display an amiable and accommodating manner to strangers'.

> In no case must Jewish provocateurs get a chance of creating incidents which will add grist to the mill of hostile propagandists abroad. For this reason all signs posted in the fight against Jewry must be removed for the period in question.

In shameless acknowledgment of the fact that these innovations were temporary, and no more than skin-deep, the circular added: 'The fundamental attitude of the German people towards Judaism remains unchanged.' This last remark was almost certainly true, but in a sense opposite to the one intended. Most rural Germans were hospitable and rational; it was only their rulers who had taken leave of their senses and become obsessed by racial hatred.

City-dwellers also received special instructions. Orders went out to Nazi guards, stormtroopers and members of the Motor Corps, telling them to be civil to foreigners. Men were to give up their seats to women in buses, trams and trains, 'even if the woman looks like a Jewess'. They were not to discuss anti-semitism between 30 June and 1 September; nor were they to inquire into the origins of 'any exotic-looking stranger' who might catch their eye. In Berlin, as in the country, signs insulting Jews were taken down, and in the final weeks before the Games copies of *Der Stürmer* were no longer posted in the reading-cases on street corners.

Countdown in Berlin

At the beginning of July, Goebbels's publicity machine for once over-reached itself with a serious miscalculation. Through the office of the German State Railways, a poster had been designed, and distributed all over the world, depicting the torch run from ancient Olympia to Berlin. By some prophetic error, which must have been deliberate, the German-Czech frontier had been moved southwards so as to include within the Reich the German-speaking districts of north and west Czechoslovakia. When protests began to pour in, the German Ministry of the Interior ordered the poster's immediate confiscation – and nobody was much impressed when the publicity office claimed that the design was an artistic one and did not pretend to topographical exactitude.

Besides pumping out information, the Nazi leaders also used the effective weapon of inviting notable foreigners to Germany and then entertaining them in style. One prize catch was the American air ace Charles Lindbergh – the first man to fly non-stop from New York to Paris – who arrived in Berlin with his wife Anne Morrow towards the end of July and proved beautifully gullible. As a guest of the regime, he received star treatment, especially from General Milch, head of the Luftwaffe. On 23 July, for instance, Lindbergh was guest-of-honour at a luncheon given by the Air Ministry, and then, after a tea-party for press correspondents at Tempelhof airfield, he went for a flight in a brand-new passenger aircraft. Somewhere over Wannsee he took the controls and threw the huge machine about so violently that he terrified most of the people on board. His stay was packed with high-level entertainment: lunch with the famous Richthofen Squadron, a reception given by the Mayor of Berlin, tea with former Crown Prince Wilhelm, a formal lunch with Goering, and a place in Milch's box for the opening of the Olympics. Between these social highlights he visited aircraft factories. He left Germany – as he was meant to – with a sky-high opinion of the regime's effectiveness.

From his hosts' point of view, the success of his visit was enormous, for he went away full of their praises. In the words of Harold Nicolson, with whom he had tea at Sissinghurst on his way back to the United States,

He admires their energy, virility, spirit, organisation, architecture, planning and physique. He admits they are a great menace, but denies that they are a great menace to us.

Tom Jones was more scathing, and recorded in his memoirs:

Lindbergh had found the atmosphere fraternal, the people congenial, the Press under control, officials deferential, discipline good, morals pure and morale high. It was a refreshing change . . . from the moral degradation into which he considered the United States had fallen, the apathy and indifference of the British, and the decadence of the French.

The German Government had vowed that they would show him everything he asked to see, and since he did not ask to see concentration camps, political prisoners, Jews, Communists, Socialists, social democrats or other opponents of the regime, his picture of the Nazi Reich was a decidedly favourable one.

Whatever effect Lindbergh's effusive public praise of the Nazis may have had, goodwill towards Germany in general was not enhanced by the Amsterdam newspaper *De Telegraaf* which on 1 July published a horrifying account of conditions in the concentration camp at Esterwege. The story came from a German Jew who had recently been released after more than a year's imprisonment, and it recorded – besides the usual privations – the grotesque sense of humour developed by the SS guards.

On 5 June, 1935, a Jewish prisoner called Ivanov had been shot dead 'attempting to escape'. Along with another political prisoner and an interned Catholic priest, the informant was ordered to bury the dead man. As they carried the coffin to the grave, they were ordered to sing cheerful songs, and once they had dug the grave the other Jewish prisoner was made by the SS captain to lie down on the coffin. Then the two other prisoners were told to shovel earth down onto the coffin and the prostrate man. Only when he was on the point of suffocation did the guards allow him to emerge. To them the episode was a splendid joke, and they expected thanks all round for sparing the Jew's life.

A recent innovation at Esterwege was that of 'hanging'. Prisoners were hung up on poles, with their hands tied

FACING PAGE:

Top: 1 August 1936. Hitler leads the cavalcade through the Brandenburg Gate on his way to declare the Olympics open.

Below: At the official opening, Hitler accepts a bouquet from five-year-old Gudrun Diem. On the left, Count Baillet-Latour, President of the International Olympic Committee; on the right, Dr Theodor Lewald, President of the Organising Committee.

Right: The girl who came in vain; banned American swimmer Eleanor Holm Jarrett.

Below: Film-maker extraordinary: Leni Riefenstahl in full cry.

Right: Strength through joy: Karl Hein, German gold-medallist in the Hammer.

Below: Jack Lovelock, in the black stripe of New Zealand, bides his time behind Ny of Sweden at the end of the second lap in the 1,500 Metres.

Above: Helene Meyer gives the Nazi salute from the winners' dais after taking the silver medal in the Foil.

Left: Jesse Owens with Leslie Jeffers, the British wrestler, in the Olympic village.

Below: Owens's triumphs are immortalised in stone on the pillar of the Marathon Gate.

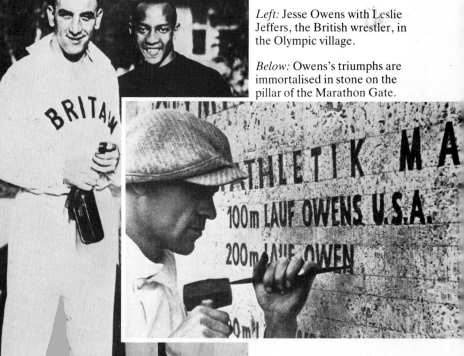

Dr Joseph Goebbels, Minister of Propaganda, weighs up some Olympic art.

Goering welcomes the guests at the Government banquet in the State Opera House.

together, so that their feet swung clear of the ground. One day a 22-year-old prisoner was asked by the Camp Commandant whether he was still a Communist, and when he answered 'Yes' he was hung up every three hours for three consecutive days. 'The pains caused by such hangings,' said the article mildly, 'are unimaginable.'

In spite of his restrained tone, the informant ended with a bitter conclusion:

> All in all, Esterwege Concentration Camp would offer naïve Olympic guests a splendid chance to see what the true Germany is like – but only if they did not have to give a day's notice of their visit, as did a Red Cross delegation which once inspected the camp. The place was cleared up the day before, and the victims of maltreatment were taken away.

This article appeared too late to have any effect on the Olympic preparations, either in Germany or abroad. In Berlin, the stadium was filled for the first time, to test the loudspeakers, on 5 July, and adjustments were made to eliminate echoes. The Olympic bell was rung to test its penetrating qualitites, and the ushers wore their light-blue uniforms to see how well they would stand out among the crowd.

By then the national teams of 52 foreign countries were committed; many were already on their way to Berlin – and indeed some had already arrived there, among them the Australians and the Japanese. In the United States, a last-minute financial crisis had been overcome by the energy of Avery Brundage and the efforts of some individual athletes. The basketball team, for instance, under its captain Frank Lubin, suffered a last-minute setback when the predominantly Jewish Universal Film Studio, which was to have been their sponsor, withdrew its backing and ordered its name taken off the players' shirts. The only way the team could reach New York in time to catch the *SS Manhattan* before she sailed on 15 July was by playing its way across the country. A game in Los Angeles raised enough money for them to reach Denver, Colorado; another match there sent them a stage further, and so on. Their persistence was handsomely rewarded – for in

129

Berlin they won the Gold Medal.

The approach of the Festival could not stop political developments in general, or Hitler's long-range scheming. On 25 July, when emissaries from a little known Spanish General called Francisco Franco were introduced to the Führer during the interval of an opera at Bayreuth, he at once gave them a sympathetic hearing. Their message was that a revolt had broken out against the Republican Government in Madrid. Franco was appealing to Hitler for military assistance: in particular, he needed aircraft to ferry loyal Moroccan troops from North Africa to Spain.

In the eyes of the Führer, the Republican Government in Spain was Red. Here was a chance to strike at the Bolshevist menace in Europe. Within 24 hours he had answered Franco's call, and Luftwaffe transport planes were on their way to Morocco. Less than a week before the beginning of the Festival on which he set such store, Hitler pitched German resources into the beginning of the Spanish Civil War.

The sole effect which the outbreak of hostilities had on the Olympics was to ensure the withdrawal of the Spanish team, some of whom had already arrived in Berlin. But the start of the war dealt instant death to the rival Games planned for Barcelona. There the city was *en fête*. Many teams had gathered, including one of nine men from the United States, and a larger one, 40-strong, accompanied by four Scots pipers, from Britain. The schedule of events included a full Olympic programme, a festival of folk art and an 800-board chess tournament. The official opening was proclaimed by the Prime Minister of Catalonia at 4pm on 19 July, but next morning, when the events should have started, the city was filled with marching troops and the sound of small-arms fire. Civil war was raging, and the rival Olympics were at an end before they had properly begun. The Berlin Festival was left without a challenger.

Protests against the Nazi regime continued until the last moment. On 29 July copies of an anonymous note were delivered to all the foreign legations in Berlin claiming that Gretel Bergmann, the recalled high-jumper, had been excluded from the German team at the last moment. A day later, in London, 18 Members of Parliament signed a letter urging the German Government to extend clemency to Edgar André, the Communist leader who had been in gaol for three years, and had been sentenced to death, after a secret trial in Hamburg.

No such pinpricks, however, could now sink the leviathan already going down the slipway in Berlin. Launched on a tide of lies and propaganda, the mighty ship of the eleventh Olympiad was about to sail.

9

THE TORCH RUN

Like the Games themselves, the torch run from ancient Olympia to Berlin was a triumph of detailed planning. The aim was that the sacred fire should reach the Lustgarten in the capital at precisely 12.59 am on Saturday, 1 August, the day of the official opening, after 3,075 runners had carried it over the same number of 1km stages. A minutely worked-out timetable was thus essential.

Planning had begun in 1935, when two members of the Organising Committee travelled out to Greece and drove home along the route to make a thorough survey. This journey in itself was no mean undertaking, for the prospectors soon discovered that on one part of the Greek section there was no road, so that the physical problems of getting each runner out to his station, and protecting him from sun, wind and rain, were formidable, especially as some of the passes to be crossed were nearly 5,000 ft high. The planners allotted an average time of five minutes for each kilometre, and required each runner to know not only his own stretch but the next one as well, so that if need be he could carry on in an emergency.

Much research went into the torches themselves. The original idea was to go all-out for authenticity and imitate the ancient Greeks, whose torches were said to have been made from bunches of narthex – a plant found especially in the highlands of Ephesus, the pith of which retained fire for long periods. When latter-day narthex proved elusive, however, resort was had to Krupps of Essen, who produced stainless-steel torches

28 inches long, weighing 1½lbs, with magnesium heads that would burn for 10 minutes regardless of rain, wind or sudden shocks produced by (for instance) the runner falling.

The run began on 20 July. At Olympia that morning buglers heralded the rising of the sun, and at noon the sacred fire was kindled in the ancient sanctuary by means of a conical steel reflector which concentrated the vertical rays of the sun onto inflammable material. Spectators were excluded as 13 Greek girls clad in short, belted smocks of rough serge, said to represent the robes of priestesses, lit the fire and kindled the first torch. Then, in solemn procession, they bore it through the arched stone doorway of the ancient stadium to the point where dignitaries of Greece and Germany were assembled. There they lit a new fire in the altar bowl. A gun boomed, and Pindar's Olympic Hymn was chanted to the accompaniment of ancient instruments. A ridiculously long message from Baron Pierre de Coubertin, founder of the Modern Olympics, was read out in French, followed by speeches from the Greek Under-Secretary of State and the German Ambassador. At last the first runner, the powerfully built Kyril Kondylis, wearing only shoes and a pair of shorts, walked up to the altar to kindle the first torch – and the greatest relay-run in history was under way.

Among those present was Leni Riefenstahl, who had come with her film crew to record the historic scene – and she did indeed capture some unforgettable images. None was more haunting than that of the fire travelling at night beside the sea: a crescent of sand, waves breaking, moonlight on the water, and the bare feet of the runner pounding along the shore.

All through Greece excitement mounted as the run stirred memories of the nation's distant past. In the white marble stadium at Athens – rebuilt for the first modern Olympics in 1896 – a huge crowd saw King George II receive the torch and light a flame on a special altar, flanked by 30 maidens in ancient costume and by 52 guards, each bearing the flag of one of the nations due to compete in Berlin. Far out in the plains and mountains, dropped off by bus, car and motorcycle, the chain of runners was waiting – and on hardly any stage did the torch-bearer travel alone. Almost always he was accompanied by a small flock of other runners, determined to give him moral support and join in the great enterprise. As one contemporary account put it, the fire was carried by runners whose names the world will never know, but who were content to be modest servants of a great idea.

For as much of the way as possible, the torch was followed also by the German radio team, who had travelled to Greece at enormous expense to make broadcasts of the run. Three reporters, three engineers and three drivers were accommodated in a 5½-ton cross-country transmitting vehicle and a touring car. Their problems were formidable, not the least being that Greece then had no broadcasting network. The terrain made severe demands on the drivers, who often found they could crawl along at only 10mph, and frequent rainstorms, particularly in the north of the country, kept reducing the roads to quagmires. At one stage the temperature inside the transmitting vehicle reached 122°F, and the discs used for recording became so soft that the needle cut deep into them. Resourceful as ever, the team sacrificed their drinking water to pour over them. In spite of their difficulties, they managed to make broadcasts from Athens, Delphi and Salonika, and their efforts contributed in no small measure to the Olympic excitement building in Germany. There, as in other countries, ancient Olympia (in the Peloponnese) was widely confused with Mount Olympus (in northern Greece), so that many newspaper readers and radio listeners got the impression that the fire was being borne down from the mighty peak traditionally inhabited by the gods of antiquity.

By day and night it crept northwards, into Bulgaria, into Jugoslavia, where for a distance it followed the railway line travelled by the Orient Express. Once in Jugoslavia – horror of horrors – the flame went out, an event never reported in Germany. One of the torches began to flicker and, as it was obviously faulty, it was whipped into a car and driven quickly to the next runner, but expired before contact could be made, so that the next torch had to be lit afresh with a match. At many of the ceremonies memories were evoked of Alexander the Great, born in Macedonia, now part of Jugoslavia.

At every frontier the fire was handed over to runners of the next country with due ceremony. In Hungary the run was seen as an event of great political significance, and the runners were required to increase their speed slightly so as to leave more time for celebration between stages. At night people could see the fire approaching from great distances across the vast Hungarian plain. Everywhere gypsies serenaded the passing torch with music, and in Budapest their chief Magyari performed during a special ceremony. Between Budapest and the Austrian frontier a detour was made through mining districts so that the runners could bring an Olympic greeting to the miners. In Kecskemét, famous for its fruit, an altar was erected in the market square and decked out with Olympic rings fashioned from apricots. In the words of the official German report, 'accompanied by jubilant cries of *Elyen!*, the runners hastened through the Hungarian landscape'.

At the Austrian frontier the fire was taken over by Dr Schmidt, the President of the Austrian Olympic Committee, who himself carried it for the first kilometre in his own country. With his balding head, corpulent figure and baggy track-suit trousers, he cut an eccentric but sporting figure among the escort of fit young men in football gear who accompanied him. Excitement mounted steadily as the torch drew near Vienna, and when it reached the city pandemonium broke loose, for local Nazis seized on the occasion to launch the biggest demonstration against the government that the Austrian capital had ever seen.

By 7.30pm, long before the torch was due to arrive a vast crowd had gathered inside the Hofburg, the centre of government. Locals noticed that the mob looked poor, ragged and half-starved, but the point was that they were in good voice, and the insidious beat of the forbidden Horst Wessel Song, named after a young Nazi martyr, marched repeatedly through the packed square.

Die Fahne hoch, die Reihe fest geschlossen,
SA marschiert mit ruhig, festem Tritt.
Kam'raden die Rotfront und Reaktion erschossen
Marschiern im Geist in unsern Reihen mit . . .

(Raise high the flags, close up the ranks
The SA marches with stealthy, steady tread.

Comrades shot by the Red Front and Reaction
Are marching with us in spirit, in our ranks.)

Again and again the German national anthem, *Deutschland über Alles*, surged up among the throng. As darkness fell a chant of '*Heil Hitler!*' began to burst out, and the police, who should have taken steps to quell such mutinous expressions, stood by doing nothing. At nightfall the setting became still more spectacular, for searchlights picked out the upper storeys of the Baroque buildings all round and etched their outlines against the black sky. When the runner bearing the torch finally came through the gates of the Hofburg, the single word 'Hitler' mounted into a continuous deafening roar.

With the sacred flame lit by the gates, Dr Schmidt began an address of welcome, but the instant he mentioned the name of President Miklas there was a storm of catcalls and booing. Even this, however, was nothing beside the eruption of hostility which greeted Prince Starhemberg, the Vice-Chancellor and head of the *Heimwehr*, or Home Defence Force. Uproar broke out the moment he stepped onto the platform and, even though he had an exceptionally powerful voice and the loudspeakers were turned up to their limit, not a word of his speech could be heard. President Miklas, by contrast, was received in silence, but, when Starhemberg lit a torch of his own and left the Hofburg on the next stage of the run, 10,000 Nazis waiting outside blasted him with a thunderous broadside of hatred and derision. Non-Nazi Austrian athletes taking part in the ceremony were booed, and all members of the pro-Nazi Athletic Association given a rousing welcome.

The message of the evening was clear. In a place as politically volatile as Vienna, the Olympic Games were an explosive subject. No doubt the Nazi leaders in Berlin were delighted to hear that the passage of the fire had been so heartily saluted.

By the time the run reached the Czech-German border on 31 July, anticipation had reached such a pitch that 50,000 people were waiting on both sides of the frontier in the village of Hellendorf to see the torch pass from the last Czech to the first German bearer. As the exchange was made, at 11.45am, tremendous cheering broke out, and according to later German reports people shouted, 'We salute the youth of the world!' Whether or not these words were uttered, the news that the fire was on German soil provoked a nation-wide outburst of trumpet-sounding and band-playing. In many a market square fanfares were blown by Hitler Youth groups, and as the trumpet-voices died away church bells began to peal.

From that point, the ceremonies were continuous. In Dresden and Meissen – indeed all through Saxony – the route was lined by phalanxes of athletes, school-children and members of the Nazi Party ordered out to increase the sense of occasion. Still the run was precisely on schedule, and so it was that at 11.38am on 1 August a runner of the Berlin Brandenburg District 3 accepted the torch at Kilometre Stone 7.3 on the southern boundary of Greater Berlin. The fire had reached the capital on time, and a further short journey through the suburbs would bring it to the Lustgarten.

10

THE SCENE IS SET

The deception was phenomenally thorough. Old hands returning to the city after a spell abroad were astonished at the transformation, and those who had never seen Berlin before were delighted by its brilliance and vivacity. For a start the whole of the Via Triumphalis, the east-west axis of the city, was stunningly decorated. Black, red and white were the dominant colours. The great government buildings lining Unter den Linden were draped with immense banners. People who had known Berlin in earlier days were horrified to find no sign of the famous limes that had given the boulevard its name. The trees had gone; in their place was a forest of huge Swastika banners, 45ft high, and between them sprouted lower masts bearing 20ft banners of German towns. Attached to the bottoms of the masts were shields 5ft in diameter that bore oil paintings of German towns and cities. As the visiting American novelist Thomas Wolfe remarked, the decorations were on a really grand scale – not just miles of looped-up bunting, but banners 'such as might have graced the battle tent of some great emperor'. Everywhere among the black, blood-red and white of the Fatherland fluttered the flags of the nations who were coming to compete in the Games, and at night all this colour took fire under the glare of searchlights.

The Brandenburg Gate was festooned with green garlands and Swastika flags. Greenery had also been used to camouflage ugly building sites. Wreaths suspended above the Charlottenburgerchaussee attracted much favourable comment.

138

The Scene is Set

In the Adolf Hitler Platz – the last important square before the Stadium – concentric circles of flag-poles ringed a central round tower 65ft high, which itself was covered with oak leaves and crowned with 20 Swastika flags. Altogether some 70,000m of oak garlanding had been prepared, the leaves fixed in a preservative that kept them looking fresh throughout the Festival. New paint gleamed everywhere, and householders had taken to heart the official instruction to plant flowers in their window-boxes, each one competing with the neighbours.

All this display, striking though it was, represented no more than the tip of a gigantic effort. Less obvious was the fact that all potentially offensive advertising – including the notices abusing Jews – had been taken down. The copies of *Der Stürmer* normally exhibited in reading-boxes on street corners had disappeared. Conversely, foreign newspapers and magazines which had not been available for years suddenly reappeared in shops and kiosks, giving the impression that censorship did not exist. The German papers for the moment shed their normal rabid chauvinism and made a show of reporting events objectively. Writers whose work had been burned in the Opera Square, opposite the University, on the night of 10 May, 1933, suddenly reappeared in the city's bookshops for the first time.

Nor was the abrupt liberation only intellectual: there was relaxation on the moral front as well. Jazz, allegedly degenerate, was once again allowed in dance-halls and night-clubs. To the great delight of patrons, the Swiss Teddy Stauffer and his Original Teddies were allowed to play swing in the Delphi Palast, while in the Mocca Efty bar in Kurfürstendamm Jack Hylton held sway. The ranks of the city's prostitutes – severely thinned out by the Nazi Government – were stiffened by means of reinforcements drafted in from the provinces.

Every native, official or civilian, was under positive orders to be pleasant to foreigners. The enemies of the Reich might be quiescent for the moment, warned Dr Gerhard Krause, head of the official press office for the Games, but they were still lying in wait for incidents,

for strange behaviour on the part of the spectators which could be

139

interpreted as unsporting . . . So we shall keep ourselves strictiy under control and always remain conscious of our duties as hosts and of our own worth. We shall approach our guests in an open manner, for we have nothing to hide from them. Our hospitality should be winningly heart-felt, but free of obsequiousness.

For most of the population, such instructions were entirely superfluous. Ordinary people were longing to meet foreigners – a pleasure scarcely ever granted them – and as a result visitors found themselves almost overwhelmed with friendliness and hospitality. Often the reception was made still warmer by an element of relief: many Berliners had secretly feared that people would shun the Games, put off by the excesses of the regime, so that they were overjoyed when foreigners actually arrived.

Newcomers were bombarded with helpful advice. People arriving by sea at Bremen discovered an Olympic office established there, ready with help and information. Those approaching Berlin by train found representatives of the German Transport Office on board, and anyone who had not yet secured accommodation was able to make a booking during the final stages of the journey. Those coming by car were similarly cosseted, being met on the outskirts of the city and given advice about the best route to their destination. In Berlin itself the visitors found official interpreters everywhere, distinguishable by their badges, who had been hastily trained for the occasion. The programme had been launched on 15 April, and by 1 August over 4,000 people had applied for the temporary posts. Of the applicants, 500 were put through a six-week course; the only real linguistic weakness was in French, which only about 20 of the 500 could speak fluently. To help make visitors feel at home, a Committee of Berlin Ladies was set up under Frau Margarete Frick, with offices in the Adlon Hotel and the task of organising visits to theatres, museums or places of special interest like Frederick the Great's rococo palace at Potsdam.

Excitement rose as people poured in by road, rail and air. Tempelhof Airport, which in 1935 had handled the unprecedented number of nearly 200,000 passengers, now broke all records; even so, most travellers came by train. Police statistics showed that over 1.2 million visitors arrived in Berlin before or during the Games, some 150,000 of them foreigners.

The city they found was much to their liking; a great capital in festive array, with all the amenities they could imagine – grand hotels such as the Adlon and the Bristol, the Esplanade and the Excelsior, elegant cafés, bars and restaurants along the pavements of Unter den Linden, another mass of bars and night-clubs packed elbow-to-elbow along Kurfürstendamm, stylish stores such as Wertheim in Leipziger Platz (like Harrods, only bigger) and the Kaufhof des Westerns in Wittenberg Plazt, a fine opera house, splendid museums and concert halls . . . and, of course, the central attraction, the new Olympic Stadium. For everyone who saw it, the stadium was initially dumbfounding: it was so big, so beautiful, conceived on such an heroic scale. Especially when empty, it made a thrilling impression: the red cinder track, green grass and grey stone rising tier-on-tier combined to produce a design both harmonious and majestic.

The number of people in Berlin was swelled by the fact that many ancillary events had been organised to coincide with the Games. An immense youth rally brought thousands of boys and girls from 28 foreign nations. A physical education congress – described by the authorities as a Pedagogical Olympiad – drew experts, and 4,000 gymnasts to demonstrate national characteristics, from as far afield as India. An aviation rally brought aircraft, pilots, maintenance crews and enthusiasts to Tempelhof, and a car-rally set hundreds of motorists heading for the capital.

In spite of these extra attractions, interest naturally centred on the 52 national teams. Some of these had already been in residence for weeks – five members of the Japanese team, for instance, had reached Berlin on 20 June after a 12-day journey on the Trans-Siberian Railway, and the Australian team had come a few days later, bringing their inevitable mascot, a kangaroo. But the majority arrived during the last few days of July, and as each one reached the capital it was met with a succession of formal ceremonies. Whenever a team came in, the railway station – generally the Tiergarten – was closed to all other people. Flags, flowers and garlands made the platforms festive for the official greeting, and a band played the national anthem of the arriving country. In an attempt to reduce delay, the authorities had devised a system of coloured luggage labels which they had sent out to all the countries in advance: red was supposed to denote bags destined for the Olympic Village, green those of the rowing and canoeing crews, who were accommodated at Grünau, blue those of the yachtsmen bound for Kiel, violet those of the women, who were to be housed separately on the Reich Sport Field itself, and so on. In practice many teams were idle about using the labels, so that delays often occurred, and, although it was flattering to be so fêted, not everybody was in the best of tempers for the next official welcome, at the Town Hall. With that over, teams bound for the Olympic Village were driven in coaches out to Döberitz – a journey of half an hour. There, at the gates, they found a detachment of Hitler Youth and the Village's own band drawn up waiting. Yet another address, this one by the Commandant of the Village; another rendering of the national anthem; a ceremonial hoisting of their flag – and at last they were free to proceed to their accommodation, where the keys were handed over to their leader. If they happened to arrive after dark, the ceremonies were torch-lit.

All this Teutonic formality was by no means welcome to athletes who had already been travelling for many hours, or even many days. The British men, who had a relatively short journey, left London by train from Liverpool Street at 8.30pm on 29 July and reached Berlin at 4.30 next afternoon. Sleeping-berths had been reserved on the boats; each competitor and official received a free ticket and vouchers for meals during the trip, but otherwise everyone was expected to pay for his own training and equipment. (So strict was the segregation of men and women that the girls in the team travelled separately.) At Döberitz the British found that the dormitory bungalows reserved for them were named Düsseldorf, Duisburg, Emden and so on. Undaunted by being dumped in the industrial wasteland of the Ruhr, they settled in, and afterwards were full of praise for the arrangements in the camp, where almost everything functioned perfectly. Their one serious criticism was that the Village had been sited too far from the stadium: although fleets of vehicles were laid on, and the drivers often worked 14 hours a day, there were so many people continuously wanting to make the nine-mile journey that organisation became a nightmare for the teams' officials.

At once the British realised that they would have done well to reach Berlin sooner (why they did not, it is now impossible to determine). In fact they were one of the last teams to arrive, and they left themselves only a single clear day – 31 July – in which to get acclimatised before the official opening. Their improvidence led to a short, sharp panic on the first day of the events when, because there had been no time for a proper reconnaissance, some of their team got lost in the bowels of the stadium and could not find the changing-room assigned to them.

But at least the British did not arrive with a row blazing in their midst – which was what happened to the Americans. As their liner *Manhattan* docked in Hamburg, Avery Brundage announced to the assembled reporters that the American Olympic Committee had suspended their champion swimmer, Eleanor Holm Jarrett, for misbehaviour during the voyage. The news caused a sensation. Not only had Jarrett been hotly tipped for the Gold Medal in the Backstroke, she was also exceedingly attractive, with a lovely face and a still more exciting figure, both of which she knew how to deploy. Besides, she was exceptionally popular with her team-mates, over 200 of whom signed a petition demanding her reinstatement.

She was already an Olympic Gold Medallist, having won the 100m Backstroke at Los Angeles in record time at the age of 19. Since then she had flirted with Hollywood but had blighted her career in films by refusing to swim for the camera, preferring to keep her speed through the water for the real business of breaking world records. Although in 1933 she had married a singer called Art Jarrett, she had maintained her training, and went aboard the *Manhattan* not only fully fit but fully expecting to defend her title.

The trouble was – as everybody knew – that she disliked Avery Brundage as much as he disliked her, and when he assigned her to a third-class cabin, which she had to share with two other young swimmers, she retaliated by going on a drinking spree in the first-class bar. After an emergency meeting of the AOC, she was warned to keep to the rules of the handbook specially compiled for the guidance of the American team, and in particular to observe the prohibition on alcohol while in training. Although she did not take much notice, she might well have survived had she not gone on another blind the night before the ship reached Europe. Rolling back towards her cabin, she had the misfortune to run into the team's chaperone, who at once sent for a nurse and two doctors; and then, having delivered herself of a few well chosen words of advice, she passed out so comprehensively that nobody could rouse her. The committee felt they had no option but to suspend her, and they confirmed their decision after yet another meeting, held aboard the Hamburg-Berlin train, claiming that they had been severely criticised by members of the Olympic party and by other passengers on the liner for not taking action sooner – particularly after a mock-marriage and mock-trial which many people had thought in extremely bad taste.

In Berlin Jarrett sought to defend herself with her usual effervescence, saying that she had never let pleasure interfere with her training, and that she needed some stimulation to prevent her becoming stale. 'I've never made a secret of the fact that I like a good time, or that I'm particularly fond of champagne,' she told the representative of the London *Daily Telegraph*. 'Everyone knows that, including the Committee.' Although ordered to return to the United States on the first available ship, she declined to obey and was instantly hired as a reporter to cover the Games by the International News Service. Forbidden to go anywhere near the women's hostel, she stayed in a hotel and swam out into Berlin society with the same confidence that she normally displayed in slicing through the water of the pool. And yet, even though she was widely fêted, and appeared in Goering's box at the stadium, she broke down in tears when she saw her own team-mates pass by.

Shorn though it was of its most glamorous member, the American team was still the largest present, with 384 members. Next came Germany with 300, then Hungary with 200,

Italy and Japan with 190 each, France with 188 and Britain with 150. In all more than 4,000 athletes and officials were accommodated in the Olympic Village. Every competitor was required to sign an *Amateurerklärung*, or 'amateur declaration', which read:

> I the undersigned declare on my honour that I am *an amateur* according to the Olympic rules of amateurism.

The women competitors, numbering only 600, lived in the Frisian House, a brand-new dormitory for students of the Reich Sports Academy, hard by the Olympic installations. The organisers were keenly aware that in Los Angeles the girls had lived in one of the city's best hotels, but they did not try to emulate any such luxurious arrangement; better, they thought, for the women to be close at hand, in walking-distance of the stadium, and out of the main city traffic. The girls' welfare was under the supervision of Baroness Johanna von Wangenheim, a hefty and formidable lady whose many years of organising the Red Cross had rendered her impervious to frivolous complaints about poor food and cold. She was renowned for her command of foreign languages, but not for her kind heart, and the atmosphere was by no means harmonious. Nothing could be done to soften the harsh, barrack-like impression which the building made on some of the girls, and although they slept in small, two-bedded rooms they were all obliged to eat in a single communal dining-hall, where one nationality did not always appreciate the table manners of another. A further source of irritation was the resounding clatter that footsteps made in the passages. It helped lower the tension when some of the competitors volunteered to join in routine household tasks such as the peeling of potatoes and the preparation of other vegetables.

If the athletes were the centre of attention, they were not by any means the only visitors to Berlin. For members of the Nazi regime the Games were the means to an end, and the end was to impress as many foreign governments as possible. Dozens of important people had therefore been invited – diplomats, politicians and social leaders – from all over the world. As Ribbentrop put it, with typical naïvety, 'sporting functions presented very favourable opportunities of staying in touch with politicians and important personages from widely scattered locations', and he himself invited a 'small invasion' of friends from France, Italy, Spain, the United States and Britain, among them Lord Rothermere, Lord Beaverbrook and Lord Monsell, with whom he had signed the naval agreement the year before. Hitler, who knew dangerously few foreigners, had invited Unity Mitford, together with her elder sister Diana, and given them free passes for the stadium. Goering had imported friends from Scandinavia. Many foreign diplomats had gathered, and German ambassadors had returned from their stations for the Festival. Royalty was represented by King Boris of Bulgaria, who had come ostensibly as non-playing captain of his national team, but mainly to increase his prospects of siring an heir by arranging for his wife to have an operation. Also present were Crown Prince Umberto of Italy and Prince Gustaf Adolf of Sweden, the latter a member of his country's equestrian team, who was photographed in the Olympic Village, with his fiancée, wearing a pair of voluminous Oxford bags.

The contingent from Britain was particularly strong. Apart from Ribbentrop's own guests, it included a key figure – in German eyes – in the form of Sir Robert Vansittart, who came with his wife Sarita. Lord and Lady Kemsley had brought their yacht to Kiel and travelled on by train; among their private guests were Sir Austen and Lady Chamberlain, but as Sir Austen refused to set foot on German soil, he missed the Games entirely. Lord Jellicoe was there, and so was Kenneth Lindsay, MP. But no visitor from London came to join the Nazis at play more enthusiastically than Henry Channon, always known as 'Chips', the American millionaire who had carved a larger-than-life-sized niche for himself in British social and political life. With his wife Honor (a Guinness) he travelled to Berlin in the style to which he was accustomed, flying to Tempelhof and being met there by a personal ADC, Baron von Geyr, and by a government car which drove him straight to the Eden Hotel, where a 'magnificent suite' of rooms had been reserved.

Conspicuous absentees, who might have been expected, were King Edward VIII and the British Fascist leader Sir

Oswald Mosley. But in any case there were so many British people in Berlin (Channon reported in his diary) that they all became jealous of each other's activities and privileges. His own included the use, whenever he wanted it, of a large car driven by a stormtrooper in a brown shirt, and continuous entertainment. Although he found Berlin an ugly city, he was greatly taken by the social life and made a perfect target for propaganda and hospitality: already pro-German to an extent that maddened friends such as Duff Cooper and Harold Nicolson, he now became a fervent admirer of the Nazis' achievement in putting the country back on its feet, and thus was worth every pfennig that the regime spent on him.

Many foreigners came not as official guests, but for their own amusement. One such was the American writer Thomas Wolfe, whose novels had achieved enormous success in Germany. *Look Homeward, Angel*, in particular, had earned him handsome royalties, which currency restrictions had prevented him taking out of Germany. The solution, he decided, was to spend the money *in situ*, on a great blow-out during the Olympics. He set to with gusto, aided and abetted by his publisher Ernst Rowohlt and by the many other German friends he had made during earlier visits, including the Dodds at the American Embassy. His stay was made all the more hectic by the fact that as it began he launched into a passionate love affair with the artist Thea Völcker. Later he drew a vivid picture of Berlin *en fête* in his novel *You Can't Go Home Again*.

Also in town was an unprecedented swarm of journalists. The official count listed 693 foreign sports reporters, 730 German sports reporters, and altogether some 3,000 pressmen of all descriptions. For the Ministry of Propaganda, used to having a captive press on a tight rein, this invasion of cynical, critical, suspicious and uncontrollable sensation-hunters was a nightmare. Goebbels addressed the whole lot at an inaugural press conference, but, apart from uttering general exhortations, there was little he could do except trust in the efficacy of the immense deception which he had taken such trouble to arrange.

On the afternoon of 29 July the IOC held its thirty-third Congress in the auditorium of the Friedrich Wilhelm University,

147

where Tschammer und Osten welcomed the Olympic dignitaries with fulsome congratulations. 'Only too often in the world have noble human tendencies risen and fought against each other through the tragedy of circumstances or through bungling,' he said. 'Therefore the highest recognition and greatest respect are due to the IOC for the way it has succeeded . . . in guarding the noble fire of sport.'

The first official event of the Festival took place that afternoon – the opening of the exhibition 'Sport in Hellenic Times' at the German Museum, where the members of the IOC gathered, wearing their new chains of office. That same evening they were guests of Frick, Minister of the Interior, at the Pergamon Museum, where in a programme described by the authorities as 'particularly solemn and impressive' classical Greek and German art were blended. A surviving photograph shows the guests and their ladies lolling glassy-eyed on chairs at the foot of the mighty Altar of Pergamon.

Next morning, the IOC dealt privately with one or two outstanding matters at a Committee meeting. Fate had already removed from the scene one of the American members – General Sherrill, who had died suddenly in Paris on 25 June; but another was still uncomfortably alive and intransigent in the form of Commodore Lee Jahncke, who had resolutely maintained his opposition to the holding of the Games in Berlin. Already, at the earlier meeting, it had been recorded that Jahncke had 'clearly infringed upon the status of the IOC in betraying the interests of the Committee', and that he had failed 'to preserve a sense of decorum towards his colleagues'. Now, as the festival was beginning, the Committee unanimously decided to expel him.

No doubt the move made the IOC feel more comfortable; but they could do nothing to forestall a disagreeable event which took place in Vienna on the evening of 31 July when, in pouring rain, the Fatherland Front held a mass demonstration against the way the Nazis had behaved during the torch ceremonies on Wednesday. Yet so small a protest could have no effect on the high spirits of the vast gathering in Berlin. It was the first time that Nazi Germany had put herself on show to the whole of the outside world, the first time the country had (apparently) laid itself bare to inspection by foreigners.

The Scene is Set

As things turned out, it was not only the first time but also the last. Yet nobody knew that at the end of July, 1936, and it was with excitement and high spirits rather than with apprehension that the multitude looked forward to the opening of the greatest show on earth.

11

GRAND OPENING

The one factor which the Nazis could not control was the weather. The last few days of July were gloriously clear and hot, but on the night of the 31st the sky above Berlin clouded over, and Saturday, 1 August, dawned overcast and drizzly, with the wide thoroughfares of the city glistening under fine rain. Nothing, however, could dampen the excitement already building along the Via Triumphalis, where thousands of people had camped out for the night. The centre of the city awoke to the thud and blare of martial music: everywhere, it seemed, soldiers marched with colours flying and bands playing in a stirring reveille. From that moment no visitor could doubt the predominantly martial nature of the regime and the Festival: uniforms and marching feet were the images left uppermost in thousands of minds as the Nazis gave full rein to their predilection for bringing out colossal numbers of human beings in massed array.

At 8am the band of the Berlin Guards Regiment came swinging up to the Adlon Hotel, where the International Olympic Committee had its headquarters, and blasted out what was officially described as a *Grosses Wecken*, or 'grand awakening'. Count Baillet-Latour's finest hour was at hand. After rousing the Adlon, the band marched off along Unter den Linden to the War Memorial, and then back. Already thousands of people were on the move, either staking out positions along the route to the stadium or heading for the Lustgarten, the long square at the eastern end of Unter den Linden where the Olympic flame was to be welcomed by an

immense youth rally. The fire itself, after yet another con-
secration ceremony early that morning in Luckenwalde, was
bobbing along through Trebbin, Grossbeeren and Marien-
felde on the last stretches of its great journey. At his office in
Hardenbergstrasse Carl Diem was taking a hundred last-
minute decisions, and all over the city his long-laid plans were
at last being put into action. Between 5am and 7am, for
instance, 20,000 carrier pigeons were taken to the Reich
Sport Field and transferred from vans and lorries into temporary cages under the terraces of the stadium, whence they
could all be released at a single moment during the opening
ceremony. They had been selected from 80,000 birds offered
by the most successful breeders in the country, and each
owner whose pigeons took part received a commemorative
medallion.

Between 8am and 10am more than 100,000 boys and girls
turned out on school playing-fields all over Berlin for a
programme of gymnastics, sports and dancing designed to
salute the opening of the Games. The first official functions of
the day were two religious services, both at 10am, one in the
Berlin Cathedral and another in the Hedwig Cathedral. Then
at 11am came an impressive ceremony at the War Memorial.
Special units of the army, navy and air force marched from
the Brandenburg Gate, followed by detachments of foreign
students and youth groups. When they were all drawn up in
formation in Unter den Linden, Count Baillet-Latour, in
sombre morning dress, moved out in procession with Dr
Lewald to lay a wreath before the memorial to those who died
in the First World War, on behalf of everybody about to take
part in the Games.

During this ceremony, by a prodigious feat of organisation,
28,000 young people were being assembled and lined up in
the Lustgarten for the youth festival due to begin at midday.
The official hosts were the Hitler Youth and its female
equivalent, the *Bund Deutscher Mädchen*, the boys in Brown-
Shirt uniform, the girls in white. To foreign spectators they
appeared to have been specially selected for their Aryan
physique: almost all were tall, fair-haired and blue-eyed.
Photographs show the fanatical precision of their alignment –
rank upon rank dead straight, stretching for hundreds of

yards. The event was exhausting for those who took part, for although the festival itself lasted only 50 minutes, the participants were on parade for several hours.

When all was set, the members of the IOC assembled in the rotunda of the Old Museum, where Goering received them and led them out onto the front steps. The ceremony began with trumpet fanfares, the raising of flags, and community singing of the Flag March, with its menacingly business-like first verse:

> Hoist up our flags
> In the wind of the morning.
> To those who are idle
> Let them flutter a warning.

The setting was sombre and impressive. Under the grey sky, the huge, neo-classical buildings loomed dark and massive, framing the vast crowd. Flanked by prancing equestrian statues, Baldur von Schirach, the Reich Youth Leader, greeted the assembly with the words, 'We, the Youth of Germany, we, the Youth of Adolf Hitler, greet you, the Youth of the World!' Another community song ('Now Let the Flags Fly'), a speech by Schirach, yet another song ('Forward! Forward!'), addresses by Tschammer und Osten, Dr Rust and Goebbels . . . throughout all this the waiting multitude was sustained by the knowledge that the Olympic torch was approaching. At exactly 12.58pm Goebbels ended his speech by flourishing his arms like a conjuror and crying, 'Holy flame, burn, burn, and never go out!'

Dead silence fell on the mighty gathering. Then, from the far distance, came a murmur of sound. The noise of cheering came rapidly closer, and suddenly, like a forest fire, it was into the ranks of boys and girls in the Lustgarten, surging through them in a solid roar.

Punctual to the minute, 12 days and 11 nights out of Olympia, the sacred flame appeared. Nor was the last runner alone: hundreds of unofficial supporters had fallen in behind him, and the police were scarcely able to control the crowd. Thirty thousand right hands shot up in the Nazi salute as the torch came first to the stand housing the guests of honour, where the runner lit a flame in a small altar, and then on to the main altar in front of the Schloss. The ceremony closed with a mass rendering of *Deutschland über Alles* and the Horst Wessel Song – the first of innumerable occasions on which the two tunes thundered out in harness during the next fortnight.

By then, it was estimated, more than half a million people had crowded into Unter den Linden alone. 'Never did I see a whole town so carried away with enthusiasm,' wrote Howard Marshall of *The Daily Telegraph*. 'Cup Final day in London is a trifle by comparison.' Loudspeakers mounted on lamp-posts kept them abreast of Olympic developments. British journalists found the behaviour of the crowd rather subdued, with none of the Cockney humour which erupted at home whenever some trifle like a stray dog or a paper bag blowing across the road, and chased by a portly constable, enlivened a delay. Nevertheless, everyone waited eagerly for the passing of the Nazi leaders, who occasionally drove up and down. Of these, Goering got by far the loudest cheers and responded most warmly; Goebbels, in contrast, remained rigid and remote. But the biggest ovation of all was accorded a contingent of Indian youths, who marched past in pink-and-grey turbans.

In London, that same day, the Conservative MP Julian Amery was addressing the House of Commons. He had received letters, he said, from panic-mongering friends who claimed that Germany had 20,000 aeroplanes and could make a ruin of England within 72 hours; even so, he did not think war with Germany was inevitable.

Almost as he delivered himself of this comforting opinion, the German Führer was receiving the members of the IOC for lunch at the Chancellery in Wilhelmstrasse. He could not escape a marathon speech by Count Baillet-Latour, but in his reply he had the satisfaction of being able to announce that the Greek Government had complied with his suggestion that excavation at ancient Olympia should be resumed under German direction.

By then, out to the west of Berlin, a fleet of 170 buses had started ferrying the athletes in to the Reich Sport Field from the Olympic Village. The stadium itself was already packed to its uppermost rim with more than 100,000 spectators who, as they waited, had music to entertain them: the Olympic Symphony Orchestra, formed from the Berlin Philharmonic and the National Orchestra, with other reinforcements, played the overture from Wagner's *Die Meistersinger* and Liszt's tone-poem *Les Préludes*.

For the crowds both inside and outside the stadium, another welcome entertainment – and a focus for patriotic sentiment – was the airship *Hindenburg*, which cruised over the city with big Swastika emblems in red, white and black emblazoned on its tail-fins and towing an Olympic flag. Largest and latest of the Zeppelins, 900ft long and 160ft wide, the biggest and most modern aircraft in the world, the *Hindenburg* offered flying proof of German inventiveness and workmanship, and so embodied in its great, sleek shape the revival of the nation's economy and morale.

Sheer novelty increased the airship's appeal. As LZ 129 it had made its first flight scarcely five months earlier, on 5 March, and after proving trips to South America had repeatedly broken the record across the North Atlantic. Cruising at 75mph, staffed by a crew of 40, with 50 passengers accommodated in two-berth cabins, and a grand piano in the lounge, the *Hindenburg* had been hailed as a flying hotel. Its quickest crossing – from Lakehurst, New Jersey, to Frankfurt – had been accomplished in 49 hours, less than half the time taken by the fastest ocean liner of the day; and now, as the Zeppelin cruised over the Olympic city through skies cleared of all normal traffic, it seemed the harbinger of a whole new era of air travel, in which the Reich would take the lead.

Airship-fancying helped pass the time; but what everyone really wanted was to see the Olympic torch, and then, above all, the Führer. Tens of thousands of people had poured into Berlin from surrounding villages and towns, and a great many of them had never seen Hitler in the flesh. To catch a live glimpse of the man who had rescued Germany from the pit was the summit of their ambition.

1500 Uhr. ABFAHRT DES FÜHRERS announced the daily programme in bold type – and on the stroke of three a cavalcade of big, open, black Mercedes-Benzes pulled out of the Chancellery to head along Wilhelmstrasse and into Unter den Linden. Hitler, in army uniform, rode standing in the

front seat of his own car, next to the driver, with his left hand
resting on top of the windscreen and his right arm free for
returning the innumerable salutes that greeted him along the
way. Another shower had just passed over, but as the heavy
cars turned through the Brandenburg Gate the swish of their
tyres on wet tarmac was drowned by the wave of cheering that
swept along with them. Through the eyes of his fictional hero
George Webber, Thomas Wolfe drew a memorable picture of
the Führer's passing;

> At last he came – and something like a wind across a field of grass
> was shaken through that crowd, and from afar the tide rolled up
> with him, and in it was the voice, the hope, the prayer of the land.
> The Leader came by slowly in a shining car, a little dark man with
> a comic-opera moustache, erect and standing, moveless and
> unsmiling, with his hand upraised, palm outward, not in Nazi-
> wise salute, but straight up, in a gesture of blessing such as the
> Buddha or Messiahs use.

At the same moment as Hitler left the Chancellery, the
Olympic flame, carried by a last short relay of runners, set off
from the altar in the Lustgarten, travelling the same route as
the Führer, but more slowly, so that it followed the official
cars at an ever-increasing distance. The torch-bearer, dressed
all in white, was escorted by a V-shaped phalanx of up to 24
other runners in white and black. For much of the way the
whole party ran in step, so that their advance was both
thrilling and hypnotic.

Repeated practice had made all the timings perfect. At 3.58
Hitler's car pulled up by the Bell Tower on the edge of the
May Field. There to greet him was a guard of honour drawn
from the three armed forces, the International and German
Olympic committees, and all 52 national teams, lined up on
the huge, flat expanse of turf. Trumpets braying from the
towers of the Marathon Gate signalled his arrival; escorted by
Baillet-Latour and Lewald, he advanced between the ranks
of the athletes and entered the stadium. As he appeared there
burst out a roar so gigantic that many people present felt the
arena was not so much a stadium as a crater, liable to erupt at
any moment.

For months Ribbentrop and Schirach had been begging Hitler to wear civilian dress for this momentous occasion: it would, they rightly pointed out, make the whole event seem less military, less daunting to foreigners. But Hitler, doubtless aware that he cut a nondescript – not to say ridiculous – figure when not bolstered by peaked cap, Sam Browne and Swastika armband, would not hear of it. He looked tanned and plump, but also dowdy in his brown uniform. Goebbels and Tschammer und Osten both appeared in white.

On his way across the centre of the arena the Führer paused to receive a bouquet from a small girl dressed in blue – Gudrun Diem, the five-year-old daughter of the man who had organised this great day – and then, to further fanfares and Wagner's March of Homage, took his place in the box of honour, where he was flanked by Hess, Goebbels, Blomberg, Frick and Crown Prince Umberto of Italy. When he raised his arm in greeting, *Deutschland über Alles* and the Horst Wessel Song roared out from the massed crowd.

Then came a powerfully emotive moment: the hoisting of the flags. All round the rim of the stadium flag-poles poked skywards; each was manned by two sailors, and at the call '*Heisst Flagge!*' over the loudspeakers, they slowly ran up the flags of the competing nations. As the banners rose into position the great Olympic bell began to toll, gently at first, then ever louder, as it boomed out its message for future generations: *Ich rufe die Jugend der Welt*.

The stage was set for the march-past of the teams. In they came, to a succession of rollicking marches. The Greeks led, as original founders of the Games and hosts of the first modern Olympiad. At their head, bearing the blue-and-white flag, was Spiridon Louis, winner of the Marathon in 1896, and now a sprightly 60-year-old, clad in traditional dress. Behind the Greeks came the Egyptians, because the German name of their country (*Ägypten*) began with 'Ä', and all the rest followed in alphabetical order, save for the Germans themselves, who as hosts brought up the rear.

The volume of noise in the stadium was stupendous. As each new team appeared, fresh cheering broke out, and the roars surged round like thunder constantly recurring. Yet nobody – least of all Hitler – was prepared for the frenzied

156

adulation which greeted the French. At their appearance an unprecedented eruption of sound rocketed into the sky. Some people supposed that it was because they gave Hitler what looked like a Nazi salute, raising their right arms as they passed. Most, however, knew instinctively that this was an impromptu mass demonstration of affection – an acknowledgement by the German people that they were prepared to bury past differences and accept the French as friends. One Parisian journalist thought he was witnessing a great moment in history. 'Never was the war threat on the Rhine less than during these moments,' he wrote afterwards. 'Never were the French more popular in Germany than on this occasion.' Hitler, in contrast, was not amused. Speer, standing at his elbow, saw that he was jolted by the reception of the French. In the prolonged cheers, Speer wrote, the Führer sensed 'a longing for peace and reconciliation with Germany's western neighbour', and he was more disturbed than pleased.

The British team – under 'G' for *Grossbritannien* – was led by the veteran oarsman Jack Beresford, whose fifth Olympics this was. They had decided, after earnest debate, not to give Hitler the Olympic salute because it looked so like a Nazi one. When they greeted him instead with a smart eyes-right, they drew only modest applause. The Americans, officially listed under 'V', for *Vereinigte Staaten Nordamerikas*, made a better show by whipping off their straw boaters and clapping them smartly to their chests, but it was not until the appearance of the German team, who entered all in white to the stirring tune of the Hohenfriedburger March, that the roar of approval climbed back to its earlier level. Every German in the packed tiers rose to his or her feet, and the entire aspect of the stadium changed as 100,000 arms went up in the Nazi salute, the sea of sun-tanned faces suddenly converted into a mass of small white stripes.

With the teams drawn up in the centre of the arena, a message from Baron de Coubertin was read out over the loudspeakers. Though still alive, the founder of the Modern Olympics was too old and infirm to come to Berlin, and so sent his exhortation on a gramophone record:

The important thing at the Olympic Games is not to win, but to take part, just as the most important thing in life is not to conquer, but to struggle well.

Nobody had time to reflect that this message was diametrically opposed to everything which the host of the Games had said and done during the past three and a half years. After a brief pause, Dr Lewald took the microphone to welcome the contestants. Impelled no doubt by the grandeur of the occasion, he spoke for far too long, and while he droned on the British radio commentator, Tommy Woodrooffe, committed a series of *faux pas* that led to furious recrimination in the British press. As many people later remarked, it was idiotic of the BBC to appoint someone who knew so little German. Unable to understand a word that Lewald was saying, Woodrooffe sought to fill the time with a stream of facetious banalities about the stadium, the weather, the *Hindenburg*, and so on. Several times he repeated, 'I don't know what it's all about, but I'm getting rather tired of this speech-making,' or words to that effect, and he maddened listeners especially by his observation that the grass in the middle of the cinder track was green. Then, at the critical moment, he was gazing skywards so steadfastly that he missed the most important event of all. Failing to realise that Lewald had at last stopped speaking, he failed also to notice that Hitler had moved to the microphone and declared the Olympics open.

It was Woodrooffe's bad luck, but everyone else's good fortune, that the Führer did this very quickly, with one brief but awkward sentence: 'I declare the Games in Berlin, to celebrate the eleventh Olympiad of the modern era, as open.'

On the high pole in the centre of the arena sailors ran up the huge, five-ringed Olympic flag. Artillery boomed out a salute. The 20,000 pigeons, suddenly released, wheeled and climbed away out of the stadium in clouds, each carrying a coloured ribbon representing one of the participating nations. Then the venerable composer Richard Strauss appeared on the rostrum to conduct his own Olympic Hymn. That he was there at all represented something of a miracle, for he had long since fallen out with the regime over his opera *Die Schweigsame Frau*. At the premiere of this work the year before, the government had insisted that no mention be made of the librettist, Stefan Zweig, on the grounds that he was a Jew. A letter from Strauss to Zweig was intercepted by the Gestapo; because it contained criticism of the authorities, the composer was obliged to resign from his post as President of the Reich Chamber of Music, and afterwards was forbidden to appear in public for a year. Yet he was too well known and important a figure for the Nazis to suppress entirely, and his participation in the Olympiad represented a compromise on both sides. His appearance in the stadium provoked a wave of patriotic sentiment, which was rendered none the less sincere by the fact that it was based on ignorance of his immediate past.

As the last verse of the hymn died away, all eyes again turned to the eastern gate . . . and there he was! The final torch-bearer, the 3,075th in the chain, a flaxen-haired Berliner called Schilgen, appeared in the gap against the sky. As he paused for a second, a tremendous gasp rose from the serried tiers. Then he ran lightly down the steps, left-handed round half the track, and up the steps at the far end to the tripod bearing the fire-bowl. For people whose emotions were already heightened, it was easy to imagine that some mythical runner had magically appeared from antiquity and come speeding straight from ancient Olympia. Reaching his destination, Schilgen again paused, then lifted his torch high. As the Olympic flame blazed up, another great cheer broke forth.

Two further ceremonies remained to be completed. In the first, Spiridon Louis was presented to the Führer, and in return handed him a symbolic olive branch plucked from the sacred grove at Olympia. In the words of one high-flown German account, 'Past and future shook hands, as the great ideals of mankind bridged the millennia.' At last it was time for the declaration of the Olympic Oath. The flag-bearers of all the nations formed up round a rostrum at one side of the track, as the oath was spoken on behalf of all the competitors by Rudolf Ismayr, the German Gold Medallist weightlifter from 1932:

> We swear that we will take part in the Olympic Games in loyal competition, respecting the regulations which govern them and

desirous of paticipating in the true spirit of sportsmanship for the honour of our country and the glory of sport.

Then, to the exultant beat of the Hallelujah Chorus, the teams marched out past the Führer, and at 6pm Hitler himself left, sent on his way by new trumpet fanfares. Later that evening the stadium filled again for a Festival of Olympic Youth: thousands of children, elaborately rehearsed over the past few weeks, danced and sang on the grass. A great procession of flags was borne in, to the Grand March from Verdi's *Aida*. Then 1,500 male and female voices joined in a rendering of Beethoven's Choral Symphony, while searchlights mounted round the rim of the stadium projected a vast tent of light into the sky.

Everyone who saw the opening ceremony agreed that it had been magnificently planned and executed. Foreign visitors were astonished and not a little unnerved by the colossal scale of the stadium and all the arrangements – by the huge numbers of soldiers lining the route to the stadium, by the continuous saluting, by the overt military nature of the regime. Another feature which shook strangers was the hysterical adulation accorded to the Führer wherever he went: men who saw him yelled themselves hoarse, women gave piercing screams, wept with excitement, fainted. To reserved British people especially, the sheer force of patriotic emotion was unsettling – and suddenly it became clear that, if this white-hot feeling could be converted into athletic performance, the German team would take some beating in the stadium.

The official printed programme for 1 August included a quotation from Herodotus. In this the historian described how, as Xerxes and his Persian army were sweeping down upon Greece in 480BC, messengers from Arcadia arrived in the king's camp. When asked what the Greeks were doing to oppose the invasion, the envoys replied that they were holding the Games at Olympia, watching athletic contests and chariot races. The Persians, astonished, asked what the prizes were, and on being told 'An olive wreath' made no effort to conceal their contempt.

The implication of the story – that the Olympic Games had been and still were a great force for peace – was hammered home at every opportunity in Berlin. But to some visitors it did seem strange that a Festival strenuously dedicated to youth, peace and international friendship should be presented in such a ferociously martial framework. Nor did it escape those who spoke German that their hosts used the same word – '*Kampf*' – for a struggle of any kind, be it athletic or military. Just as '*ein Kampf*' could mean, equally, a battle or a sporting competition, so '*kämpfen*' could mean either to fight or to compete, and the stadium was often described as '*die Kampfbahn*' – the arena where battles could take place. It was only a slight difference from English, but even so the similarity of the two notions seemed uncomfortably close.

12

FLYING START

The weather remained obstinately dull, with cloud that persisted all day, high humidity and an unseasonably cold wind Nor was it only Germany that suffered. In England the Bank Holiday weekend was so cold that at Southend-on-Sea some 5,000 people who had elected to sleep out on the beach spent most of the night walking about in efforts to keep warm. In Berlin there was at least Olympic excitement to generate heat, and by the time the track events began, at 10.30 on Sunday morning, the stadium was again packed out.

The first heats, appropriately enough, were those of the 100m – for many people the most glamorous event of all, whose winner would be truthfully proclaimed as the fastest man on earth. The enormous German, Borchmeyer, was much fancied by the home crowd, as was the Dutchman, Martinus Osendarp. But the man everyone wanted to see was the 22-year-old black student from Ohio University, Jesse Owens. It was common knowledge that on a single afternoon – 25 May, 1935 – less than a week after falling downstairs and hurting his back, this man had equalled one world record and broken three others. It was true that later in the summer of 1935 he had been beaten by his fellow-Blacks Eulace Peacock and Ralph Metcalfe – the second of whom was here in Berlin – but Owens, because of his four world records, was the focus of attention.

Although born James Cleveland Owens, he acquired the name that made him famous when a schoolmistress, hearing him give his initials as 'J.C.', thought he had said 'Jesse'. In

Berlin he came by yet another version, for to the German crowd he was inevitably 'Yesseh Ohvens', and once they had seen what he could do a terrific chant of '*Oh—vens! Oh—vens*' would start up whenever he appeared. That the Nazi regime considered Blacks *Untermenschen* was of no consequence to thousands of German schoolboys, whose imagination was immediately captured. Not lucky enough to get tickets for the stadium, they spent hours with ears glued to radio sets, thirsting for further news of their new hero.

Films show that, in technical terms, Owens was a 'scuttler' – that is, he ran with a very low action, not picking his knees up much; and it was a curious fact that although he had a close and good relationship with his trainer, Larry Snyder, he improved very little with coaching. In 1933, while still only 19, he had run 100 yards in 9.4 seconds – a world record that remained unbroken for 21 years. He was in fact a wonderfully gifted natural athlete, with a most beautifully proportioned body, and everyone who saw him agreed that he moved with incomparable grace.

In Berlin the crowd had to wait until the last of 12 heats before they saw him in action. Before that, they watched Borchmeyer win in 10.7 seconds, Wykoff, the white American, in 10.6, and Osendarp in 10.5. Preparation for each heat took some time. As blocks were not yet allowed in competition, every runner dug himself starting-holes in the cinder track, and for this purpose the authorities issued small silver trowels, which the athletes were allowed to keep as souvenirs.

At last came Heat 12, and with it a sensation. Owens did not merely win. He won by yards, and, without being challenged at all, equalled the world and Olympic record of 10.3 seconds. The crowd roared and sports-writers reached for their superlatives. 'Owens exceeded all expectations and swept down the track like a whirlwind,' said one. 'It is inconceivable to think of him being beaten,' said another. He was described as a black panther, a black bullet, a black arrow. 'The first glimpse of Owens was astonishing,' wrote an experienced British observer.

It left no doubt in people's minds that here was true athletic genius . . . No sprinter I have ever seen . . . has run in such effortless style. He was in a class above all other competitors; his arms and legs worked in perfect rhythm, and he carried his running right through the tape.

The second round of the heats began at 3pm. This time Owens was drawn in Heat 2. With 100,000 pairs of eyes glued to him, he again electrified the stadium by storming through to win in the unbelievable time of 10.2 seconds. Had there not been a slight following wind, this would have been a new Olympic and world record. Metcalfe and Borchmeyer also won their heats, but both in 10.5 seconds. Owens's pre-eminence, and the apparent effortlessness of his style, were the talk not only of the stadium but of Berlin – for the whole city was continuously receiving Olympic news broadcast from loudspeakers ranged along the streets, each announcement preceded by a bark of '*Achtung!*'. In the arena itself the crowd quickly took Owens to their hearts, for even from a distance they could see that he was a delightful person, cheerful, easy-going, and generous in victory.

Another man who quickly established himself as a favourite was Herr Miller, the starter, whose absolute steadiness and reliability, reflected in his broad face and stocky frame, gave the athletes such confidence that he contributed substantially to the smooth running of the Festival. Again and again, dressed from head to foot in white, holding the .380 pistol high in his right hand, he called the start-sequence with perfectly timed two-second pauses: '*Auf die Plätze*' . . . '*Fertig*' . . . *Bang*! What the runners could not see, but what endeared Miller to the crowd, was his habit of bobbing his knees in the middle of every sequence, always at exactly the same point, on the first syllable of the word '*Fertig*'.

If no other event on the first day could match the glamour of the 100m, there was plenty more excitement, and nothing gave the crowd more satisfaction than the fact that the first Gold Medal of the Games fell to a German girl, Tilly Fleischer, the effervescent and popular javelin-thrower, who rose magnificently to the occasion and broke the Olympic record. Fourteen girls came out to throw, and at first all eyes were on Hermine Bauma, the Austrian champion, who had already exceeded the old Olympic mark. To begin with, Fleischer did not shine. Inhibited by nerves, she threw only 38.60m in the first round, well behind her compatriot Luise Krüger and the Polish girl Maria Kwasniewska, who led. In the second round, however, she overcame her stage fright and improved prodigiously with a throw of 44.69m, a new Olympic record, which put her well in front. The crowd, gripped by feverish excitement, set up a tremendous chant of '*Til—ly! Til—ly!*'. Krüger responded to this nationalistic fervour with a throw of 43.29m, which overtook the Pole and put her in second place. Still, it seemed, Bauma might snatch victory at the last moment, but in the final round Fleischer made the throw of her life and achieved 45.18m, to break the Olympic record again and take the Gold Medal. Krüger, unable to improve further, won the Silver, and Kwasniewska the Bronze. The dreaded Bauma came forth. A contemporary German account recorded that after 'the proud double victory' for the host nation 'the jubilation in the tiers of spectators knew no bounds'.

The Führer, busy with affairs of State, did not witness his girls' triumph. But when he did arrive, late in the afternoon, he was just in time for the final of the men's Shot Put. His movements throughout the Games showed that he had been well briefed on which events Germany was likely to win, and he tried to make sure he was present for every Aryan success.

The Germans had trained intensively for the Shot Put; but by some hideous mischance a printer's devil had got into the daily programme, and both of Germany's leading pair – Hans Wöllke and Gerhard Stöck – had been listed as representing the United States. Nothing could have been more inappropriate, for nakedly nationalistic hopes had been piled on the broad shoulders of the two men. Never in the history of the modern Olympics had Germany won a Gold Medal in any of the main track or field events, and this was her first real chance to gain one.

Formidable opposition included the giant American Jack Torrance, who had set a new world record in 1934 with a distance of 17.40m. But the Germans were encouraged by rumours coming back from the practice-areas of the Olympic Village that Torrance was far below his best form – and so it proved. In the early rounds the pace was set by the Finn Sulo

Bärlund, who established a new but short-lived Olympic record with a throw of 16.03m. Wöllke, however, was only seven centimetres behind him, and in the final – spurred on no doubt by the presence of his Führer – he surpassed all his previous efforts with a heave of 16.20m. When the crowd saw that he had overtaken Bärlund's marker they roared so loudly that for a few moments the loudspeakers could make no impression on the din. Then came the announcement: '*Wöllke stiess* [threw] *16.20 Meter, neuer olympischer Rekord!*' Another eruption. Up in the box of honour Hitler battered furiously with his programme on the rail in front of him, grinning with excitement. But still Bärlund had one more throw, and the stadium fell deathly silent as, in the words of a German report 'the colossal Finn put the whole of his native energy' into his last chance. A hundred thousand pairs of eyes followed the shot through the air, and agonised silence prevailed when the missile was seen to have passed the 16m mark. Then, at the announcement that Bärlund had managed only 16.12m, there was an uninhibited explosion of relief and jubilation.

For Hitler and all his people, it was a tremendous moment: at last a German had broken a barrier which had started to seem impregnable. What was more, Stöck came third, and the Americans nowhere, Torrance finishing a disappointing fifth. It is hardly surprising that the Führer himself wanted to congratulate his men: he summoned them to his box and shook hands before the multitude – a process which he repeated with the medal-winning javelin girls, and with the winners of the 10,000m, which took place that evening. Strictly speaking, he should not have done this, for his position as Patron of the Games put him outside the framework of Olympic officials, and, as Count Baillet-Latour pointed out to him, he should congratulate either every winner or none. Since he could not be present all the time, it was clearly not possible for him to receive them all, and so after the first evening he decided to receive no more.

The 10,000m, which he stayed to watch, was a Finnish affair throughout, as everyone expected it to be. Among the crowd was the Flying Finn himself, the great Paavo Nurmi, who in his day had set 22 world records and single-handedly had revolutionised the business of middle- and long-distance running. One of his main innovations had been to run holding a stopwatch, which contributed enormously to his development, both in training and in competition. He won his first Gold Medal at the 1920 Olympics, in the 10,000m, and four years later had a prodigious haul at Paris, carrying off golds in the 1,500m, 5,000m, 3,000m team race and the cross-country. Annoyed at being excluded from the 10,000m that year, because he was running in so many other events, he is said to have gone out on a training spin during the race and covered the distance in a shorter time than the winner in the stadium. That same year – 1924 – he set a world record for the 10,000m that was not beaten for quarter of a century, and in 1928, at Amsterdam, he won the event yet again.

Now, in Berlin, he was present only as a guest of honour and as a trainer, but his experience and example, and the tradition he had created, inspired the Finnish trio of Ilmari Salminen, Arvo Askola and Volmari Iso-Hollo to a wonderful concerted display. When the race went off to a fast start, the Finns lay back together and let another group make the running. Prominent among these was the Japanese Kohei Murakoso, who led for lap after lap, setting such a pace that after four kilometres only five other runners were still in contention – the three Finns, a Pole and the Englishman James Burns. Murakoso passed the half-way mark in the potentially record-breaking time of 15 minutes 0.9 seconds, and held his lead so gallantly that the crowd rose to him, scenting a miracle. It made a bizarre but thrilling spectacle – the small and slender man from the East being hounded by a whole formation of lanky giants from the North.

Then, with six kilometres behind them, the Finns put in their long-expected mass-attack, and in a flash the Japanese found that instead of leading he was fourth. Yet still he hung on. At the end of eight kilometres he seemed to find new energy and suddenly went ahead again, to hold the lead for another circuit. But as they entered the last lap the Finns played their trump card. Led by Salminen, they swept past and kept going in an irresistible sprint. Murakoso was beaten. Two hundred yards from home Iso-Hollo fell back slightly, and at the tape Salminen came in half a pace ahead of Askola.

The time of 30 minutes 15.4 seconds was four seconds outside the Olympic record, but the race was a triumph of teamwork for the Finns, brilliantly planned and executed.

That day – as on all days of the competition – the victors were presented with their medals and crowned with olive garlands on a dais beside the track just below Hitler's box. The flags of the winning countries were run up, and the band crashed out the national anthem of the gold medallist. If this happened to be *Deutschland über Alles*, the crowd generally burst into song, and the great tune – known to the British as 'Glorious Things of Thee Are Spoken', but stemming in fact from Haydn's Emperor Hymn – came rolling down the stands, followed more often than not by an impromptu rendering of the Horst Wessel song. The crowning ceremonies were performed by girls dressed in white – members of the Honorary Youth Service, specially recruited from Berlin sports clubs and trained for two years to perform this kind of duty in the stadium.

After receiving the victorious Finns, Hitler departed, not waiting for the result of the High Jump, which he could see would hardly be to his liking. The competition, which had run late, had begun in the morning, and as anticipated had produced fireworks. In the final Olympic trials in the United States two Blacks, Cornelius Johnson and David Albritton, had both unofficially broken the world record with heights of 2.078m. For the first round in Berlin 50 of the world's best jumpers were divided into two groups, and all those clearing 1.85m went through to the final. The power of Johnson was immediately apparent: fast and confident in his approach, tremendous in his spring, he cleared all the intermediate heights with contemptuous ease, and did not bother to remove his track-suit until the final jump-off. He won the Gold Medal with 2.03m; Albritton won the Silver with 2.00m, in spite of an injury to one ankle; and such was the standard that the first four all comfortably surpassed the former Olympic record. After taking the Gold, Johnson, not satisfied with his achievement, went on to attack the world record of 2.06m (6ft 10in), held by Bill Marty of the United States. In the gathering dusk he had the bar set at 2.08m, but failed to clear it with all three attempts.

So ended a first day packed with interest and excitement. As on all the days that followed, Leni Riefenstahl and her camera teams were much in evidence. Her Olympic Film Company had been granted sole rights to the Games, but her freedom of action had been severely limited by the International Amateur Athletics Federation, which had written to her in July laying down the conditions under which she was to operate. She was allowed three towers in the centre of the arena, two pits for cameramen at the High Jump, one five metres from the start of the 100m and another by the finishing tape. The taking of motion pictures directly in front of runners was forbidden on principle, as was the filming of anyone who did not want his or her picture taken. All cameramen were required to operate sitting or prone. In spite of these limitations, her cameras seemed to be everywhere – gliding along rails, in balloons, under water. She herself sometimes appeared with Hitler in his box, but more often than not was to be seen urging on her crews from point-blank range.

On the first evening an announcement was made of the awards in the art competitions which had been held to enhance the Games. In the section for buildings the Gold Medal went to Werner March for the Reich Sport Field, which also won the Silver Medal in the architectural section. On the whole, however, the entries were uninspiring, and when an Honourable Mention was given to the 'swimming-pool of the Mussolini Forum in Rome', the foreigners present became still more cynical.

An event more relevant to the Olympics – although it had been devised only at the last moment – was the despatch of another torch run, this time to Kiel, scene of the sailing contests. The big relay from Olympia had evoked such interest and excitement that Diem had quickly planned an extension of it. On the evening of 2 August the first of a fresh chain of torches was kindled from the fire blazing in its bowl by the Marathon Gate, and runners set off for the port on the Baltic, over 300km away to the north-west. Later in the week yet another run was launched, this time to Grünau, in the east of Berlin, where the rowing events were to take place. To eke out the short distance (scarcely 20km in a direct line), a zig-zag route was adopted, and each torch-bearer ran only 200m.

The one disappointment of the day was the performance of the television cameras, which had been set up with a great deal of publicity. Television was then in its infancy, and this was the first occasion on which it was used to cover a sporting function. In the race to establish a regular service the Germans were slightly ahead of the British, who were working all-out to have their new station at Alexandra Palace, in North London, ready to transmit some simple demonstration programmes to the Radio Exhibition due to open at Olympia on 26 August. Transmission of real programmes was not expected to start before October.

In Berlin transmission had already started, and two rival systems were in action: the Farnworth camera of the Fernseh company, which needed a team of six men to operate it, and the Ikonoscope developed by Telefunken, which usually needed only three men. Both cameras were enormously cumbersome, the Ikonoscope being over 6ft long. Before the Games only two hours of television broadcasts had been put out every day, usually from 8pm to 10pm, but now 15km of special cable had been laid to public viewing rooms in the city, and coverage was greatly extended. Altogether there were nearly 30 small theatres or halls in which the transmissions could be viewed, and after the Games authorities claimed that 162,000 people had watched the Olympics on television. What they saw is another matter. The Ikonoscope 'makes 90,000 pictures every hour', explained one contemporary account, seeking to impress, but the quality was extremely variable. In the van used to relay some of the broadcasts pictures could be quite clear. 'It was easily possible to distinguish individual runners, jumpers and officials,' reported one journalist with a note of slight surprise. At the Post Museum in Leipziger Strasse the signals were projected onto a large cathode-ray screen, but often all that could be seen were occasional shadowy outlines. Even on an ordinary receiving set the pictures were scarcely recognisable: they resembled very faint, over-exposed film, and were so hard to follow that many people turned away in disappointment. Jesse Owens might well be winning a heat of the 100m, but viewers had to take the word of the commentator for it.

Television apart, the technical facilities devised for the Games seemed faultless. The photo-electric timing mechanism, activated by the starting pistol, worked perfectly, and a constant source of fascination for the crowd was the immense stop-watch mounted on the left-hand tower of the Marathon Gate. Made by Siemens, the largest stop-watch ever built, this had a face 11ft in diameter. It, too, was activated by the starting pistol and, as one observer remarked, 'as a race starts, this writes, and once it has writ no luckless runner can cancel its message'.

For the British team, the day was something of a shock. They had come expecting high standards, but what they found took their breath away. 'Great Britain has played a brave, if in most cases inconclusive, part in the first meetings in the stadium,' reported *The Times* – and that was about all that could be said. In the 10,000m, it is true, Burns had hung on gamely to finish fifth. Two of their best sprinters – Pennington and Sweeney – had got through into the semi-finals of the 100m, but their chances of reaching the final, let alone of winning a medal, seemed exceedingly remote. McCabe, Handley and Powell had come safely through their heats in the 800m; but in this event, which for the past four Olympics had been dominated by British runners, the team was unsettled by the absence of J. C. Stothard, who had seemed by far the brightest prospect until a severe loss of form put him out of contention. In the Shot Put, High Jump and Women's Javelin, Britain's athletes had been outclassed.

The main reason for their relative weakness – as they knew – was the fact that they were all still true amateurs, in the best of British tradition. Several, like the 400m specialist Godfrey Brown, were students; some, like the team captain Don Finlay, were in the armed forces. Others were working. But all had trained in their spare time, with their own resources, and it was disconcerting to find that many of their competitors had not only been excused work for months but had had their training organised and paid for by the state.

The middleweight wrestler Leslie Jeffers was a typical example. A constable of the London Metropolitan Police, he had to bicycle to and from his station at Southwark for shift-work, which might be from 6am to 2pm, 2pm to 10pm or 10pm to 6am. Because he was given no special dispensation to prepare for the Olympics, he had to train at home, whenever he could. Imagine his apprehension, then, when he arrived in the Olympic Village at Döberitz to find that his neighbours, the Turkish wrestlers, had spent the past six months at a camp in the mountains, paid for by the government, with nothing to do but train and take muscle-building exercise such as logging. Women and alcohol had been banned, and fresh teams of wrestlers had been sent up every fortnight to take on the Olympic hopefuls. How could a part-timer, however good, compete against this kind of preparation?

Godfrey Rampling, the 400m specialist, had more experience, having already represented England at Los Angeles in 1932; but he too had trained on a shoestring – 'If you could call it training,' he said 50 years after the event. 'By today's standards we scarcely trained at all.' In 1936 Rampling was 27 and an army officer. At the Royal Military Academy in Woolwich, known as 'The Shop', he *had* had a bit of instruction from an old man called W.G. George, who had once held the mile record; but after that he had been left to his own devices. In those days, to have professional coaching was regarded as poor form – the sort of thing a true amateur did not do – and an essential part of the philosophy still governing British sport was that one should not take things too seriously. Thus Rampling's preparation for Berlin had been minimal, and the casual approach of him and his colleagues in the relay team, when they sauntered out on to the practice track of Döberitz for a bit of baton-changing drill, astounded the Americans.

13

BLACK MAGIC

For the second day of the field and track events, Monday, 3 August, the weather was still dull. After a cool, cloudy morning, two heavy showers passed over Berlin at lunchtime, one at about 12.30 and the other at 2pm. The rain left the cinder track damp and heavy, and may have marginally affected the times in the sprints, which took place during the afternoon.

Several events were held outside the stadium – wrestling in the Deutschland Halle, the épée section of the Modern Pentathlon in the Turnhalle, and the first round of the Polo on the May Field. (A note in the daily programme entitled '*Das ist Polo*' described the game as '*eine Art Hockey zu Pferde*' – 'a kind of hockey on horseback' – and explained that the game, which had originated in Persia, had been brought to England by officers of the Anglo-Indian army in the first half of the nineteenth century, since when it had spread all over the world.) In the stadium itself, the only morning activities were the early rounds of the Hammer, and the first track events, the heats of the 400m Hurdles, did not begin until 3pm. By then the great bowl was again packed to its rim – but not out of curiosity about the hurdlers. What everyone had come to see were the semi-finals and final of the 100m.

The Hurdle heats duly took place and produced no surprises. The favourite for the Gold Medal, Glenn Hardin of the United States, went through as expected to the semi-final, but in a comparatively slow time, and the German runner Nottbrock put the crowd in high fettle by winning a well judged tactical race. All this, however, was merely an appetiser before the feast.

173

This time Owens was drawn in the first of the two heats. In spite of the palpable tension he looked as cool as ever, and prepared his starting-holes without fuss. Silence fell as starter Miller raised the pistol high in his right hand and went into his invariable sequence. *'Auf die Plätze'* . . . *'Fertig'* . . .

At the gun Owens was away to a good start. As one observer remarked, he did not seem to come fully upright until he had covered the first 30 yards. Again the miracle happened. Without apparent effort, without extending himself, he pulled away from his team-mate Wykoff and the Swedish Strandberg to win in 10.4 seconds. According to the representative of the London *Morning Post*, his victory 'drew from the stands one of those sudden shouts, high-pitched and sharply accentuated, which the Berlin crowd reserves for a specially popular win'. Amid a storm of cheers he pulled up grinning, then returned to swaddle himself in track-suit and heavy blanket. But for the damp track, he might well have equalled the Olympic and world record once more.

In the second semi-final the times were again a fraction slow. Metcalfe won in 10.5 seconds, followed by Osendarp in 10.6 and Borchmeyer in 10.7. The two British runners, Sweeney and Pennington, both came fifth in their heats and, as only the first three went forward to the final, both were eliminated.

The scene was set for a thrilling final, due to be run at 5pm. First, however, came the final of the Hammer, and whether by chance or design the Führer arrived in time to witness another German triumph. An immense roar of excitement heralded his coming, and today in his box he had with him a rare collection of celebrities, among them Max Schmeling, Leni Riefenstahl and Julius Streicher.

Hitler appeared just as the German Erwin Blask had stepped into the circle to launch his second throw of the elimination round. Galvanised by the presence of the Head of State, Blask surpassed himself with a distance of 55.04m, a new Olympic record. The turf of the stadium was so soft after the rain that the heavy ball of the hammer vanished out of sight as it landed, driven underground by gravity and its own momentum. Blask's compatriot Karl Hein was suffering from nerves and managed only 52.5m, which put him in third place, behind the young Swede Fred Warngård. In the final, however, Hein suddenly came into his own; with his confidence restored, he produced three tremendous throws of 54.7m, 54.8m and finally 56.49m, thereby beating by nearly two metres the Olympic record which had stood for 24 years before Blask had broken it earlier in the day. Though Leni Riefenstahl herself was beside Hitler, she had her cameramen well organised; they caught the Führer grinning and gasping with excitement. Blask came second and Warngård third, so that Germany carried off another Gold-and-Silver double. Nobody can have watched the final with more mixed feelings than Dr Patrick O'Callaghan of Ireland, who had won the Gold Medal for the Hammer in both 1928 and 1932, but now was in Berlin merely as a spectator.

Heats of the women's 100m, begun at 4pm, brought yet another sensation. The holder of the Olympic record, the Polish girl Stanislawa Walasiewicz, was drawn in Heat 3, but the runner with by far the greatest curiosity value for the crowd was Helen Stephens, the tall, bony farm-girl from Missouri, who the year before had set a new world record – so far not ratified – of 11.5 seconds, well below the best Olympic time of 11.9.

Like Jesse Owens, Helen Stephens was a natural athlete. She had been running for pleasure since she was a young girl, and had been taken up by a professional coach at the age of 15, but she had not a tenth of the grace of her black contemporary. Almost six feet tall and strongly built, she was described in one German account as 'outsized and almost as effective as a man'. Certainly she had amazing speed, and on her first appearance exceeded all expectations, leading right down the course and finishing ten yards ahead of the next runner in 11.4 seconds – a new Olympic and world record, which was disallowed because of a slight following wind. Walasiewicz won the next heat easily enough, but only in 12.5 seconds, and at once it was clear that Helen Stephens could outrun all opposition as easily as Owens. (In due course she did indeed win the 100m title.)

Her electrifying first appearance perfectly set the scene for the men's 100m final. The stadium buzzed with expectation as the six men formed up on the track, Owens in lane 1 and

Metcalfe in lane 6, the two Blacks framing the four white runners – Borchmeyer of Germany, Strandberg of Sweden, Osendarp of Holland and Wykoff of the United States. Everyone fell quiet as they prepared to get on their marks. Only the fair-haired Osendarp betrayed any sign of nerves, pattering about in front of his starting-holes and rubbing his hands on his shorts. Owens looked perfectly calm as he went into his easy, alert crouch, balancing on the tips of his fingers, with his eyes focused in absolute concentration along the tunnel of the track ahead.

By the time Miller raised his right hand, the vast stadium had gone dead quiet, but the crack of the starting pistol let loose a terrific roar. The runners went off in a bunch. At 30 yards they were still all together. Then, inexorably, Owens drew ahead. His speed was devastating, his fluency sheer delight. He broke the tape a yard ahead of Metcalfe, equalling the Olympic and world records of 10.3 seconds. Third came Osendarp, who was so thrilled to have won a medal that he turned round and sprinted back down the track almost as fast as he had run the race. Obviously the crowd had wanted Borchmeyer to win, but they had known he had little chance, and they gave Owens a generous ovation.

Then followed an incident which is still debated 50 years later. The medal-giving ceremonies for the Hammer and the 100m were held one after the other. First Hein, and then Owens, ascended the winner's dais in full view of Hitler and his guests. For a moment a white-clad girl held the wreath symbolically over Hein's bent head. Then he straightened up and gave Hitler the Nazi salute. The band began to play *Deutschland über Alles*, and the crowd to sing. Once again the entire aspect of the stadium changed as 100,000 right hands went up in salute. Then it was Owens's turn. He too was crowned, and as the band launched into 'The Star-Spangled Banner' he bowed to Hitler, who acknowledged the gesture with a formal salute and turned away.

What was the Führer thinking at that moment? What was in the mind of the other monster who stood at his elbow – Streicher? Did Owens remind him of Jim Wango, the black wrestler whose death he had brought about a year ago? Did his public vilification of Blacks begin to haunt him?

Whatever Hitler was thinking, he did not invite Owens to his box – and it was his failure to do so which gave rise to the legend that he had snubbed the greatest athlete of the Games. In one way this is unfair, for, as has already been made clear, after his *faux pas* the day before the Führer had been specifically requested *not* to congratulate the athletes. In not receiving Owens, he was thus only doing what Baillet-Latour had asked him to do – and he did not publicly congratulate Hein, either. Nobody noticed anything untoward at the time. On the other hand, there is strong evidence to show that he had fallen victim to his own racial propaganda, and was not going to demean himself by shaking hands with the sub-human which he considered Owens to be.

With Hitler in the box of honour was Baldur von Schirach, who later recorded that after Owens's victory the Führer said, 'The Americans should be ashamed of themselves, letting negroes win their medals for them. I shall not shake hands with this negro.' Tschammer und Osten, who was also there, pleaded with him to meet the hero of the hour 'in the interests of sport', and later, Schirach claims, he himself sought to keep up the pressure in the Chancellery:

> 'America will see the treatment of Jesse Owens as unfair,' I said. 'He is an American citizen, and it's not for us to decide whom the Americans let compete. Besides, he's a friendly and educated man, a college student.'

Hitler's response was violent. For only the second time in the 11 years that Schirach had known him, he shouted. 'Do you really think,' he yelled, 'that I will allow myself to be photographed shaking hands with a negro?'

With typical naïvety, Schirach recorded that he considered the Führer's behaviour unfair. Hitler, he said, had failed to recognise the Olympiad's potential for uniting nations because of a question of race. What Schirach could not see was that Hitler was entirely cynical: he had no intention of uniting nations unless he derived some benefit from doing so. The Owens incident gave a strong hint of what was going on behind the Olympic façade. Obsessed by his own racial theories, bent on the armed physical expansion of the Reich,

Hitler was merely using the Games as a means of gaining prestige and time.

During the Festival, while not in the stadium, he was doing all he could to foment the civil war in Spain – and it was no accident that on the evening of 3 August, at the very moment when he was perfunctorily returning Owens's salutation, a mass demonstration was being set up in Moscow to express solidarity with the Communist forces in Spain. In the Soviet capital, as factories and offices closed for the day, with the thermometer standing at 97°F, some 120,000 workers were marched to Red Square where they formed up under banners proclaiming WOE TO THE TRAITOR REBEL GENERALS OF SPAIN and HAIL, SPANISH PROLETARIAN FIGHTERS. It was proclaimed that a compulsory levy would be made in all State offices and factories to raise the equivalent of £1 million for the Spanish Popular Front, and four days later Mr Shremik, Secretary of the Russian All-Union Council of Trade Unions, announced that the Soviet Gosbank was handing over to the Spanish Government the sum of nearly £500,000, which had already been collected.

If the horde of journalists in Berlin had discovered the depths of Hitler's duplicity, they would have had the scoop of their lives. As it was, they got an unrivalled view of him whenever he came to the stadium, for the large press gallery was right above the box of honour, and they could look straight down on him and whatever cronies he might bring with him. An enormous number of press seats had been allocated – nearly 1,000, all fitted with writing-desks, in the stadium alone, as well as 18 cabins for the agencies – and every effort had been made to humour the newsmen. Even so, they soon became suspicious of the arrangements made on their behalf. Rumour went round that every second seat in the press box was occupied by a secret-service agent. New correspondents seemed to appear every day, and very few of them ever made any notes. The system of reserved seats, so carefully maintained at first, went by the board, and people sat wherever they liked. No doubt many of the newcomers were simply impostors, who muscled in on the pretence of being reporters, but some genuine journalists did feel uneasy, as one despatch shows:

Today, when one of the many charming telephone girls informed me that the *Daily Herald* wished to speak to me, a total stranger asked me why I typed my stories when I was also telephoning to London. I carefully explained that I did so to speed up dictation, but he seemed dubious. He wanted to know if I posted my work, and if I sent it by airmail. Having completed my call, I laid my typewritten material down while I went to seek further details. On my return both my unknown neighbour and my story had disappeared.

No doubt secret agents of all kinds were fully extended during the Olympic fortnight, as the Ministry of Propaganda and the Gestapo tried to keep check of all the foreign reporters loose in the city. As the Games progressed there inevitably occurred one or two unfortunate incidents which would normally have gone unreported but which now became grist to the visiting newsmen's mill. The leading Austrian glider pilot Ignaz Stiefsohn was killed when a wing came off his aircraft as he was doing stunts above Staaken military aerodrome. There was a row among the wrestlers, when Britain, Canada and Australia clubbed together to protest against the judges and their methods. An inexplicable error of communication caused acute embarrassment to the British wrestler Leslie Jeffers, who did well to beat Terry Evans of Canada, the Empire champion, in the third round of the middleweight freestyle, but was then defeated by Poilvé of France, the eventual Gold Medallist, in the fourth. Somehow, in transmitting the news to London, two agencies credited Jeffers with having already won the Gold. Telegrams began to pour in on him at the Olympic village, one of them from Sir Philip Game, the Commissioner of the Metropolitan Police, congratulating him on behalf of the entire force. For the moment there was nothing he could do but squirm, and it was never established how the mistake had come about.

Such odd scraps of news kept the journalists on their toes. What most of them did not realise was that, as the athletes competed in the stadium, visiting diplomats were extremely active about the city, and none more so than Sir Robert Vansittart, who met all the Nazi leaders for informal but important discussions. The constant theme of every man and woman in Berlin, he reported afterwards, was Communism.

'Indeed, they can think and talk of little else. The obsession is in any case endemic, but Spanish events have reinforced their thesis.'

To show Vansittart how efficiently the Nazi had driven the Red menace underground on their own territory, Hess took him on a drive, without any escort, through the Communist quarters of Berlin, and they completed the trip 'without seeing a sour look'. Goering, similarly boastful of his achievement in cleaning up the Reich, offered Vansittart a large bet that he would drive him alone to the roughest spot in Germany, that they would get out of the car and stand there, and that nothing would happen. His guest declined the wager on the grounds that he had practically given up betting on certainties.

Vansittart's diplomatic round included some clandestine encounters, one of them with King Boris, who, because he was trying to remain *incognito* when not at official functions, suggested that they should meet in the middle of a wood. (In fact they met in an hotel, and the king became bold enough to visit the Olympic Village wearing a loud, double-breasted pinstripe suit and a trilby hat.) In general Vansittart found that 'an Olympic truce lay thick above the city', putting the Nazi leaders in a sunny mood and making him disinclined to push any of his discussions too hard. All the same, he found 'the whole dominant caste completely confident of their hold over the people', and his hosts would hardly have enjoyed the descriptions he gave of them when he returned to London. Of Ribbentrop, whom he met many times during the fortnight, he wrote:

> I fear that he is shallow, self-seeking and not really friendly. No one who studies his mouth will be reassured . . . To him one has to listen without much chance of interruption . . . for he is guided by his command of English.

Goering he described as a 'primitive, bounding creature' who had never grown up:

> General Goering enjoys everything, particularly his own parties, with the gusto of Smith Minor suddenly possessed of unlimited

tick at the school stores. The world is his oyster, and no damned nonsense about opening it.

On the other hand Vansittart fell for the fat general's second wife, the blonde and attractive Swedish filmstar Emmy Sonnemann, whom he had recently married in a ceremony so extravagant as to attract much unfavourable publicity. 'Goering's really nice wife is a young lady of Riga,' wrote Vansittart, 'likely to keep her seat as well as the smile on the face of the tiger.' Yet the person he got on best with was Goebbels, who seemed to him the deepest of the hierarchy. 'I found much charm in him – a limping, eloquent slip of a Jacobin, quick as a whip in quotes and often, I doubt not, as cutting.' In spite of the rumours which ascribed unbridled lechery to the Propaganda Minister, Vansittart saw that Goebbels's marriage to Magda was a happy one, 'with attractive devotion on both sides'.

A formal meeting with Hitler got off to a difficult start, for some ill-informed staff officer had told the Führer that he probably would not like Vansittart, as he was short, dark and Jewish-looking, and spoke no German. When Hitler found himself confronted by a man of 6ft 1in, with medium-brown hair, who praised the Olympic arrangements in faultlessly idiomatic German, he was so taken aback that for a few moments he could not utter. When he recovered, he was friendliness itself, and the talk became a real conversation, not a monologue. In the 'prevailing and remunerative lull' provided by the Games, Vansittart saw Hitler as

> an amiably simple, rather shy, rotundly ascetic bourgeois, with the fine hair and thin skin that accompany extreme sensitiveness, a man of almost obvious physical integrity, very much in earnest, not humorous, not alarming, not magnetic, but convinced of a variable mission and able to impress himself so strongly that he impresses himself on those around him.

This, Vansittart wrote, was the sunny, August aspect of the Führer, which 'underlined rather than effaced' the other aspect,

> the harder, more violent, mystically ambitious, hotly and coldly

explosive traits which flare capriciously and keep everyone . . .
in such a state of nervous tension that I more than once heard the
stadium compared with a crater.

Like his colleagues, Hitler complained to Vansittart that he was
misunderstood in Britain, but his visitor was not impressed. Almost every day, amid the flood of hospitality which he was receiving, came a forceful reminder of what he called 'the reverse of the
medal' – a 'thin, almost transparent profile with a high forehead
and frightened eyes whose name was, too appropriately, Israel'.

> He came in by the back door of the Embassy, plainly terrorised;
> indeed, he murmured – he never raised his voice above a
> murmur – were it known that he had come to see me, it would be
> the end of him. He mentioned a common friend who had recently
> committed suicide, looked nervously over his shoulder and asked
> if nothing could be done to alleviate the lot of his co-religionists.

Vansittart's description of this encounter was a generalised
one; not one Jew but many came to solicit his help, and he
always interviewed the supplicants in the bathroom, that
being the only room in the Embassy which he felt confident
the Germans would not have bothered to fit with microphones. Although there was little he could do immediately,
he did in the end arrange the escape of several families
through the Swiss Red Cross.

For most Jewish families still living in Berlin, the Olympic
fortnight was a horrible time. Some were optimistic, believing
that the sudden intense interest of the outside world would
force the regime to ease religious persecution permanently
rather than just for the duration. The majority, however,
were nauseated by the ease with which the Nazis conned their
visitors into thinking Germany a civilised country. At least
one woman who took her daughter to the stadium has never
forgiven herself. She did not want to go (and so tacitly
indicate support of the Reich), but somehow felt she ought to
see what was happening. Then, when the crowd rose to sing
Deutschland über Alles for some home victory, she remained
ostentatiously seated. The man next to her leaned over and
asked, 'What's the matter? Aren't you Germans?' – and to
save herself serious trouble she was forced to shake her head.
It was, and always remained, the bitterest moment of her life.

14

NEW PEAKS

Quickly the city settled into an Olympic routine: the stadium packed every day for the track and field events; Hitler attending the Games whenever he could, or whenever there seemed a good chance of a German victory; vast crowds lining the Via Triumphalis to see him come and go; and in the evenings merrymaking on a scale which Berlin had not seen since before the Nazis came to power.

For visitors like the Channons, bent on pleasure, the time was one of continuous parties. Yet even on his social rounds Chips soon became aware of an atmosphere of political intrigue. 'We are told that Ribbentrop is a waning star,' he wrote after only 48 hours in the German capital, 'that Goering and Goebbels hate each other; that Hess, the deputy leader, is Hitler's favourite. There is talk, too, of a Hohenzollern, or perhaps Brunswick, restoration.' Such gossip added spice to the Channons' non-stop entertainment: they were invited not only by the Nazi leaders, but also by royalty and the remnants of the aristocracy. They had tea with the Duke of Saxe-Coburg Gotha (a grandson of Queen Victoria and a fervent Nazi), lunch with the Crown Princess and her son Prince Friedrich of Prussia, dinner with the Bismarcks. In conversation with Philip of Hesse, Channon found that the talk turned to English nannies, and the fact that they had given most of the royalty of Europe Cockney accents.

Between these festivities he fitted in occasional visits to the Games. The athletics bored him, but he found the stadium itself 'terrific':

Suddenly the audience was electrified. Hitler was coming, and he looked exactly like his caricature – brown uniform, Charlie Chaplin moustache, square, stocky figure, and a determined but not grim look . . . I was more excited than when I met Mussolini in 1926 . . . and more stimulated, I am sorry to say, than when I was blessed by the Pope in 1920.

Thomas Wolfe was similarly impressed – to begin with, at any rate – and he left a vivid account of how the crowds thronged ceaselessly through 'those tremendous banner-laden ways', and the whole city had become 'a mighty Ear, attentive, focused on the stadium':

> Everywhere the air was filled with a single voice. The green trees along the Kurfürstendamm began to talk; from loud-speakers concealed in their branches an announcer in the stadium spoke to the whole city . . . the *Vorlauf* [heat] was about to be run – and then the *Zwischenlauf* [intermediate round] – and at length the *Endlauf* [final] – and the winner: 'Owens – Oo Ess Ah!'

Another visitor who found the athletics tiresome was Diana Mitford. She and Unity had been given free passes for the stadium by Hitler, but fortunately their seats were a long way from the box of honour, and they were able to slip out without causing offence. The only man they really enjoyed watching was Owens, and Diana recorded graphically how he outdistanced everyone else:

> After Owens came the runners of other countries, bunched together, and far behind them all an Indian with his hair done up in a bun. 'Oh!' cried the Germans near us as Jesse Owens got further ahead and the Indian further behind. 'Oh, *der Inder! Der arme Inder!*', the poor Indian.

Alas for the author's powers of observation – no Indian took part in any race in which Owens competed.

In Döberitz, the 'womanless village', life soon fell into a regular pattern. Most of the athletes became fond of the place. The accommodation was excellent, the food good, the service first-class, the surrounding woods and fields delightfully rustic. Few of the competitors were worried by the presence in every bedroom cupboard of a block for a helmet to rest on – a sure sign that the place was to become a barracks as soon as the Games were over. An imaginative programme of entertainment was laid on in the evenings: cabarets, variety shows, animal acts, films, newsreels of the previous day's Olympic events, and, on one memorable occasion, a concert given by the Berlin Philharmonic Orchestra, followed by fireworks. One Norwegian sent home a postcard saying he wished he could stay in the village for ever. 'We dread our return to normal life,' he wrote. 'We are living in the midst of paradise.' The only drawbacks were the distance of Döberitz from the stadium and the continuous scrum of traffic heading both ways, most of it generally in the same direction at any particular moment.

In seeking to cater for the tastes of 52 nations, the cooks of the Norddeutscher Lloyd company faced a formidable task, and they soon discovered that there were as many dietary fads as countries. Several national teams not trusting to German supplies, had brought mountains of their own rations with them. The Argentines imported 8,000 lb of meat, which they demanded three times a day, in large helpings. The Bulgarians brought special cheese made of sheep's milk, the Finns large quantities of smoked ham and bacon, the Latvians their own sausage and grey bread. Milk was easily the most popular drink, and constantly demanded, in every form. The consumption record was held by the Indians, who put away two litres (3½ pints) per person per day. Endless special requests bombarded the kitchens. The French always wanted *hors d'oeuvre* instead of soup. The Dutch liked cheese for breakfast, and hot meals only in the evening. The Chileans proved moderate eaters, but the Czechs demanded pancakes for breakfast. The only teams to drink wine were the French and the Italian; the French took it straight, but the Italians cut theirs with water. 'The French sportsman is also an epicure, paying less attention to practical nourishment than to tasty and varied dishes,' said a German report with a hint of disapproval. The French weightlifters lived on a diet of steaks and white bread washed down with red wine. The Germans lowered huge quantities of steak tartare, chopped raw liver, cream cheese with oil and enormous numbers of eggs, often four per meal. In comparison the British seemed poor trenchermen, calling often for grilled meat, while the Americans went for huge breakfasts of eggs with ham or bacon, oatmeal or hominy grits and orange juice, with a specific prohibition on kippered herrings.

In the stadium Jesse Owens remained the centre of attention; on and off the track, he continued to perform with exemplary skill. He gained his second Gold Medal – in the 200m – with a grand slam, winning every heat and setting a new Olympic record. He broke the old record in the first round with a time of 21.1 seconds, equalled that in the second round, and in the semi-final ran 21.3. But as his fellow-Black Robinson ran 21.1 in the other semi-final it was clear that the final would be a thrilling battle.

Before that took place, the crowd was treated to a brief address by the Swedish explorer Sven Hedin, who was famous in Germany for his exploits in crossing Central Asia. A burly, commanding figure with close-cropped hair, he spoke from a small rostrum in the middle of the arena and addressed his remarks to the youth of the world. Fortunately he had the sense to keep his speech short, and included some memorable exhortations. 'Do not be content with what you are able to do,' he cried. 'Strive to achieve what you are not able to do, and, if possible, the unattainable.' He concluded with a stirring allusion to Sophocles: 'At the conclusion of the Games, go forth again to all quarters of the earth as heralds serving the good.' Few of the 100,000 people present realised how fortunate they were to escape another talk which Hedin gave a couple of days later, in the Prussian Academy of Sciences. There, given a free rein, he spoke at stupefying length on 'The Part Played by the Horse in the History of Asia'.

The final of the 200m took place at 6pm. The two Dutch finalists, Osendarp and van Beveren, were drawn on the inside. Then came Owens and Robinson, and on the outside Hänni, the Swiss, and Orr of Canada. At the gun Owens, Osendarp and Robinson were quickest off the mark. By the beginning of the final straight Owens had established a slight lead, which he steadily increased to about four metres at the tape. Behind him there was a fierce battle for second place.

Osendarp almost won it, but Robinson overtook him in the
last 20m. Responding to the pressure of the final, Owens
again broke the Olympic record, with a new time of 20.7
seconds.

For many people, however, his most memorable triumph
came in the Long Jump. Here the loyalties of the crowd were
under strain. By then they loved Yesseh Oh-vens, but they
also loved their own Luz Long, the student from Leipzig who
had out-jumped everyone in Germany, and they yearned for
him to win. For 40 years since the inception of the Modern
Olympiad the event had been dominated by Americans, who
had only once failed to take the Gold Medal; but now, the
home crowd knew, they had in Long a man capable of
breaking the pattern. The Olympic record stood at 7.73m, the
world record at 7.98m.

Both Owens and Long passed the old Olympic mark in the
penultimate round, the first with 7.87m, the second with
7.84m. That distance also gave Long a new German and
European record, and, when Owens cheerfully congratulated
him on it, the crowd roared its approval. Owens's manifest
good nature, and the friendliness of the rivalry between the
two men, contributed powerfully to the appeal of the final.

This produced a riveting duel, made all the more absorbing
by the fact that each man had a quite different style. Long
flew high, with both hands flung straight up above his head;
Owens travelled on a lower trajectory but gave a hitch-kick in
mid-flight, as though running in mid-air. Long went first with
a jump of 7.73m. Owens did a no-jump. Long went again – an
enormous distance, which made the crowd bellow even before they knew what it was. '*Sieben comma Sieben-und-
Achtzig,*' announced the loudspeakers. Seven eighty-seven!
Long had equalled Owens's distance. The applause was
stupendous. Again Owens smiled and congratulated his
opponent. Then he waited patiently for the noise to die down
as he prepared for his second jump. As at the start of a race,
his concentration closed out the world around him. For a few
seconds he leant easily forward, in a half-crouch, with only his
fingers moving as he sought for absolute balance. Then he
was sprinting for the take-off board . . . and as always he
landed so perfectly that his impetus carried him forwards and

upwards in a second, bouncing hop.

Seven ninety-four! Another record. Now Long needed a superhuman last effort. Utter silence gripped the crowd as he lined up for his final attempt: the arena went so still that members of the English team became aware of a sound they had never noticed before – the flags of the nations slapping against their poles high on the rim of the stadium. In this mighty hush Long gathered himself for a supreme effort. Trying to put everything into it, he over-ran the board. No jump! From all round the arena there arose a mighty groan, an earthquake of disappointment. The chance of a home victory had gone. But at once another miracle made some amends for the one the Germans had been seeking. Freed from any possibility of defeat, Owens flew into his final jump and soared over all the earlier marks, through the allegedly invincible eight-metre barrier, to a new Olympic and world record of 8.06m. For the spectators the tension had been scarcely bearable, the excitement never to be forgotten.

Objective observers saw that Owens was a relative novice in the art of long-jumping, and that he achieved what he did mainly through sheer speed. His hitch-kick action was nothing like as refined as the method of his rival, and had he been able to improve his technique he might have gone a good deal further. All the same, nothing could detract from the fact that he had won a third Gold Medal and set a new standard in that event.

The sunny demeanour which endeared Owens to the crowd was not put on: it was his nature. Loaded though he was with medals and acclaim, and hideously pestered by autograph-hunters, he remained unaffected and friendly towards everyone. Few people remembered him more warmly than Ina Beyer, who in 1936 was 13. Because she was of impeccably Aryan appearance – tall, blonde and blue-eyed – she was chosen as one of the many thousand schoolgirls who were ferried in by bus and lorry every day to give mass dancing and gymnastic displays in the stadium. One morning she met Owens, who took a fancy to her and asked her to teach him German. This she proceeded to do, in the short time open to them, and in a few days the two had become firm friends. But Jesse was not a quick learner, and one word in particular defeated him absolutely. 'Come on,' he would say every morning, taking hold of Ina's long plaits. 'Tell me again – what are these?' '*Tsöpfe*,' she would answer. '*Tsöpfe*.' But still he could not get it.

The morale of the British team rose sharply on the third day of the track and field events when Harold Whitlock, a tall, slender motor mechanic from London, won the 50km Walk. This was a true triumph of amateur effort, a great victory for individual determination and courage.

Whitlock was already 32, married and the father of three small children. He was working as the manager of a garage in New Cross, and got no special leave for the Olympics. Far from it: the time he took off to go to Berlin was considered holiday, and his wages were stopped while he was away. He had no coach, but did all his training on his own, with only the support of his family and the advice of friends to help him. The one advantage he had over other members of the British team was that, as a mechanic to a car-racing team, he had already travelled a good deal in Europe, and so was not put out as much as some by the novelty of his surroundings in Berlin.

Seeing that the only way to get picked for the Olympics would be to prove himself the best long-distance walker in Britain, he had set out in 1935 to do just that, and by dint of ferocious training had won all the important races – the Liverpool to Manchester (34 miles) in May, the Bradford Walk (32 miles) in June, the Nottingham to Birmingham (55 miles) in July, and the London to Brighton (51 miles) in September. In October his club, the Metropolitan Walking Club, and the newspaper *Sporting Life* decided on the spur of the moment to attack the eight-hour record, so he volunteered for that as well and broke it, by covering 51 miles 1,042 yards round the track at the White City. After that he 'put himself out to grass' until Christmas to build up for the next season, and then in early spring went into training again.

The result was that he came to Berlin in top condition. His main rival, he knew, would be T. A. Schwab, the Swiss holder of four world records. Other dangerous men were Stork of Czechoslovakia and Dalinsch and Bubenko of Latvia (in

German, *Lettland*). His plan was to let them set the pace and come at them from behind when he judged the moment right. He preferred, he said, to walk as a hound rather than as the fox; being a hound made him 'eager in the chase and voracious for a kill.'

On Tuesday, the day before the race, he deliberately stayed away from the stadium, for he knew that if he watched other events the excitement would drain off his nervous energy. Wednesday was again cool – ideal for hard walking – and when the 35 contestants left the stadium after a preliminary lap Whitlock was last but unworried. The only thing that concerned him was that he had not had time to reconnoitre the course – the manager of the British team had not even been able to find out where the course *was* – so that as they headed out through the Grunewald over a variety of terrain (asphalt, gravel, grass and in one stretch tree roots) everything was new to him.

Whitlock's hope was that he and the other two British entrants – Joe Hopkins and Lloyd Johnson – could stay together and walk as a team. But before they reached the 15km mark the pace had proved too hot for Hopkins, who fell back. Three kilometres later Johnson also started to flag, and Whitlock had to go on alone to keep in touch with the leaders.

Before the race elaborate arrangements had been made to provide the walkers with whatever special refreshments they wanted at feeding-stations along the route. But when Whitlock reached the 20km mark there was no sign of the glucose drink he had ordered or the British attendant who was supposed to have brought it. He therefore pressed ahead, eating the two glucose tablets he carried with him.

Now he began to overtake others. At the 25km mark he spotted the attendant, but instead of his glucose mixture the man could offer him only sweet, sickly tea made with condensed milk. Whitlock drank some but found it disgusting and threw the rest away. Now there were only two men ahead of him – Stork and Dalinsch. The fiasco of the refuelling had made him angry and full of fight, and he soon caught Stork and passed him. Dalinsch was further ahead and, because Whitlock knew him to be a doughty fighter, he stalked him carefully, easing his pace down as he closed so that he hardly seemed to be gaining. Then, having provoked no response, he accelerated past, surprised to find that Dalinsch did not react.

Thus after 31km Whitlock took the lead, only to find soon afterwards that he was feeling queasy. Perhaps Dalinsch too had been affected by the tea, he thought. Maybe that was the reason he had not counter-attacked. Was it going to finish him too? He began to feel really uncomfortable, as if he had a hard lump in his stomach, and for a couple of kilometres the pain forced him to reduce his pace. Word came from behind that Schwab was closing on him fast, and that Bubenko was also back in the hunt, hard behind the Swiss. Whitlock's lead had been reduced to 30 seconds. The pain increased and his saliva dried up – and then suddenly he was sick, throwing up all the tea. In a few strides he was back to normal.

By the 45km mark he had increased his lead again, and he lengthened it still more up the incline from the Wannsee towards the stadium. A burst of cheering greeted him as he emerged from the tunnel into the arena. The finish lay to his right, but as he checked left he saw to his consternation a line of sprinters on their marks, all set for the gun in one of the 200m semi-finals. Providentially the starter saw what was about to happen and lowered his pistol, so that Whitlock went on unobstructed to the tape. He finished in 4 hours, 30 minutes and 41.4 seconds, beating the former Olympic record by the prodigious margin of 20 minutes, with Schwab coming in second a minute and a half behind him. It was a magnificent achievement, which put new heart into the British team.

Another epic struggle developed – unexpectedly – in the Pole Vault, which began in the morning but lasted so long that it went on far into the night, developing into a tremendous battle between the Americans and the Japanese. When darkness fell the struggle continued under floodlights, and some 30,000 spectators were so gripped by it that they stayed on, though half-frozen, until the end. After breathless excitement the Gold Medal was won by the American Earl Meadows, who touched the bar at 4.35m, but did not dislodge it, and so set a new Olympic record. Behind him came the two Japanese, Nishida and Oe, both with 4.25m. By the finish all the competitors were utterly exhausted, for they had been jumping intermittently for almost 12 hours.

The British scented another chance of a Gold Medal in the 400m, an event in which they were particularly strong. Godfrey Brown, Godfrey Rampling and William Roberts had all previously beaten 48 seconds and were undoubtedly the best European runners at the distance. In Berlin, however, they had to contend with a new dimension in the shape of the Blacks Archie Williams and James Lu Valle.

Brown, who ran in spectacles, was then 21 and at Cambridge, where he was President of the University Athletics Club. Though dogged by bad draws – in the early rounds he got lane 6 once and lane 5 twice, putting him in the disadvantageous outside positions – he came safely through to the final. Rampling went out in the semi-final, but Roberts also got through. Realists saw that for sheer speed no one could touch Williams, but Brown was not disheartened, and on the day of the final went off before lunch for a quiet walk on his own.

The final proved a desperately exciting race. Again Brown was unlucky and drew lane 6, on the outside. At the gun he was away fast and held a short lead for the first 100m. Then Williams passed him and established a lead of nearly three metres, which seemed decisive. But on the final straight Brown launched a thrilling counter-attack and closed up fast. Fighting tenaciously, he all but caught the leader. At the tape Williams was faltering; Brown was only a couple of feet behind, and gaining fast. Ten more yards – *five* more yards – and he would have won. At his shoulder another tough duel had been fought out: Lu Valle (third) and Roberts (fourth) were so close that both were timed at 46.8 seconds. Brown was so exhausted by his effort that for a few moments he collapsed on the grass, but he quickly recovered.

A silver medal in the 400m did much for British morale – and soon another came in the 110m Hurdles. Don Finlay, an army officer, was Captain of the British team, and had returned outstandingly consistent times; he was also supremely fit, for when on duty in England he would punish soldiers who had committed minor misdemeanours by taking them with him on fiendishly fast cross-country runs. Yet here again form showed that in Berlin he was up against someone a yard faster – as usual, an American, but this time white, in the shape of Forrest Towns. When, in the semi-final, Towns broke both Olympic and World records with a time of 14.1 seconds, the result of the final seemed a foregone conclusion. So it was – but Finlay finished powerfully to come second, and defenders of British standards could justifiably point out that his time of 14.4 equalled the former Olympic record.

Another gripping struggle came in the 1,500m, or metric mile. A fast time was guaranteed by the presence of the Olympic record-holder, Luigi Beccali of Italy, and the ace American miler Glen Cunningham. For Britain, it was a severe disappointment that Sydney Wooderson, their be-spectacled and gawky-looking mile champion, had not fully recovered from an ankle injury, and, although he ran in one of the heats, he was eliminated. A dark horse – in the sense that he ran in the all-black strip of his native New Zealand – was 27-year-old Jack Lovelock, who had three times been beaten by Wooderson, but was known to have trained excep-tionally hard for the Olympics. With his crinkly brown hair parted straight down the middle, his bashful grin and slight physique (he weighed only 9 stone 7 lb), Lovelock looked hardly robust enough to take on such powerful competition.

An amusing story was told of an evening he spent in Cambridge. At the time of the Olympics he was a student at St Mary's Hospital, Paddington, training to become a doctor, but before that he had been to Oxford University. Visiting Cambridge one evening, he was spotted at large in the town by two of the Bulldogs – the bowler-hatted officials who enforce university discipline. Because he appeared to be breaking the rules by not wearing a formal gown, they gave chase. Lovelock took off and led them a high-speed dance. Little realising they were behind one of the fittest men in the world, the Bulldogs ran until they were nearly done-for – whereupon Lovelock suddenly pulled up unruffled. When his gasping pursuers demanded to know whether or not he was a member of 'the University', he answered, 'Yes.' But when they invited him to go along with them, he declined, since to him 'the University' meant Oxford.

In Berlin he was drawn in Heat 2 of the 1,500m, and ran a canny race, content to coast in third. Then in the final he showed himself a master strategist.

The race began just after 4pm on Thursday. As the runners were lining up, Hitler appeared, and they had to wait while the German and Olympic flags were hoisted. The crowd, having cheered the Führer, turned back to the athletes. 'Cun – ning – HAM!, Cun – ning – HAM!' they bellowed, rooting for the likely winner – and for most of the race their fancy looked safe. All through the first three laps Lovelock lay back, letting others dispute the lead, but keeping tucked in close behind the front-runners: Cunningham, the swarthy Beccali, and Ny of Sweden in vivid blue shorts. As the gun went for the last lap. Ny sped briefly ahead. Beccali put in a spurt and overtook him. But then a brilliantly aggressive move brought the crowd howling to their feet. The last time Lovelock had raced against Cunningham, he had waited till 60 yards from home before sprinting. Now he suddenly launched a blistering spurt 300 yards out and took the American by surprise. The crowd roared themselves hoarse as Lovelock held his sprint right to the tape, which he broke in the world and Olympic record time of 3 minutes, 47.8 seconds. Cunningham, five yards behind, also beat the old world record, and five of the twelve finalists surpassed the former Olympic best.

The B.B.C. commentator on this race – as on all the track events – was none other then Harold Abrahams; but although he had gained a Gold Medal in the Olympic 100m, he would never have won one for his performance on the radio. His commentaries were amateurish in the extreme, full of empty pauses, repetitions and mistakes; and unfortunately for British listeners he was at his most erratic during the 1,500m. As the race started he announced, 'There's an American leading. I can't see who it is . . . I'll tell you who's leading in a moment . . . Oh, it's the German, Böttcher. I'm so sorry.'

As the runners finished the second lap, he said, 'Time for the 800 metres . . . I missed it. I'm sorry: it's the excitement. Ha, ha!' When Lovelock took the lead 300 yards from home, Abrahams did convey this vital information, but then became more and more incoherent:

'Lovelock leads! Lovelock leads! Cunningham's leading. No, no! Lovelock leads by three yards. Three hundred yards

to go. Lovelock! Lovelock! Come on, Jack! A hundred yards
to go. Come on, Jack! My God, he's done it! Jack, come ON!
Lovelock wins! Five yards, six yards. He wins! He's won!
Hooray!'

This great victory went some way towards restoring the
prestige of white athletes; but so many medals and records
had already fallen to coloured men that the Berlin spectators
had become decidedly partisan. 'There is no feeling against
them as individuals,' reported Howard Marshall of *The Daily
Telegraph*, 'but these American negroes are not popular with
the German crowd.' Goebbels's own newspaper *Der Angriff*,
though not resorting to its normal hysterical abuse, put the
matter with characteristic generosity. If the American team
had not brought over 'black auxiliaries', it said, 'things would
look badly for it . . . Long would have won the Long Jump,
Lanzi the 800m, Osendarp the 100m . . . and everyone would
have considered the Yankees a great disappointment.' All
correspondents agreed that organised heckling went too far
during the 5,000m, which was won by Hoeckert of Finland,
with his fellow-countryman Lehtinen a close second. A storm
of whistling and concerted shouts became so distracting that
immediately after the race the authorities appealed to the
crowd to moderate their outbursts.

The official British attitude, as expressed by the British
Olympic Association, was that 'a spirit of good sportsmanship
and complete friendliness' had prevailed. This may have been
true of the athletes themselves, but it was certainly not true of
the crowd, which was described by Godfrey Brown as 'one of
the most unpleasant before which athletes have ever had the
misfortune to compete'. Soon after the Olympics Brown
wrote a sharp attack, both on the ponderous nature of all the
organisation – 'we could sense a huge, remorseless machine
rolling relentlessly towards its predestined goal' – and on the
behaviour of the crowd:

When the Head of State sets the example by applauding any
competitors from his own nation, people may find it difficult to
be well mannered . . . but on the afternoon when Jack Lovelock
breaks the world record for the 1,500 metres, to reserve your
largest roar of applause for an unfortunate Swede who happens

to conclude the javelin-throwing with a moderate effort, because it means your compatriot has won, to whistle and hoot United States competitors in the pole vault because you want their coloured Japanese rivals to win – all this deserves stronger language.

Nationalist feeling became more rampant with every German success, and *Deutschland über Alles* seemed to erupt from the crowd with ever-increasing frequency. When Gerhard Stöck – big, blond, beautiful, and of admirably Aryan appearance – won the Javelin, he sprang to attention and gave a rigid Nazi salute, there where he was, on the track, and during the national anthem he bawled out his own version from the winner's rostrum.

Several times the Jewish question came perilously close to the surface. One was when the German high-jumper Gretel Bergmann failed to appear for the event. She had – it will be recalled – been ostentatiously recalled from exile in England, at the same time as the fencer Helene Meyer had been summoned back from the United States. Her name was listed on the German team, but at the last minute she did not turn out, so that only two German girls took part in the High Jump, instead of three.

The reason, carefully concealed by the authorities, was shameful in the extreme. On the morning of 29 July – two days before the official opening of the Games – she called on the American Consul General in Stuttgart, ostensibly to enquire about a visa, and told the following story.

On 17 July she had received a letter from the German Olympic Committee in Berlin telling her that because of her mediocre performance (*mittelmässige Leistung*) she would not after all be required to participate in the Games. This was nonsense, for in the German qualifying championships she had jumped 10cm higher than the next best girl. She therefore telephoned the head of the Jewish athletic organisation in Berlin, and he protested vigorously to the Olympic Committee. The only result was that he found himself ordered to report twice daily to the Gestapo, so that he could not slip out of the country to spread the news. The dishonesty of the authorities was confirmed when the Olympic High Jump was won by Ibolya Csak of Hungary with a height of 1.60m. As Gretel Bergmann had cleared 1.64m in the qualifying championships, she must – had she competed with anything like her normal form – have won the event. It cannot have pleased the Nazis, hungry as they were for medals, to realise that their own racial phobia had deprived them of a Gold.

Helene Meyer, in contrast, did take part, and what is more won the Silver Medal in the Foil. When she mounted the rostrum in the stadium for the crowning ceremony, she smiled proudly, gave the Nazi salute and received an ovation. Nevertheless, her motives in taking part were the subject of much uncharitable gossip. One friend of hers claimed that her main purpose in returning to Germany had been to see her ageing mother, who was suffering from diabetes. Another colleague said that on being invited to represent Germany she had demanded full citizenship, but she herself denied this. Some people took the view that her decision to participate was immensely courageous, and that she was trying to strike a blow for Jews; others, that she was merely seeking personal glory, and should never have come within a thousand miles of Nazi Berlin. Certainly by agreeing to appear she handed the regime an ace, which they lost no opportunity of playing.

Racial overtones also cast a blight on the record-breaking American 4 × 100m relay team. On the morning of the heats, the two Jewish members of the team, Martin Glickman and Sam Stoller, found that they had suddenly been replaced by Jesse Owens and Foy Draper. That Owens was the fastest man in Berlin had already been proved beyond doubt, but Stoller had also run 100m in 10.3 seconds, and was at least as fast as Draper, who replaced him. The official reason for the switch was that the Germans were going to spring some sort of surprise with *their* team, but nobody found this convincing. There were only two credible explanations: one, that Glickman and Stoller had been dropped simply because they were Jewish; and the other, that the United States was determined to win at all costs, even at the expense of disappointing men who had trained for months to run in the event. Neither reason did the team managers much credit.

In spite of the last-minute upset, the new team performed spectacularly. To beat the 40-second barrier, reached by the

American team at Los Angeles in 1932, was widely considered impossible, yet the *ersatz* squad in Berlin managed it,
thanks not least to their perfect baton changes. Owens, drawn
in lane 4, gave them an ideal start and established a lead of
nearly five metres by the end of his leg. Metcalfe increased
the gap to seven, Draper to ten and Wykoff to twelve,
breaking the tape in 39.8 seconds. The Italians came second,
and the Germans, by a fluke, third: in spite of a brilliant run
by Borchmeyer, who made up a lot of ground, they were
hampered by poor handovers and would have come fourth if
Osendarp of Holland had not dropped the baton only 30
yards from the tape.

The final day of the track and field events – 9 August –
contained a vintage programme, but for most people *the*
event was the Marathon. Hailed by the Germans as *der
klassische Lauf*, the 'classic race', with its direct evocation of
ancient Greece, the Marathon was seen as the ultimate test of
strength and stamina, and so as an event carrying unequalled
prestige. By the time the 56 competitors came out on to the
track at 3pm, the stadium was overflowing, and it was estimated that more than a million people had assembled along
the 42km course, which wound out and back through the
Grunewald and the western fringes of the city, taking in part
of the Avus motor-race track.

At last the clouds had burned away and the weather was
what it should have been all the time. With the sun blazing
down out of a clear sky, many of the runners wore hats, for
they knew that there was little shade along the route. Just
before the start Hitler arrived with most of the Reich Government in tow, his party including the veteran Field Marshal
von Mackensen, who wore the uniform of the Death's Head
Hussars.

The favourite, in more senses than one, was the little
Argentine runner Juan Carlos Zabala, who had set a new
Olympic best time in Los Angeles and was already a familiar
figure in Berlin, where he had spent the past few months
training. The next most likely winner seemed to be the short
and wiry Kitei Son, who was officially listed as a Japanese,
and ran with the emblem of the red rising sun on his white

vest, but who in fact came from Korea, then part of the
Japanese empire. During the previous winter he had completed a marathon in a time five minutes faster than the
Olympic best. Also to be reckoned with were a trio of Finns
coached by the immortal Nurmi.

The race started on the stroke of 3pm. Zabala, wearing a
hat, at once took the lead as the runners did one lap of the
stadium before heading out through the Marathon Gate to
the west. For the first few kilometres he steadily increased his
advantage, setting a phenomenal pace. Spectators who had
often seen him training along this very route greeted him like
an old friend, but the more knowledgeable among them were
worried, for they could see that, going at the speed he had
chosen, he must either finish in an unprecedented time or
blow up. Still, they supposed that with his great experience he
must know what he was doing.

After 12km he was a minute and a half ahead of the next
man, Dias of Portugal, and next behind him came an
improbable-looking pair: the short, dark, bow-legged Son,
and the much taller Englishman Ernest Harper from York-
shire, whose neatly parted fair hair remained unruffled
throughout. The crowd was intrigued by Son's white shoes,
which he wore without socks and which were made with the
big toe separated from its neighbours in a compartment of its
own. People also noticed that he and Harper kept talking –
though what about, no one could be sure. Behind them, at a
distance, the three Finns also maintained a running conversation; and the public, who had been led to believe that all Finns
were endowed with almost supernatural tactical guile, reckoned that they must have the race under control to be chatting
so composedly.

As the long battle developed, every move was reported
over loudspeakers to the crowd in the stadium. They, however, were thoroughly spoilt, for they had other thrilling events
to entertain them as they waited. One was the final of the
women's 4 × 100m Relay, which the German girls had an
excellent chance of winning: they had justified all optimistic
predictions by setting a new world record in their heat, so
that, when they came onto the track for the final, native
excitement and anticipation were intense.

The draw was not ideal for the Germans, who found themselves in lane 4, next to their most dangerous rivals, the Americans, and just ahead of them in the staggered start. All the same, the race began perfectly for them. On the first leg, round the curve, Emmy Albus made ground on all opponents. A perfect handover, and on the straight Käthe Krauss went clear ahead. Another perfect exchange, and away into the second curve went Marie Dollinger, a veteran who had competed in the two previous Olympiads. She knew that she must leave her last colleague Ilse Dörffeldt with a lead of several metres to give her a chance against the United States' final runner, the all-conquering Helen Stephens – and she did not fail. With the sprint of her life, she opened up a gap of 10 clear metres.

Like 100,000 of his subjects, Hitler leapt to his feet shouting with excitement. The stadium roar was cataclysmic. But then came disaster. Dörffeldt, accelerating to full speed before she had a proper grip of the baton, could not keep hold of it, and it tumbled onto the track. The poor girl hesitated and pulled up. Helen Stephens swept past to victory. Hitler sat down with a thump, lost for words. Though comforted by a colleague, Dörffeldt buried her face in her hands, and everyone could see that she was crying. Afterwards the Führer made a special effort to comfort her, but speculation raged as to whether, even if she had not dropped the baton, Helen Stephens would have overtaken her. It seems unlikely. Stephens was much faster, but the German girls had built up a formidable lead, and were heading for another record, whereas the American team's time turned out half a second slower than that of the Germans in their heat.

The other relay held during the Marathon was the final of the men's 4 × 400m. Here was another short, sharp fight, in contrast to the long, grinding struggle out in the suburbs. The British had known all along that this race would offer them their best chance of a Gold Medal, and when it came, they took it. All four members of the Relay squad – Frederick Wolff, Godfrey Rampling, Bill Roberts and Godfrey Brown – excelled themselves, but none so outstandingly as Rampling. Wolff, the weakest of the four, finished the first leg eight metres behind Limon of Canada and three behind Cagle of the United States. With the great Black sprinter Phil Edwards going second for Canada, it seemed impossible that anyone could catch up – yet Rampling did. In the words of Howard Marshall, 'his glorious stride and immense power set us shouting deliriously. He pounded round the first bend, accelerated amazingly, strode past Young of America, overhauled Edwards and hurled himself unbelievably into the lead. This was tremendous racing.'

Rampling's run swung the race decisively in Britain's favour. He handed over a three-yard lead, which Roberts and Brown increased, to take the Gold Medal with a time of 3 minutes, 9 seconds, eight-tenths of a second outside the world record. The Americans took the Silver Medal and the Germans the Bronze.

For Rampling, it was one of those golden days on which he managed to transcend the state of deliberate concentration which can sometimes be inhibiting, and passed through on to a higher plane, almost of trance, which released all the power latent in his body. 'If I was *too* concentrated, too much aware of details, I never did well,' he recalled nearly 50 years later. 'If I noticed the stitching on the shorts of the chap in front of me, it was no good. But on that day in Berlin I just seemed to float round the track, passing people without effort.'

After the British victory, as the Marathon struggle continued outside, 2,000 German gymnasts took to the turf in the stadium to demonstrate their national system. But by then, as the loudspeakers made clear, dramatic changes were taking place in the race. At the half-way mark Zabala still had a lead of about a minute over Son and Harper, who rounded the turn together; but then, on the blazing-hot concrete of the Avus straight, Son raised his pace. Harper stayed with him, and the two began to close on the Argentine. At the 28km mark Zabala was appalled to find them suddenly level. Drained by the heat, by the unyielding concrete surfaces, and by his own excessive speed in the early stages, he could scarcely respond. For 100m he stayed with the leaders, then fell back, and after three more kilometres staggered out of the race. Several other runners did the same, and Leni Riefenstahl's cameramen caught their agony, dwelling on it with almost obscene relish.

The Finns were still going well, but now, too late, they realised that they had been nursing their strength excessively. Though they speeded up, they could not get back into contention with the leaders. By then Dias had also crumpled, so that third place was being disputed between the Finns and another Japanese-Korean, Shoryu Nan. In the final stages of the race Son drew away from his long-time partner Harper, and when the trumpets sounded his approach from the towers of the Marathon Gate, he emerged from the gloom of the entrance-tunnel alone. A great storm of applause greeted him. Gathering his strength, he sprinted valiantly for the last 200m and broke the tape, his face twisted by strain, in a new Olympic best time of 2 hours, 29 minutes and 19 seconds. There followed a long pause of more than two minutes before Harper appeared, with Nan close on his heels. Two of the Finns finished fourth and fifth, one minute and two minutes behind Nan, but the third of their trio could manage no better than ninth.

After his triumph Son was at pains to make it clear that both he and Nan were Koreans, obliged to run in alien colours only because Japan had conquered their country in 1910. He made a point of signing his name in Korean script, and drawing maps of his homeland beside it; but the distinction meant little to western reporters, and the Nazi propaganda machine was able to get away with ascribing the victory to Japan – a country which Hitler was keen to cultivate and support in its struggle against the Bolshevist menace of the Soviet Union in the Far East.

He cannot have been pleased to learn that, even as Son was fighting his way through the Berlin heat to victory, a large Communist demonstration was taking place in London. There several hundred people gathered in Hyde Park and marched to the German Embassy in Carlton House Terrace to protest against the Reich's supply of arms to the insurgents in the Spanish Civil War. For the moment, however, the Führer could return to the Chancellery replete with the knowledge that the final day of the Olympic track and field events had been a great success.

15

ENTERTAINMENTS

Many thousands of ordinary people were being suitably entertained and impressed by events in the stadium, by parades and displays outside, by exhibitions and theatres, by the city itself. But it was above all the *Ehrengäste* – the guests of honour – whom the Nazis wanted to court, and for the delectation of important strangers the leaders arranged a series of magnificent parties. If lavish hospitality alone could have forged a link between Germany and Britain, the Olympic fortnight would have done the trick, for the entertainments were on a prodigious scale, and carried out with a degree of taste which agreeably surprised even the most critical of the visitors.

Some of the guests, like the Channons, did nothing except enjoy themselves. Others, however, were active behind the scenes, and none more so than Sir Robert Vansittart, who had come to Berlin with his wife on what he later described as a busman's holiday. The Olympics, in German eyes, provided *the* opportunity of cracking Vansittart's apparently unreasoning hostility and prejudice against them. From the moment when Goebbels had a foot-bath of orchids delivered at the British Embassy to greet Lady Vansittart on her arrival, they did everything they could to convert him, with the result that he was more often out of the stadium than in, not merely going to all the parties but having private audiences with the leaders as well. That they failed entirely was not only a measure of the gulf between their intelligence and his but also a striking demonstration of how blind they were to the evil of their own practices: they simply could not see that it was impossible for a man as honest and clear-sighted as Vansittart to go along with them.

Whatever manoeuvring might be going on in the background, on the surface all was gaiety, and the pressure of entertainment relentless. The principal victims were the members of the International Olympic Committee, who had scarcely been in Berlin an hour before they found themselves invited to at least one formal banquet or reception at every lunch-time and dinner-time for the next 16 days. It seems a miracle that they survived, for their schedule was appalling: lunch given by the City of Berlin in their honour; lunch given by the Reich Sport Leader at his home; dinner arranged by the President of the Organising Committee in the White Room of the Berlin Royal Palace; gala dinner in the House of German Fliers, given by the Commissioner of Berlin's Metropolitan Police; gala dinner in the Golden Gallery of Charlottenburg Palace, given by Baron and Baroness von Neurath; gala dinner and reception given by General von Blomberg; lunch on board various warships at Kiel; gala dinner given by the City of Kiel; lunch party given by Dr Lippert, the Commissioner of State; lunch in the stadium's terrace restaurant, given by Dr Diem . . . And so it went on.

Not to be outdone, the British gave a reception for nearly 1,000 guests at the Embassy on the evening of Saturday, 8 August. The host was the Ambassador, but because Lady Phipps was ill at the time her place as hostess was taken by her sister, Lady Vansittart. The guests included not only the whole British team and its officials, but many of the leading German politicians as well, among them Goebbels, Ribbentrop, Frick (Minister for the Interior), Baron von Neurath (Foreign Minister) and Prince August Wilhelm. Almost half a century later, Lady Vansittart retained undimmed her most vivid memory of the evening. As she stood receiving guests by one of the open windows, she heard a sudden commotion outside – a man yelling violently. She looked out and saw a horrible figure, dressed from head to foot in black, white-faced, spectacles glinting, with a revolver at his waist. It was Heinrich Himmler, head of the Gestapo, abusing the police on duty for having stopped his unnumbered car in the wrong place. It does not sound as if the party was an unqualified success, for Channon described it as 'boring, crowded and inelegant'.

Between these minor diversions came the really serious engagements – the parties given by the senior members of the hierarchy which brooked no refusal. Predictably enough, no host was more ostentatious than Goering. A lunch for the committee at his private house, described as being 'of German baroque cuisine', began with melons stuffed with *foie gras* and mushrooms, followed by kangaroo-tail soup, before progressing to more mundane fare. At an evening garden-party in the grounds of the enormous new Air Ministry, he had the lawns illuminated by searchlights mounted on buildings all around and the swimming pool strewn with floating lilies lit from underneath. A miniature replica of an eighteenth-century village had been built for the occasion, with an inn, a bakery and many craft shops. Goering and his wife received their guests sitting in front of a tea-pavilion. During dinner the *corps de ballet* from the Berlin Opera danced on the lawn; afterwards, long screens were suddenly withdrawn to reveal a full-scale Viennese fun-fair, complete with merry-go-rounds, shooting galleries, wine and beer-booths, all staffed by pretty young actresses in Tyrolean costume. Entering fully into the spirit of the occasion, the Reichsmarschall himself delighted his guests by taking a ride on one of the roundabout horses. Chips Channon found the evening enchanting:

> The end of the garden was in darkness, and suddenly, with no warning, it was floodlit, and a procession of white horses, donkeys and peasants appeared from nowhere . . . It was fantastic, peasants dancing and *schuhplattling*, vast women carrying pretzels and beer, a ship, a beerhouse, crowds of gay, laughing people, animals . . . 'There has never been anything like this since the days of Louis Quatorze,' someone remarked. 'Not since Nero,' I retorted . . . Goebbels, it appears, as well as Ribbentrop, was in despair with jealousy.

Another *pièce de résistance* master-minded by Goering was the government dinner, at which he acted as host, in the State Opera House in Unter den Linden – a magnificent occasion, perfectly executed, for which the preparations were immensely elaborate. Under the direction of the Munich architect Oswald, the seats were removed from the floor of the theatre, and the auditorium, orchestra pit and stage were boarded over to make a level arena. Here the guests dined at round tables, while the Nazi leaders occupied the boxes, beaming down on the assembled throng. Red and white were the colours of the evening, the decor being of Pompeiian red offset by tall vertical banners of white velvet, with the ladies all asked to wear long white dresses. Flunkeys in pink velvet and powdered wigs lined the entrance, holding tall poles with lanterns on the tops. Goering himself, also in white and loaded down with decorations, welcomed the guests as they arrived. In the foyer he and Emmy – according to Channon 'a tall, handsome and seemingly almost naked woman' – moved easily among 'an obsequious crowd of Royalties and ambassadors'. When the company went into dinner, Goebbels and his party took the box on the right of the proscenium, Goering – with the Crown Prince of Sweden and the King of Bulgaria – that on the left. During the meal ballet dancers swirled between the tables, and opera singers sang from positions high up in the amphitheatre, so that their voices came floating ethereally down from the gods.

Afterwards Goering addressed the gathering in fulsome terms, hoping that every visitor might take with him or her the impression of a nation whose sincerest object and wish it was to join hands in the spirit of genuine friendship and fellowship with every other nation of the earth. Those close to the official host could not help noticing that, although his fat face was smiling expansively, his blue eyes remained very cold. Then Goebbels addressed the guests on behalf of the government, and Goering, circulating among the tables, presented the ladies with small porcelain replicas of the Olympic bell. The style and splendour of the evening put Channon in mind of

> the fêtes given by the Directoire of the French Revolution, with the upstarts tipsy with power and flattered by the proximity and ovations of the ex-grand, whom once they wished to destroy.

The French Ambassador, André François-Poncet, reflected

on a more immediate paradox: that men who clearly enjoyed such civilised entertainment could at the same time be directing a brutal campaign of racial and political oppression.

That such a campaign was in progress would have been revealed by one visit to Oranienburg, less than an hour's journey from the Olympic stadium, on the northern outskirts of Berlin. There, at the point where the suburban electric railway ended – the equivalent in London's terms of Enfield – behind walls topped with barbed wire, lay *Konzentrationslager der Standarte 208* – Concentration Camp of District 208.

The inmates of this establishment, none of whom had been convicted of any crime, were leading a rather less luxurious life than the Olympic dignitaries dining and dancing a few miles from them. They slept in what had been the cooling-rooms of a brewery, packed like rabbits into long, vaulted chambers. Damp ran down the walls, and there was practically no ventilation. The wooden bunks, in three tiers, were so low that the prisoners had to creep into them head-first, from the end. One man calculated that he had three cubic metres of air-space – less than a third of the minimum granted to convicted prisoners.

Their day began at 5.30, with *ersatz* coffee and a piece of grey bread. They were then marched out to work on whatever project was in hand – swamp-draining, road-building, forestry, the hacking-out of tree-stumps – until sundown, for although they were supposed to be in *Schutzhaft*, or 'protective arrest', they were in fact no more than slaves of the State. Their food consisted mainly of mixed macaroni and potato; they called it pig-wash, and most of them threw it away, half-starved though they were. Back in the camp, the SS guards made every effort to humiliate and demoralise them; for the slightest offence, often imagined, they would beat men up with rubber clubs or whips, or drive them over the obstacle course on the back parade-ground until they collapsed. Another favourite practice was the systematic frustration of the need for free time and relaxation; when the prisoners were exhausted in the evening, the guards would arbitrarily call them out to do drill or perform futile, unnecessary tasks, and this perpetual harrying, like a form of Chinese water-torture, reduced people to a state of terrible nervous tension.

This, however, was nothing beside the physical torture inflicted by the notorious stone coffins, built to his own design by an earlier commandant, Sturmbann Führer Schafer of the SA. The coffins were a form of upright cell, just big enough for a man to stand in, but too narrow to allow even a slight bending of the knees. The agony produced by incarceration in one of them was vividly described by an inmate of the camp:

> These standing berths are the product of a torturer's imagination of an absolutely mediaeval type. The prisoners penned into them underwent terrible hours, nights of inexpressible torment . . . to feel the limbs becoming numbed from below and beginning to ache, the knees beginning to sag and graze the walls, eternally wondering where to put one's arms and how to go on standing; and besides these things the no less dreadful spiritual torment, the fearful stab of one's thoughts . . . it is simply a hell, and the man who devised it is not a human being but a beast.

Such was the bestial treatment being given to innocent citizens by agents of the German Government while the Olympic Games were in progress. As the Nazi leaders moved among their international guests at the dazzling parties, they knew perfectly well what was going on – not only in Oranienburg, but also in Dachau, Esterwege and many similar camps. Some of the guests, some members of the International Olympic Committee, must also have had a good idea, but they closed their minds to reality and carried on with the Games.

No one, it can safely be said, gave much thought to concentration camps on the evening when Hitler held his own grand dinner in the Chancellery. This was the first party given in the new dining-room which he had just had built, extending the Chancellery out into the garden. According to George Ward Price, the correspondent of the *Daily Mail*, he had changed the decor six times before he was satisfied; eventually he had settled on rows of dark-red marble pillars, which formed an arcade down each side of the room, rising to a ceiling of light-blue and gold mosaic. For this special evening the

Führer dispensed with his normal young servants, who wore brown-and-white jackets, and replaced them with elderly footmen in a livery of blue and silver, with white stockings. As guests came in, they were announced by a major-domo in black livery and knee breeches, with a cocked hat under his arm and wearing a court sword.

Two hundred people were invited, and it was noticeable that the visitors outshone the locals. Since the Nazi regime discouraged jewellery and make-up, most of the German women lacked glamour; and Hess (for example), in plain khaki uniform, looked downright dowdy beside Vansittart, the principal guest, who was resplendent in full evening dress and decorations. One notable exception among the home team was Emmy Goering, whose sun-tan (acquired from much tennis) and fine Nordic colouring made her lack of make-up irrelevant. It was during this meal that Count Baillet-Latour startled Henriette von Schirach by saying that there would be a war within three years.

Sarita Vansittart, placed on Hitler's right, was surprised by the courtliness of his greeting: he kissed her hand and took her by the arm to lead her into dinner. He wore ill fitting evening dress, the jacket tending to slide off his narrow, sloping shoulders; refusing wine and all the other food offered, he ordered spinach and a poached egg, and Lady Vansittart, feeling she should keep him company, did the same. Because her German was limited, she at first felt nervous about the conversation, but soon she found that Hitler was happy enough to chatter away on his own. When eventually she plucked up courage and said, '*Kein Fleisch? Kein Wein? Keine Männer? Keine Frauen?*' (meaning that if everyone became vegetarian teetotallers, life would be awfully dull), he burst out with a hoarse bark of laughter so loud that her husband, sitting opposite in the bend of the horseshoe table next to Emmy Goering, looked up startled, wondering what on earth she could have said.

Whether because of that remark, or because of her attractive appearance, Hitler took such a fancy to his neighbour that after dinner he led her off to his study and spent half an hour there with her, alone except for Schmidt, his interpreter. He kept telling her how much he admired England, and said,

You should come to Berlin more often. Come every month! I can't talk to the British Ambassador, but I can talk to your husband.' (It seemed to escape the Führer that the Ambassador whom he disparaged was the brother-in-law of the lady to whom he was talking.) In his eagerness to find out how Britain had won her Empire, he said, he had seen the film *Lives of the Bengal Lancers* five times. When his guest tried to tell him that the film was not renowned for its historical accuracy, he seemed crestfallen.

Sitting so close to him, Lady Vansittart had plenty of time to observe how extraordinarily smooth the skin of his face was, how the little moustache and hanging forelock looked as though they had been stuck on (exactly as in the cartoons drawn by Low), how his slaty-blue eyes were red-rimmed and seemed to gaze hungrily at her. She stared back, secretly rather amused to be knee-to-knee with a creature so awful, but also thinking that he was a made-up man, an actor with nothing behind the façade, very vulnerable, and not a real person at all.

The talk turned to the Olympics, and Hitler said, 'You saw all the young men in the stadium today. Do you think I'd let them die in battle?' When Lady Vansittart replied that she thought it was always the youngest who went first, the Führer again seemed taken aback; and as he went on talking he began to think about the black side of the regime, the people who were in concentration camps at that moment. Seeing her face change, Hitler at last suggested that they should go back to the party, where people were beginning to wonder what had become of them.

The Führer's clumsy attempts to establish new friendships among the British were reinforced ham-fistedly by those of Ribbentrop, who gave an immense and very stylish party at his own home in the suburb of Dahlem. As the house could not possibly accommodate the 600 guests, he and his wife Annalies transformed the garden into what he called a 'small festival field' by pitching a marquee over the lawn and tennis court, which was covered with coconut matting for dancing.

The party was held on 10 August, and on that morning, after intensive manoeuvring inside the German Chancellery and Foreign Office, the announcement was made that Ribbentrop had been appointed Ambassador to London, in succession to the late Leopold von Hoesch. As he himself remarked, this gave his evening a particularly German–English note, and although the guests of honour included the Goerings, the Hesses and the entire Olympic Committee, the one man whom he really wanted to impress was Vansittart.

After one set-back, when Countess Baillet-Latour arrived unexpectedly, and thereby threw the entire seating-plan into chaos, everything went well. The setting looked perfect, the swimming-pool covered with water-roses and the rhododendrons in exceptionally fine bloom. Vansittart was civility itself, congratulating Ribbentrop handsomely on his appointment. After dinner people danced to the strains of the popular Hungarian violinist Barnabas von Geczy, and the festivities lasted until dawn was breaking. Both the Vansittarts danced a lot and appeared to enjoy themselves greatly. 'Was this a good omen?' Ribbentrop wrote later. 'Did Sir Robert not find Berlin so repulsive after all?' Channon also enjoyed himself – so much so that he drank rather too freely:

> The lovely evening, the fantastic collection of notabilities, the strangeness of the situation, the excellence of the Ambassador's (or more correctly Frau von Ribbentrop's) champagne, all went somewhat to my head.

Emboldened by the success of the party, Ribbentrop invited Vansittart to lunch with him alone in the Hotel Kaiserhof. Alas, the idea proved disastrous, even though the host 'turned on every facet' of his power to convince, insisting that only a close union between Germany and Britain could put Europe to rights, that only Hitler had the power to bring such a union about, that the Führer was ready for an 'upright and equal understanding'. Although Vansittart listened politely, he baffled his host by remaining completely non-committal. 'During my life I have conducted conversations with hundreds of Englishmen on this topic,' wrote Ribbentrop, 'but never was a conversation so fruitless, so lacking in response and commitment.'

One thing, he concluded, was absolutely clear: no German-English understanding could ever be brought about with

Vansittart. 'With him, every word fell on stony ground.' To Ribbentrop, Vansittart was 'the man from the Foreign Office, with totally preconceived ideas', and even when Hitler later suggested that Nazi ideology might have something to do with the Englishman's attitude, Ribbentrop would not believe it. The full depth of his incomprehension was revealed in his own autobiography, published posthumously in 1953, after the Nazis had brought about the deaths of nearly 30 million people and he himself had been executed for war crimes. Describing his attempts to win British hearts and minds during the Olympic Games, he wrote:

> When people today maintain that Vansittartism and all the hatred of the Germans inherent in this word were a result of Hitler's policy, I say this to them, and I believe it is true: Hitler's policies were the result of Vansittart's policies of 1936!

In spite of what amounted to a severe diplomatic rebuff, Hitler presented Vansittart with an Olympic medal, whose tag he had signed. Not long afterwards, when Lady Vansittart showed the medal to a Hungarian graphologist, he took one look at the barely legible signature, not knowing whose it was, and said, 'One day that man will commit suicide.'

The final official party of the Olympics, and one of the most spectacular, was that given by Goebbels, who took over the Pfaueninsel (Peacock Island), a nature reserve in the middle of the Wannsee. Because the party was called a 'Sommerfest', the men did not wear evening dress, but the sheer scale of the occasion made up for any slight lack of style.

Army pioneers had built a bridge of boats to connect the island with the mainland, and on the night they lined it as a guard of honour, presenting oars while the 2,000 guests streamed over. As people arrived, they were welcomed by girls dressed as Renaissance pages and shown to their dinner-places in brilliantly coloured marquees. Vintage champagne flowed, and Goebbels was at his most ingratiating as he limped among the huge assembly. The one discordant note was struck by the firework display, which began at about 10pm and was so violent that many people found their thoughts turning involuntarily towards war. 'Cannon roared and fireworks began on a scale which would have impressed the Romans,' wrote Channon. For half an hour the sky was ablaze with light. Several of the guests complained that this was a form of military propaganda, and Ambassador Dodd reported: 'The people at our table were shuddering at the fearful noise of the explosions, which shook the earth.' Eventually the noise died away and peace returned to the clear, warm summer's night.

16

OTHER EVENTS

In the many ancillary events arranged to bolster the Olympiad, the accent was strongly on youth. Just as the great Olympic bell summoned the youth of the world, so the attention of the visitors was constantly drawn to the fact that this was a festival for young people, and strenuous efforts were made to involve as many as possible. Easily the greatest concentration was the vast concourse of boys from 25 countries which assembled in a tented camp off Heerstrasse for the duration of the Games.

The British contingent, 30-strong, was gathered from many sources, including schools, the Boys' Brigade, boys' clubs and the YMCA. They were selected by the Home Office, and one of the few rules laid down was that all must wear grey suits. When the party assembled at Croydon Airport for the flight to Germany, it became apparent that grey suits could take an amazing number of shades and shapes, and in Berlin the British boys found themselves at a severe sartorial disadvantage, outsmarted by fancy new uniforms and various styles of national dress.

The routine of the rally was highly organised: reveille at 6.30am, physical training, breakfast at 8am, a march to the stadium for the day's events, and always a sing-song in the evening, with no leave to go outside the camp except on organised excursions. Needless to say, such regimentation was too much for the decadent British boys, who first struck back by attending the early-morning parades in their pyjamas, and, when this move failed to draw retribution, by ceasing to attend at all. Another area in which they were found wanting was that of the evening sing-song. Every night one country's group had to entertain the rally. Most contingents sang their national anthem, but the British thought it would be insupportably embarrassing to render 'God Save the King' or 'Land of Hope and Glory'. Eventually the decision was taken to sing 'What Shall We Do With the Drunken Sailor?', which caused a good deal of bewilderment. To their dismay, the boys found that the authorities had made a record of the performance, copies of which were later handed round. Afterwards, their main memories were of the fanatical enthusiasm with which the German and Italian boys spent their time doing drill – and they came home with their disrespect for Hitler undamaged, so ludicrous had he appeared to them when seen in the flesh.

During the Games another pseudo-military youth exercise was in progress. Twenty-four detachments of Hitler Youth were tramping across the Reich, from different starting-points, with Nuremberg and the September Party rally as their goal. One group, deeply tanned, passed through Berlin, having marched across the disputed Polish Corridor from East Prussia. They stayed a few days to watch some of the Olympics, and then pressed on; by the time they reached their goal they would have covered 550 miles in 47 days, and, as the *Berliner Tageblatt* pointed out, they were doing it for a purpose:

> They are not wandering in the manner of previous unmanaged generations, when the object was discovery and enjoyment of the countryside. They are moving in step, in an idea, the idea of a community, of the group.

At the same time, groups of foreign boys were also on the move about Germany, attracted by the Olympics and the generous fare concessions offered by the German Railways. One such party, the Britannia Youth Tour, covered 1,500 miles in three weeks, took in the Games, and finished their trip sight-seeing on the Rhine. Living partly in Hitler Youth camps and partly in private homes, they got a more immediate idea of the state of the country than visitors who stuck to

215

Berlin; and, although most people they met were well disposed towards Britain, they found Hitler propaganda intense everywhere, in villages as much as in towns. '*Heil Hitler!* is the universal salutation, at any time of day or night,' reported the group's leader. 'Even children just about big enough to walk would shout *Heil Hitler!* as I passed, and extend their arms.'

Meanwhile the Games were continuing. After the white heat of the track and field events, which flared so briefly, the fire had to some extent gone out of the Festival, and many of the athletes had dispersed to the corners of the earth; yet there was still a big programme to be completed.

One of the most continuously popular arenas was the new open-air swimming complex, outside the main stadium. The 16,000 seats were generally packed, especially when the weather turned fine, and the crowd unashamedly partisan. As expected, the men's swimming and diving events were dominated by the Americans and the Japanese, and for most of the time the spectators rooted for European competitors in vain. One exception was the Hungarian student Ferenc Csik, who won the 100m Freestyle with easily the fastest time of his life. The balance was to some extent restored by the women's events, in which Ria Mastenbroek of Holland was outstanding, taking Gold Medals (and setting new Olympic records) in both the 100m and 400m Freestyle, a Silver Medal in the 100m Backstroke, and a third Gold in the 4 × 100m Relay. So thrilled was she after the 100m record that she burst into tears of excitement as she walked back round the pool. Since it was her compatriot Dina Senff who won the 100m Backstroke, the Dutch girls altogether had a great triumph, and this was due not a little to their formidable trainer, Mother Brown. A large lady, given to urging on her girls by physical contortions performed perilously close to the edge of the pool, Mother Brown made a terrific hit with the crowd, who of course were longing for her to fall in. That would have been a great sensation; as it was, the crowd round the pool got one on 16 August, when an over-excited American fan, Mrs Carla de Vries, burst through Hitler's SS entourage and embraced him. She had only meant to get his autograph, she said afterwards, but when she came close to him she thought he looked so nice that she felt sure he would not mind if she kissed him. The Führer, though startled, seemed to enjoy the attack.

Almost within shouting-distance of the swimming-pool, in the northwest corner of the Olympic grounds, lay the Dietrich Eckart open-air theatre. This fine amphitheatre, whose potential had been pointed out to Hitler by Werner March during the Führer's first visit to the site, proved an admirable setting for the gymnastics, and accommodated a crowd of up to 25,000 people on ringed stone tiers, as though at some festival in ancient Greece. A large tent covered the main stage, but another stage had been built out into the orchestra, or circular acting area, and there was room for several competitors to perform simultaneously. Fortunately the gymnastic events did not begin until the weather had cleared up, on 10 August, and the spectators were able to bask comfortably in the heat. To the great delight of the predominantly German crowd, their men carried off most of the honours, Alfred Schwarzmann winning the individual Combined Exercises, and Konrad Frey proving supreme on the Parallel Bars and the Pommelled Horse. The German girls' team also triumphed, winning the Combined Exercises by a narrow margin from Czechoslovakia. In the evenings the theatre assumed the role for which it had been built, and was taken over for the production of plays and oratorios.

Gymnastics of many kinds were being discussed and practised at the Pedagogical Olympiad, in which nearly 1,000 people took part. Each participating nation had sent lecturers and a team of gymnasts to demonstrate national ideas about physical education, all housed in a special Sport-Students' Camp. For most of the participants the lectures were paralysingly dull, especially as they were delivered in the language of the expert who was speaking; but the hazards of having to sit through Major J. G. Thulin, Director of the South Sweden Gymnastic Institute, on 'The Foundations of Ling Gymnastics and their Present-Day Application in Sweden', or Dr Kalle Rikala of Helsinki University on 'The Sauna as a Training Aid in Finland', were much mitigated by the fact that everyone was issued with free transport-passes and free tickets for all events in the stadium.

Another huge ancillary festival taking place simultaneously

was that of the *Kraft durch Freude* ('Strength through Joy') organisation. In an imitation village built specially for the festival, with artificially rustic houses and beer-gardens, some 30,000 specially meritorious workers indulged in a fortnight's riotous celebration.

The Olympic yachting, meanwhile, was taking place at Kiel, on the Baltic coast. There visitors found a most attractive town, set between the lovely Holstein birchwoods and the sea, framed by cliffs and broad white beaches. The Olympic regatta was held on two separate courses – the races for the smaller boats in the *Binnenhafen* ('inner bay') and those for the bigger vessels in the *Aussenhafen* ('outer bay'), dominated by a red-and-white lighthouse tower on one shore and the monumental Marine Memorial on the other. As in Berlin, the arrangements were elaborate. The two starting ships *Undine* and *Najade* were equipped with telephones and telewriting equipment, and immediately before each race they received weather reports from four different locations. In the daily programmes, and on the quaysides, there were maps of the two bays divided up into numbered squares, so that anybody could quickly work out where each boat was at a given moment. But in spite of all the forethought that had gone into the preparations, the regatta was marred by disputes, the judges' decisions often being challenged, and the protests upheld.

The towering Marine Memorial was enough to remind visitors that Kiel was the Reich's main naval base, and the presence of warships rammed the fact home. As in Berlin, the German Government used the occasion of the Olympics to stage ceremonies extolling the theme of peace, war and reconciliation: at their invitation, the British cruiser *HMS Neptune* arrived in Kiel on 3 August, bringing with her the bell of the former German battle-cruiser *Hindenburg* which had been scuttled, with the rest of the captured German fleet, at Scapa Flow in 1919.

On the morning of 10 August Hitler flew in from the capital, and at 9.35am the *Neptune* began a 21-gun salute as the Führer's standard was hoisted on board the *Grille*. Captain Bedford of the *Neptune* called on him formally at 1pm, and afterwards he steamed round the fleet in a launch. When he departed at 4.05pm, another 21-gun salute thundered out. Then, on the evening of 17 August, came the ceremony of handing over the bell, which took place in the hall of the Commander-in-Chief's office building. At the key point, the four British sailors who had been formally guarding the bell marched away from it, allowing their places to be taken by four Germans. In his speech Captain Bedford described the return of the bell as 'a gesture of the friendship which exists between the navies of our two nations', and expressed the pious hope that the bell would ring in an era of still closer cooperation. In his reply, General-Admiral Räder said that it was only 'an ill fate' that had made the two navies opponents in the Great War.

In Berlin, meanwhile, the rowing events were continuing at Grünau, in the east of the city. There too the setting was attractive. The Germans were fond of comparing Grünau with Henley; for them, it was *the* regatta course, and the Berlin Regatta Club had been holding races there for more than half a century. The area was – and is – a leafy suburb; but, even if people might argue that its surroundings did not quite measure up to those of Henley-on-Thames, there was no doubt that it had better facilities. The Müggelsee – the lake on which the 2,000m course was laid out – was big enough to allow six boats to race abreast (compared with a maximum of two at Henley), and the new stands built for the Olympics held 20,000 spectators.

The British naturally took a strong interest in the rowing events, but their performance proved disappointing, and the only Gold Medal they won was in the Double Sculls, rowed in pouring rain. The race was a thrilling one. For most of it the German pair looked certain to win. Then, 300 yards from home, Jack Beresford and Leslie Southwood, of the Thames Rowing Club, put in a tremendous sprint. With 100 yards to go they were level, and they went on to win by three lengths. It was an astonishing achievement by Beresford, who had won his first Olympic medal (the Silver in the Single Sculls) 16 years and four Olympiads earlier, and was now 37.

The rowing was at least well organised. The same could not be said of the football competition, which was described by one British observer as 'a shambles from start to finish'. It may be that this verdict was coloured by the extreme mediocrity with which the British XI performed: having barely struggled through the first round against China, the British, the masters of the game, who had taught the rest of the world how to play it, went out 4–5 to Poland. The trophy was eventually won by Italy, who beat Austria 2–1 in the final, but not before an unseemly fracas had threatened to ruin the competition.

The riot took place during the second-round match between Austria and Peru. Accounts of what happened varied. According to one, during the pause before extra time, with both teams standing on the pitch, a mob of Peruvian supporters rushed onto the field, and during the scrummage that followed one of them produced a revolver. Certainly one Austrian player left the field pouring blood. The match was completed, and won 4–2 by Peru, but only after further invasions of the pitch had rendered the team mass-assistance. Austria lodged a protest, which was upheld. The authorities ordered a replay without spectators, to begin at 5pm on 10 August, but although the Austrian team turned out, the Peruvians never showed. Having walked out, they vainly incited all the South American teams to join their boycott. In Lima an angry crowd smashed the windows of the German Consulate and tore down an Olympic flag, but in Berlin the incident passed over without further repercussions.

To fail at football caused the British great pain, but they brought disaster upon themselves by their lack of early organisation. This was the first time the football authorities had ever tried to assemble a team representing Great Britain, and all they had done was to collect together, a few days before departing for Berlin, players nominated by English, Scottish and Welsh associations. The team had never played or even trained together, so that its early demise was not surprising.

Of far greater satisfaction to British and Imperial hearts was the hockey, which was won, with dazzling skill, by India. Commentators described the Indian players as being 'nimble as cats', and it was true that their agility left all opponents groping. Immediately before the start of the Games a sudden crisis had threatened, when it was found that the 50 dozen hockey balls procured by the Germans from India were too

big and too heavy. After frantic telephoning, a new consign-
ment was put aboard a plane from London, and fortunately
these met the requirements of the International Federation.

Even though forced to play with British balls, the Indians
carried all before them. Not until the final against Germany
did they concede a goal; and then, as though galvanised by the
sudden revelation that they could be scored against, they
raced away to win 8–1, bringing their aggregate for the
competition to 27–1. In extenuation of their team's heavy
defeat, German commentators explained that hockey in India was like football in European countries: all boys played it
as soon as they were big enough to run. The fact that eight of
the eleven Indian players were brown or black evoked no
hostile comment; for, uncomfortable though it might be to
people like Streicher, it was common knowledge that the
Indians were of Aryan descent, and therefore blood-brothers
of the Germans. When they mounted the rostrum in the
stadium to receive their medals, resplendent in light-blue
blazers, they received a warm ovation; and since their conti-
nent was still part of the British Empire, the national anthem
played for them was 'God Save the King'.

Throughout the Olympic Festival there was no single report of a foreign visitor being insulted on racial grounds.
Neither Jewish athletes nor Blacks were harassed or made to
feel in the least degree unwelcome: on the contrary, all
newcomers were received with overwhelming hospitality,
and the friendship struck up between Jesse Owens and Luz
Long seemed to epitomise the general air of goodwill. This
was certainly what Hitler and Goebbels had hoped to create,
but the fact that it did materialise was capable of two quite
different explanations. On the one hand, it could be argued
that the Nazi regime had its people under such rigid control as
to be able to govern their every response; on the other, it
could be said that ordinary Germans were friendly and hospitable by nature, and would never have persecuted Jews or
Blacks of their own accord, had they not been incited to do so
by their crazed leaders.

Although much of the friendliness was spontaneous, there
is no doubt that behind the scenes the Nazis were working
all-out to impress, and in some cases actually to subvert. The

manager of the South African team, Frank Rostron, was amazed to find himself the object of the most flattering attention even before he left Johannesburg, where a German baroness called on him to enquire what arrangements she might make on his behalf in Berlin. In Germany, he discovered that a brand-new, chauffeur-driven, cream-coloured convertible had been placed at his disposal. So lavishly were he and his team fêted that afterwards he was hardly surprised to find that one of them, the light-heavyweight boxer Robie Leibbrandt, had succumbed to Nazi overtures.

Leibbrandt was an eccentric – a vegetarian who slept on bare boards and every two weeks fasted for 24 hours, during which he ate nothing but sand and charcoal. In Berlin, he had scarcely installed himself in the Olympic Village when a man calling himself Dr Leibbrandt and claiming to be a relation came to the gate to see him. Whatever the true status of this visitor, after the Games Leibbrandt was given some sort of scholarship to revisit Germany, and he stayed there. During the Second World War, after being trained in sabotage and espionage techniques, he was landed by U-boat on the coast of South-West Africa. From there he infiltrated South Africa and led the security forces a great dance, blowing up railway lines and bridges until he was captured. At his trial in Pretoria he shouted '*Heil Hitler!*' from the dock as he was condemned to death; but his sentence was commuted by Smuts.

How many other competitors were subverted during the Games, it is impossible to say; but in the city tourists as a whole were not molested. Moving about Berlin, they noticed that the police exercised far more positive control of pedestrians than at home. Visitors were startled to find that they were supposed to cross the main streets only on recognised crossings, and that anyone who tried to move according to his own ideas was immediately reprimanded or even fined on the spot. Cedric Venables, who broadcast commentaries on the Olympic rowing for the BBC, reported in the *Middlesex County Times* that 'pedestrians in the city are thoroughly trained in the art of self-preservation, for to all practical purposes there is no speed limit, and traffic moves very fast indeed . . . Motor horns are completely *verboten* at all hours of day and night.'

The number of strangers in Berlin was certainly very high, but a great many of them were Germans who came in from not far afield, and the total of foreign visitors fell well below that predicted, and claimed, by the tourist authorities. Rooms remained available all over the city, and shopkeepers complained vigorously that the bonanza which they had been promised never materialised – in spite of the fact that tourists could exchange their foreign currency for marks at almost double the normal rate. The police were able to report with satisfaction that their stratagem of denying international criminals access to the country had worked extremely well. Advance gangs of pickpockets were caught trying to cross the frontiers, and during the whole Festival only 64 charges were brought for petty theft, 39 of them against foreigners. There were also 270 charges of ticket-speculation, and a ruthless drive was made against beggars, 104 of whom were arrested during the Games, mostly for begging under the guise of soliciting autographs. Such successes were most gratifying to the authorities, for, in the words of the official German report, they proved 'the high degree of safety' which prevailed in the country.

The final event of the Games, which took place in the stadium on the afternoon of 16 August, was the 'Prix des Nations', the show-jumping section of the three-day equestrian event. In this competition also the British found to their chagrin that their preparation had been utterly inadequate. Having decided to enter only in February, they got their own team together at the last moment, and were incensed to discover that the German team had spent the past 18 months in full-time training, struck off from all other duties. In April, 1935, Ivone Kirkpatrick, from the British Embassy in Berlin, happened to stay with Countess Görtz, the widow of a well known show-jumper, and there he found the whole German equestrian team already assembled. A replica of the Olympic cross-country course had been built in the park, and some 30 officers and men were devoting their lives to practice.

Their diligence paid off handsomely – and nowhere more than in the 23-mile cross-country section of the three-day event. The 35 obstacles were so large and difficult that many foreign riders, who had no experience of the course, came to grief. Worst of all was the water-jump, which claimed a huge number of victims: what the German riders knew, but others did not, was that the bottom of the stagnant pond into which the horses had to leap was extremely uneven, the water being reasonably shallow at one or two points, but with deep pockets in others. One after another the horses plunged into the holes and almost out of sight, sending their riders flying over their heads into the water. Even with their special knowledge one or two of the German riders misjudged it and got a ducking. The severity of the course drew stinging criticism from the captain of the British team, Lieutenant Colonel P. E. Bowden-Smith, who described the obstacles as 'ludicrous'. (He, it need hardly be said, went into the water.)

By the time the show-jumping began in the stadium on the final afternoon, in the presence of the Führer, the Germans held a clear lead, which they had no difficulty in maintaining. As each horseman entered the arena he saluted Hitler, who always lifted his hand in return. The hero of the afternoon was their rider Oberleutnant Freiherr von Wangenheim, who had broken his collar-bone in a fall the day before, but now had to ride again to give his team a chance of winning the team trophy. With his left arm in a sling he set out, and all went well until, half-way round the course, his horse Kurfürst slipped in a tight turn and went down flat on its side. A tremendous gasp rose from the crowd as horse and rider lay motionless; then Wangenheim scrambled up, got the horse back onto its feet, remounted without assistance, and finished the course. His courage was for many people one of the highlights of the Games.

The jumping lasted all evening and into the slow summer dusk. Chips Channon, usually bored by sporting encounters, found it 'very exciting, even breathless'. Once it was over, and the final medals had been presented, it was time for the closing ceremony.

This too was magnificently staged. At 9pm, with a blare of trumpets, blue-white searchlight beams lanced up into the sky from all round the rim of the stadium – vertically at first, then angling in to form a gigantic tent or dome of light. The flags of the nations were borne in procession past Hitler's box, dipping as they went by him. Baillet-Latour made a commendably short speech of thanks on behalf of the IOC and called on the youth of the world to assemble again, in four years' time, in Tokyo. A choir of a thousand sang various hymns, with many more thousand voices joining in around the stadium. Fifty-two girls in white processed forward to crown the lowered national flags with garlands. In the distance unseen artillery roared and thundered. The great Olympic flag was run down from its pole in the centre of the arena and ceremonially borne away by men dressed in white, to be delivered into the custody of the Mayor of Berlin until such time as it should be needed again. Other lights were doused, and all eyes turned to the Marathon Gate, where the Olympic flame now burned brilliantly in the dark. To the solemn tolling of the great Olympic bell, the fire began to sink and die. When it vanished, a tremendous silence fell. Then, apparently from high in the starlit sky, a deep, ghostly voice came calling, 'I summon the youth of the world to Tokyo.'

The official ceremony was at an end; but the crowd, knowing that Hitler was present, although invisible in the dark, expected him to speak. When he did not, shouts of '*Heil Hitler!*' and '*Sieg Heil!*' began to ring out. Gradually individual voices blended into a full-throated roar: '*Sieg heil!*' '*Sieg heil!*' '*Sieg heil!*' The crowd rose irrepressibly to its feet, with right arms upraised, to sing *Deutschland über Alles* and the Horst Wessel Song. A mixture of excitement and apprehension gripped the foreigners in that great gathering as the marching beat of the song pulsed out into the night:

Bald flattern Hitlerfahnen über allen Strassen,
die Knechtschaft dauert nur noch kurze Zeit!

(Soon Hitler flags will be fluttering over every street,
The days of slavery are almost over!)

Many ghosts were abroad that evening – not only the spirits of dead stormtroopers, but foreshadows of the future, too. What did this terrific show of Nazi strength portend? What would happen after the Olympiad had ended, as it began, in a blaze of nationalistic fevour?

By any system of reckoning, the Germans had done unpre-
cedentedly well. By their own system, they had easily won
the Games – although it had always been Coubertin's clearly
expressed intention that no country should win or even seek
to do so. The haul of 33 Gold, 26 Silver and 30 Bronze Medals
gave Hitler and his people incalculable satisfaction.

Purely on the athletics front, the Olympiad had been
memorable. After Los Angeles in 1932 many people had
thought that the zenith of human achievement had been
reached, and standards set which could never be surpassed;
yet here in Berlin 17 Olympic and five world records had been
broken in the men's events, and five Olympic records in the
women's. Although the Decathlon winner, Glenn Morris of
the USA, had been officially declared the outstanding athlete
of the Games, almost everybody present awarded the trophy
– in their minds, at least – to Jesse Owens. For 99 people out
of 100, it was Owens's Olympiad. In all his 14 appearances he
had never seemed extended (except possibly in the Long
Jump final), and he had broken Olympic records 11 times. In
a single week he had revolutionised the speed events and
opened up a new vista of sporting possibilities for the human
race. Everyone recognised that he was a supreme athletic
genius, the God of the Games.

For the Nazis, however, athletics were only part of the
purpose of the Olympiad. On 17 August the *Völkischer
Beobachter* boasted that in staging the Games so magnificently the New Germany had 'shown the world its true face'. Most
visitors, as they packed up and left, were ready to accept this
verdict. On the surface everything had been wonderful: the
Olympics themselves full of thrilling moments, the organisation faultless, the atmosphere one of great goodwill, the
entertainments dazzling, the food and wine as good as could
be found anywhere in the world. The people as a whole had
been polite and forthcoming. Many lasting friendships were
formed or strengthened, and many happy memories brought
away. Yet, even without seeing any direct evidence of persecution, some visitors were worried by the furious energy
manifest in the incessant parading and marching, and by the
strength of the national feeling which repeatedly boiled up in
the stadium.

One man who saw the light during his stay was Thomas Wolfe, whose earlier blind admiration of all things Nazi at last gave way to a more realistic appreciation. The Games, he thought, had been 'merely a symbol of Germany's new-won power', and behind them he was aware of an 'awful concentration' and an 'abnormal stiffness'.

Chips Channon, in contrast, returned to Britain singing the praises of the regime, only to find himself sharply rebuked by Harold Nicolson, who perceived the evils of Nazism with perfect clarity. Channon, Nicolson wrote in his diary, had 'fallen under the champagne-like influence of Ribbentrop' and the youthful sway of his aristocratic hosts during the Games, and this made it impossible for him to see the essential difference between Britain and Nazi Germany:

We represent a certain type of civilised mind, and [believe] that we are sinning against the light if we betray that type. We stand for tolerance, truth, liberty and good humour. They stand for violence, oppression, untruthfulness and bitterness.

Sir Robert Vansittart felt exactly the same, and expressed the anxiety which the Games had aroused in him with chilling prescience:

These tense, intense people are going to make us look a C 3 nation if we elect to continue haphazard, and they will want to do something with this stored energy . . . These people are the most formidable proposition that has ever been formulated; they are in strict training now, not for the Olympic Games, but for breaking some other and emphatically unsporting world records, and perhaps the world as well.

17
RETROSPECT

That the success of the eleventh Olympiad gave Hitler an enormous boost, both moral and political, nobody could deny. The world came to Berlin, and, with the exception of a few cynics, the world was overwhelmed with admiration for what it had seen. According to one American journalist, John T. McGovern, the highlight and main surprise of the Games had been the 'social achievement of the German nation', which had pulled itself up from the gutter after only three years of the new regime. In spite of the country's well-known difficulties, he wrote,

> We have just seen the German peoples play perfectly the role of a gracious, fair and generous host, literally to millions of visitors and to competitors from 52 separate nations, at the same time providing the most elaborate and magnificent architectural setting and comprehensive games facilities and equipment that the world has yet seen.

Not everyone was so fulsome. Almost all, however, agreed that the host nation had done a magnificent job, and 99 out of 100 people who went to Germany that summer came away thinking the Nazi regime could not be as bad as rumour claimed. Both at the level of the ordinary tourist and in the highest diplomatic circles, the regime had scored a triumphant success.

It is tempting to speculate on what might have happened if attempts to boycott the Games had succeeded. If the worst had occurred (from Hitler's point of view), and the International Olympic Committee had moved the Festival to some less rebarbative country, Nazi prestige would have suffered a serious blow, and the rest of the world would have been made to think much harder about what was happening in Germany. Whether or not that would have achieved any practical result is another matter. By the end of 1936 German rearmament had so far outstripped that of the western allies that the chance of halting Hitler physically had gone for the time being; but his lead was itself partly the product of the Olympic Pause, and it is at least open to question whether concerted, resolute action against him early in 1935 might not have done something to inhibit his policy of expansion and damage, if not destroy, his standing among his own people.

Equally, it could be argued that a severe insult from the international community might have positively accelerated his progress along a route which he was determined to take anyway. Certainly he would have been enraged – and he would no doubt have attributed a successful boycott to the villainy of world-Jewish Bolshevism. If the United States alone had withdrawn its team – and thereby diminished the lustre of the Festival – he would surely have blamed the Jewish community in that country. As it was, he had every reason to congratulate himself, the one less-than-perfect feature of the whole Olympiad being the success of the Blacks.

In this context it is only fair to point out that racial attitudes were deplorable, at that date, in the United States as well as in Germany, especially in the South, where Owens came from. It is true that the number of lynchings fell from 18 in 1935 to 8 in 1936, but on 15 August – the penultimate day of the Games – a crowd of more than 10,000 men, women and children held all-night hanging parties at Owensboro, Kentucky, waiting to get a good view of the execution of Rainey Bethea, a Black who had abducted and killed a 70-year-old white woman. Even in London a person's colour could cause ructions; the Canadian Olympic team, returning from the Olympics, were enraged to find themselves barred from the Bloomsbury hotel into which they had booked when the management discovered that two of their number (including Dr Phil Edwards, the captain) were black. The difference between

229

Germany and other countries, of course, was that the Nazis were deliberately seeking to foment and incite racial hatred, while elsewhere Governments were doing their best to damp it down.

All the same, the phenomenal performance of the Blacks in Berlin worried many people besides the Führer, and in the weeks that followed the Games gave rise to agitated controversy. Unnamed 'medical authorities' were quoted as saying that the emergence of the Blacks had introduced a new factor into sport; coloured athletes were claimed to have abnormal muscular qualities, different from those of white men, and in particular an 'elongated heel' which gave them extra spring and therefore an unfair advantage. Because of this, it was suggested, future Olympiads would have to be split into two sections, one for Blacks and one for Whites.

It was not long, however, before this theory was shot down with the derision which it deserved. In a letter to *The Daily Telegraph* the distinguished biologist Professor J. B. S. Haldane argued that there was no evidence that pure Blacks were more likely than Whites to produce champions, and pointed out that, since almost all American coloured people were of mixed origin, Jesse Owens was, if anything, an argument for *Rassenschande* (racial defilement) rather than for Black superiority. Meanwhile, he added,

> If we are going to exclude negroes, why not add Finns, who are of a rather different stock from other Europeans, and have a most 'abnormal' capacity for winning long-distance races?

The point was driven home by another reader of the same newspaper, Mr F. V. Harris, who wrote that the theory belonged to 'a type of pseudo-scientific argument which, one had hoped, had lost all credence among intelligent people':

> Of course, the potentially first-class athlete is an exceptional individual. White or coloured, he may or may not have an 'elongated heel'; at any rate his musculature is likely to be developed above the average. As a negro, I am proud of those black athletes who comported themselves so honourably in sportsmanship at Berlin.

230

A more serious matter, in England, was the relative failure of
the British team. Even before the Games were over, the Rev.
F. Brompton Harvey was writing to the Editor of *The Daily
Telegraph* from Leicestershire to deplore the country's lack of
medals:

> The failure of Englishmen in the Olympic Games should give a
> jolt to our national complacency. England is admittedly the
> Mother Country of sport; yet the pick of her athletes . . . have
> been outclassed.
>
> A century ago Englishmen in general had two convictions: 1.
> That they could not be beaten; 2. That they would have to beat
> numerically superior foes. I believe that Nelson or Wellington
> never had, and never expected to have, as many men and guns as
> the enemy. Now, a maritime people, we are beaten in rowing by
> the inland Swiss. In boxing (pre-eminently a British sport) we
> occupy a back seat . . .
>
> What are the reasons for this decline in athletic prowess – in
> skill and will to win? We have much in our favour; we have a long
> tradition of supremacy; our people are the best fed in Europe; we
> have the highest standard of living and the greatest amount of
> leisure; our climate is perfectly adapted for outdoor exercise; we
> have not been distracted by revolution nor crippled by financial
> stringency . . .

The culprit, the writer announced, was Democracy – the
'shibboleth' which encourages mediocrity and does away with
virility. 'It is not pleasant to think of the Union Jack waving
over a company of "also rans",' he concluded:

> And we need not wonder if this failure in manly sports on the
> world stage is interpreted by our rivals as another proof that
> England has 'gone soft'.

'Has England gone soft?'! The suggestion was too challenging
to leave alone. Other correspondents sprang into action,
most of them vigorously defending the performance of the
British team with the evidence that many of its members had
beaten their previous best times or distances. Lord Burghley,
invincibly patriotic, told his local newspaper, *The Peterbor-
ough Advertiser*, that the arrangements had been splendid.
When asked if he thought that harder training would have

brought more medals, he replied that people seemed to forget that the British had done their best to spread the cult of sport throughout the world, and that the rest of the world had learned to play exceedingly well.

Another defender of the faith pointed out that to judge national prestige by athletic prowess 'betrays a mentality still under the influence of public school ideals', but many people were uncomfortably aware of the fact that precisely such a judgement had just been passed in Berlin, and that Britain had come out badly. The real problem, several suggested, was that Britain had no effective system of national coaching, and until British athletes got help, in the form of money and organisation, on the scale that other countries already enjoyed, they would not begin to compete. In Berlin, things had been particularly tough for the women in the British team, for money had been 'poured out like water' on those representing other countries, whereas the British girls had got no financial support at all.

What Britain really needed, said E. R. Voigt, gold-medallist in the 1908 Olympics, was a Ministry for Health, Sport and Recreation. Although some people decried the idea of government control of sport as alien to the British mentality, it was generally agreed that the country should have far more athletics tracks, and that these could best be provided by local authorities. Indeed, if the British were not to make fools of themselves at the London Olympics in 1944, such tracks *must* be provided, and soon.

The controversy raised again, in acute form, the much-debated question of amateurism. Most of the British team who went to Berlin *were* amateurs in the strictest sense of the term: they were students and young businessmen and policemen and motor-mechanics who had trained in their spare time, with their own resources . . . and the majority of British people were glad that it was so. They clung to their traditional belief that sport should be part of the training that makes a man, but not the be-all and end-all. They would rather have Britain play the game than become hell-bent on victory.

The official line taken by the British Olympic Association was that nothing had been gained or proved in Berlin. 'With all the resources and determination of a truly national movement, what did Germany achieve in the track events?' asked the annual report scornfully. 'Third in the steeplechase, fifth in the 100 Metres, sixth in the walk, and third in each of the relay races.' Field events – hammer, javelin, discus, shot – were another matter, the report conceded – but would a tremendous national drive for Tokyo be worthwhile? 'Would the production of one 25-foot long-jumper, one 52-foot weight-putter, or one 230-foot javelin-thrower (the standard which will be necessary to place men in the first six at Tokyo) really demonstrate anything of national importance?'

It was inescapably true that the spirit of the Berlin Festival had been far from what Baron de Coubertin had intended – a verdict confirmed by Sir Robert Vansittart. He reported that, although in the past the Olympic Games had been internationally beneficial, in a political sense, they were now the opposite, because they had become so nationalistic:

> The crowd [in Berlin] was full of nationalism. There is a tendency toward competitive national advertisement, and the footsteps of prestige can almost be heard on the track. One does not feel much amateur spirit in the air, but rather a jealously-guarded political demonstration.

That tensions had run high within the British team became apparent immediately after the Games when eight of its members signed a letter to the AAA vigorously registering a number of complaints. One was that the team arrived in Berlin far too late for its members to acclimatise themselves and produce their best form; another, that the organisation of transport to and from the stadium had been inadequate. The most serious deficiency, however, had been the lack of an official coach with experience of athletics under modern conditions: a number of British athletes had felt so bereft of professional advice that they had been driven to seek unofficial help from the coaches of other countries. Bevil Rudd, Athletics Correspondent of *The Daily Telegraph* and himself a former gold-medallist (in the 400m at Antwerp in 1920), countered by saying that it was 'in the preceding months, not in the preceding days or hours, that our chances of winning ebbed'. The British had not realised how intensively other nations were preparing, he added: 'All the same, many years in an athletic camp would never have got our sprinters up to the Owens-Metcalfe standard.'

As usual, the AAA tried to sweep the complaints out of sight, but its efforts were defeated by a violent blast of criticism from Godfrey Brown, who returned to Cambridge and published a savagely sarcastic article in the university magazine *Granta* at the beginning of October. One of his targets was the small army of officials who had accompanied the team, and whom he described as 'to a great extent mere dead weight'. The swimming team of 19, he pointed out, had had 18 officials, and the football team 14 for 22 players: 'Its great feats are common knowledge.' Brown also attacked the fact that all the judges in Berlin had been German, and referred to a photograph in which all but one of them were looking down the track for an oncoming German, 'instead of at the tape which the winner happens to be breaking'. His main tirade, however, was reserved for the nature of the Festival itself:

> The fact is that some of us went to Berlin with a mistaken idea – that we were going to watch or take part in a sports meeting. Instead, we were treated to a piece of political propaganda . . .
>
> On the last day we were inflicted with the sight of thousands of gross, flabby Germans, so-called Hitler Youth, clad in nothing but shorts and performing ridiculous evolutions on the grass. We cried, 'Sweep on, you fat and greasy citizens,' and made a dash for the first train home.

Brown was by no means alone in his distaste. A few of those who competed in Berlin realised that as soon as the Games were over the whole Olympic complex would be inherited by the Reich Academy for Physical Education, which would accommodate 650 students at a time and instruct them not only in what other nations considered sport, but also in gliding, rifle-shooting, hand-grenade throwing, target orientation, pack-marches, military reconnaissance and courier work. Here, in the buildings which had just been skilfully used to lull the suspicions of 52 nations, instructors would teach the art of developing rabid chauvinism and race-hatred through sport.

The manifest health and strength of the German people, so evident in Berlin, planted many anxieties. Had the Nazi passion for physical training already had such an effect? Was there not some substance in the observations of George Ward Price, who wrote that 'in physique and appearance the boys and girls of Germany and Italy are now the finest in Europe'? They surpassed those of other nations, he claimed, as much as British boys used to in the days when they were the only ones who played games:

> German and Italian schools devote a part of every afternoon to physical training. Their exercises are a parade of bronzed, muscular young bodies like Greek statues come to life . . . There is a danger that while the people of Britain are invoking the name of freedom they may fall behind . . . Personal liberty in Britain often means the liberty to slack. The democratic countries must ask themselves whether they can hope to compete, even in the pursuit of peace, with these highly disciplined nations whose spirit has been steeled in the fire of adversity.

If the author had asked whether the British *wanted* to compete, by imitating Nazi methods, the answer would certainly have been 'No'; and typical British level-headedness surfaced in 1937 when the Reich Government invited delegates from foreign countries to study physical education in Germany. The party from Britain detected a distinct tendency 'to develop the body at the expense of the mind'. They reported that 'modern Germany has no use for a horde of young men and women carrying too much intellectual top-hamper, neurasthenics, pessimists, cranks and rainbow-chasers, a prey to *Weltschmerz* and defeatism'; but at the same time they came out strongly with the conclusion that excessive physical education in a whole nation the size and standing of Germany 'might lead to fearful consequences for her and trouble for the entire world'.

That trouble was not long in coming; and hints of it began to leak out as soon as the Games were over. On 18 August, only two days after the Festival had finished, Captain Wolfgang Fürstner, the former Commandant of the Olympic Village, committed suicide. Typically, the German press was instructed to say that he had been killed in a car accident, but foreign journalists found out what had happened and broke the story. Fürstner had been a *Mischling*, but he had done such an outstanding job in creating the Village that he had been allowed to retain his position almost to the end. Then, with the Games a few weeks off, he had been quietly demoted, and the arriving athletes found the name of the Village Commandant given as Baron von und zu Gilsa. Fürstner hung around miserably during the Games, but then, seeing that he had no future under the Nazi regime, went home and shot himself. The propaganda machine could not erase all trace of him, for issue No. 6 of the monthly magazine *Olympic Games 1936* had contained an article by him, and a photograph of him looking at a model of Döberitz; but in the official report on the Festival he was mentioned as little as possible.

On 24 August Mussolini, out with the Italian Army on manoeuvres in the hills south of Naples, made a radio broadcast to the whole nation. 'We can, at any time, in a few hours, mobilise eight million men,' he boasted. 'The armaments race cannot now be checked. We do not believe in the absurdity of perpetual peace.' In Rome the Duce had already given his returning Olympic athletes a rough welcome: although berating them for the overall mediocrity of their performances, he nevertheless bestowed presents on those few who had done any good – £80 to a gold-medallist, £50 to a runner-up, and so on.

For the time being, in the sunny interlude after the Games, Anglo-German flirtation was continued, most conspicuously by the veteran statesman David Lloyd George, who visited Hitler at Berchtesgaden in September, 1936. The visit was arranged by Tom Jones, who earlier had sought to effect a meeting between the Führer and Baldwin. This time his plans succeeded better than even he could have hoped: after the most friendly discussions, Lloyd George returned to announce that, of the many great men he had met, Hitler was one of the greatest, and that neither he nor the German people wanted war. It was widely remarked that an article which Lloyd George wrote in *The News Chronicle* not only whitewashed the Führer but blacked his boots as well.

The true nature of the Nazi regime – effectively suppressed

during the summer – reappeared at the Nuremberg rally in September. International observers had expected a fresh verbal onslaught against Bolshevism, but they had not reckoned on the extreme virulence of the attacks. Hitler's speech in particular hit a level of hysterical hatred which surpassed anything he had achieved before. As the British Consul in Munich, D. St Clair Gainer, reported, propaganda was again being focused on the people of the Reich: 'The enemy has been indicated to them in no uncertain terms. They are being taught to believe that Soviet Russia and international Jewry wish to attack and destroy them.'

Another small but telltale sign was the execution of Edgar André, which became known in London at the beginning of November. It emerged that after his arrest in 1933 he had been detained for a time in the Hamburg Stadthaus – scene of some of the most frightful barbarities. Then, after being reduced to a physical wreck in the Fühlsbuttel concentration camp, he had been transferred to a hospital in Hamburg before going to the scaffold. For poor doomed André, the Olympic Games had brought a stay of execution, but no more – and that was the effect they had in the political long term as well: a stay of execution, which gave Hitler a useful breathing space in which to further his evil and lunatic designs.

Of the characters who had played a leading part in the Olympics or their preparation, some fared better than others. Hitler – so far as is known – committed suicide in his Berlin bunker on 30 April, 1945, alongside his mistress Eva Braun, having destroyed not only his own country but much of Europe as well. To the end he blamed the Jews for all the evils that had befallen him – and them. The Third Reich, which he had boasted would endure for 1,000 years, had lasted just over 12. Next day Goebbels had all his six children murdered by the administration of lethal injections, and then got an SS guard to shoot him and his wife through the backs of their necks. Goering, though taken prisoner by the Allies and tried at Nuremberg, managed to frustrate his captors at the last moment by crunching a cyanide capsule the night before he was due to be hanged. Streicher *was* hanged at Nuremberg, at

2.08am on the morning of 16 October, 1946. As he mounted the rostrum with his hands tied behind him, he yelled out, 'Jewish holiday! Jewish holiday 1946! Now we go to God. The Bolsheviks will hang you all next.'

Ribbentrop, who duly went to London as Ambassador, consolidated his reputation as a fool by giving the Nazi salute when he presented his credentials to King George VI, and by many later *faux pas*. His appointment was so disastrous that after a year he had to be replaced. He too was condemned to death as a war crimninal and hanged at Nuremberg.

Sir Eric Phipps left Berlin in April, 1937, when he was transferred to become Ambassador in Paris. 'This pleasant Englishman and his wife will leave behind them good friends,' remarked the *Deutsche Allgemeine Zeitung*. He was succeeded by Sir Neville Henderson, who could be relied on to further the British Government's policy of appeasement. Sir Robert Vansittart was also soon removed from any post in which he could actively obstruct the cementing of Anglo-German friendship: in 1938 he was made chief diplomatic adviser to the Foreign Secretary – a position which gave him no executive power.

The Zeppelin *Hindenburg*, which at the Games had seemed so potent a symbol of the German renaissance, met a disastrous end at Lakehurst, New Jersey, on 6 May, 1937. The airship had crossed the Atlantic and was coming in to moor in the evening. Because a thunderstorm was raging in the area, it loitered around for an hour; then, as the weather cleared, it was approaching the mast at 7.30pm, and passengers were waving from the windows at people on the ground, when flames suddenly spurted from underneath the body near the tail. Instantly, with a terrible explosion, fire engulfed the whole airship, which plunged to the ground in a mass of flame. Although some of those on board managed to stagger clear of the blazing wreckage, 36 people were killed, and there was nothing left of the monster but a skeleton of twisted steel. President Roosevelt and King George VI sent telegrams of sympathy to Hitler. The cause of the disaster – variously ascribed to lightning, an electrical fault or sabotage – was never properly established, but the tragedy undermined faith in the safety of airships in general, and effectively brought their brief supremacy to an end.

Diana Mitford married Sir Oswald Mosley on 6 October, 1936, in the drawing-room of Goebbels's house in central Berlin, next door to the Chancellery. The day was bright and sunny, and the leaves were turning yellow; as the bride waited with her sister Unity, she saw Hitler walking in the garden. She wore a pale-gold tunic for the ceremony, which was kept secret to avoid press attention, and afterwards the participants drove out to Goebbels's villa at Schwanenwerder, where he had thrown his Olympic party, for a wedding feast arranged by Magda. Hitler's gift was a photograph of himself in a silver frame embossed with the German eagle and the initials 'AH'. The Goebbelses gave the couple a leather-bound edition of Goethe's works in 20 volumes.

On 3 September, 1939 – the day on which Neville Chamberlain declared that Britain was at war with Germany – Unity Mitford shot herself in the head with a pistol at her flat in Munich. In spite of the desperately tense international situation, Hitler himself arranged for her evacuation from Germany. Though she returned to England and lived on for some years, she never fully recovered.

The athletes who triumphed in Berlin were prevented from distinguishing themselves in another Olympics by the Second World War, which put paid to the festivals projected for Tokyo in 1940 and London in 1944. This was perhaps part of the reason why Jesse Owens never again touched such heights of achievement. Even before he returned to the United States from Berlin, promoters were battling to sign him up, but somehow none of the lucrative deals was ever quite clinched. He remained unspoilt but poor, and took to running exhibition races, often as a special half-time attraction in the middle of baseball matches. In the words of the writer Norman Katkov, 'He ran against cars, trucks, dogs, and baseball players with a head start. He ran against anything and anybody, anywhere, and when there were no contestants, he ran just to please the customers.' His matchless physique and speed endured wonderfully well. In 1956, at the age of 43, while on a State Department goodwill tour of India, he ran 100 yards in 9.8 seconds. He became a persuasive spokesman for the American Olympic movement, and did much good work arranging sports meetings for children, especially those from underprivileged families, all over the United States. He died of cancer in March 1980, aged 66, but memories of him have never faded in Berlin, where in 1984 the street leading to the Olympic Stadium was renamed Jesse Owens Strasse.

Avery Brundage demonstrated the depth of his commitment to athletics by devoting most of the rest of his life to the Olympic movement. He became Vice-President of the International Olympic Committee in 1945, and President in 1952 – a post which he retained for 20 years. But if his passion for sport was undoubted, so too were his racial and political prejudices; at one meeting he became so exasperating that the mild-mannered Lord Killanin, who succeeded him as President of the IOC, shouted out that he was a Fascist. His fundamental lack of human understanding was cruelly revealed at a crisis in the history of the Olympic movement – the occasion at Munich in 1972 when Palestinian terrorists assassinated 11 members of the Israeli contingent. First Brundage baffled and enraged both the German officials and his colleagues on the IOC by attempting to take charge of subsequent events himself, without consulting anyone else. Then, at the hastily organised memorial service in the stadium, he made an appallingly inept speech. All that was needed was a short message of sorrow and condolence, a decent tribute to the dead; instead, Brundage chose to deliver himself of a sharp political tirade against those African countries who had threatened to withdraw from the Games if Rhodesia – then white-ruled – took part. As in 1936, he showed himself obsessed by the belief that politics must not enter into sport, but everyone present was horrified by his insensitivity, which Killanin later described as 'truly amazing'. He died in 1975 in Garmisch-Partenkirchen, scene of the 1936 Winter Games.

It is to Leni Riefenstahl that we owe the most memorable record of the Berlin Olympics. Her film, on which she worked with exceptional intensity and devotion, pioneered new heights in the sphere of visual sports reporting, and is still seen as a masterpiece today. Far more than a mere documentary, it glorifies the human body, and man as an athlete, with a boldness of vision never before achieved in the cinema.

240

In the winter of 1936 she went to ground with more than a million feet of film, and in her own words 'lived in the editing room for a year and a half, never getting home before five o'clock in the morning'. She had her laboratory fitted with glass partitions, over which she hung long strips of film, so that she worked surrounded by her raw material. From it she fashioned an epic six hours long and divided into two parts, which was officially shown to Hitler for the first time in April, 1938.

Part 1, 'Festival of Nations', begins on an heroic, appropriately Olympian scale with heavy, Wagnerian music by Herbert Windt surging powerfully as a montage of Greek temple-façades floats and turns and fades across the screen. The camera sweeps over ancient Olympia, with huge column-drums lying fallen among the olive groves. The great buildings of the Acropolis in Athens – the Parthenon and Erechtheum – ride out and dissolve into one another. Coming down to a smaller scale, it fastens on individual marble figures; then, in a masterly stroke, the statue of a discus-thrower dissolves into a live athlete, nearly naked, in an identical attitude, who moves, pivots, and hurls his quoit.

From that moment, all is action: the lighting of the first torch at Olympia, the beginning of the run, the first hand-overs, the arrival of the fire in the Lustgarten, its appearance in the stadium, Hitler's official inauguration of the Games, the grand opening ceremony, the athletic events themselves. Throughout, the pace is varied by brilliant cutting and the skilful use of slow-motion. Always the director's attention focuses on the human frame, on muscles and sinews straining at their limit to break new barriers of pain and achievement.

Luckily for posterity, it made no difference to Leni Riefenstahl what colour an athlete might be; when she saw a beautiful body, she filmed it, whether it was black, brown, white or yellow. Thus her camera dwells hungrily on the physical perfection of Jesse Owens, and just before the bang of the starting-gun goes in to caress in close-up the gleaming muscles on his thigh. In the never-ending Pole Vault, it returns again and again to the spectacularly handsome face of Nishida, the Japanese who came second. In the Marathon, it lingers on the awe-inspiring courage of the winner, Son, and the pain of those who could not stand the pace. Small wonder that Goebbels was furious with the film's lack of racial bias, and that he forbade the German press so much as to mention the name of Riefenstahl for 18 months.

If the second half of the film, 'Festival of Beauty', is less compelling than the first, the reason is mainly that the events it portrays are less exciting: the yachting at Kiel, the rowing at Grünau and the swimming (which the film crews had great difficulty in capturing) cannot compare with Owens in full flight. Even so, Part 2 has some stunning sequences, not least that of the mass gymnastic display by women. In the words of the historian Richard D. Mandell,

> As the camera angle rises, the viewer is transported with aesthetic emotion . . . We swoon with the instinctive grasp of the pure power of these massed *völkisch* gymnasts as the camera immortalises their actions, ever more drained of fleshly beauty – for the artist in control has shown massed human motion abstracted, epitomised.

The film has often been described as a triumph of propaganda, but this is less than just. What it did was to *record* a triumph of propaganda, brilliantly capturing the militaristic nature of the organisation, particularly the opening ceremony; but its enduring merit is as a creative work of art. Even so, its director could not escape the consequences of her own close association with the Nazi leaders, which pursued her down the years with the tenacity of the Furies.

In the autumn of 1938 she travelled to Hollywood for a private showing of her film but, although it was well received, she herself was not: she found herself ignored and snubbed, and left in high dudgeon. She began the war as a camera reporter covering the invasion of Poland, but abandoned her unit when she saw German troops massacre a party of Jews, and her complaints to authority went unanswered. She returned to planning a film of her own, and in 1944 married an army officer, Major Peter Jacob. In 1945 she was arrested by advancing American troops at her house in Kitzbühel, and thereafter spent some time in detention camps. After the war she twice appeared before de-Nazification courts, and was twice cleared; nevertheless her past clung to her, and even in 1960, when the British Film Institute invited her to give a lecture, there was such an outcry that the project had to be cancelled. At the end of that year she gave a private screening of the Olympic film in London, but when she tried to defend her conduct in the 1930s she repeatedly broke down in tears. She claimed that she had always resisted the Nazis' racial theories, had never joined the Party, had refused Party medals and honours, and had never been an intimate friend of Hitler's, but had always sought to maintain her independence as an artist.

Later she found a new source of inspiration in Africa, producing handsome and imaginative photo-studies of the Masai and other tribes. When her Land-Rover turned over and she fractured her skull, she again proved herself a tremendous survivor, fighting her way back to health. Her 80th birthday found her still battling, and vigorously protesting that everyone who had ever written or said anything about her had always got it wrong.

Fifty years on, Berlin itself is a fascinating but sinister place. The western half of the city, almost completely rebuilt, once again hums and whizzes with frenetic energy, as if the local forces which originally made men choose the place for a capital have exerted themselves once more. The eastern sector of the city, in contrast, is forbidding beyond description: a grey and lifeless prison.

Fortunately for visitors, the Olympic Stadium is in the western sector, and it remains a magnificent creation. Though damaged in the war, and since repaired and partially roofed-over, it is still a building of enormous originality and power: huge, grey, monolithic and yet graceful, it sets the mind racing with a mixture of excitement and dread. The whole layout of the sports complex retains an heroic grandeur. Anyone coming up its immensely wide approach or walking in through the Marathon Gate and seeing the names of the Olympic victors carved out of its limestone pillar must feel many a ghost hovering round him.

Outside on the ground stands the great Olympic bell, which plunged to earth when its tower was shattered by bombs.

Cracked, and punctured by a single cannon shell, it still bears the legend, in gothic script, '*Ich rufe die Jugend der Welt*', a poignant reminder of what the 1936 Olympics should have been. But climb the new Bell Tower on the edge of the May Field, and you get a devastating reminder of what havoc the host of those games wrought upon the whole of Europe.

Close at hand there is a substantial hill – the only piece of ground in the neighbourhood that rises at all steeply. This is composed entirely of thousands of tons of rubble cleared from the city's ruins after the war. It is not this, however, that takes the attention: what seizes the eye and the imagination is the Wall. Whichever way you look, you see instantly that Berlin is now an island in the Red Sea. There is the Wall, circling and enclosing like a sinister white snake: to the west, it is only two miles off. Beyond it lies Döberitz and the former Olympic Village, which became an army barracks as soon as the Games were over; but Döberitz is now in East Germany, and one cannot drive to it from the stadium. Nor can one drive far towards the east along the former Via Triumphalis: the beginning of the long, straight route is in sight, lancing away through the district of Charlottenburg, but half-way along its length it is cut in two by the Wall at the Brandenburg Gate. The quadriga still prances above this symbol of the city, as it did on the Olympic posters, but the gateway itself is sealed off, and beyond it lies East Berlin, an infinitely depressing shadow of its western neighbour.

Ironies crowd in on the observer. As a direct result of Hitler's megalomania, the menace of Communism, against which he railed so frenziedly, has closed in to swallow half his former capital and to press in hard on the one sector of it that remains free. The regime which now controls the German Democratic Republic is in many ways as barbaric as that of the Nazis which it replaced. From this spot, in the balcony of the Bell Tower, that fact is vividly apparent in the form of the Wall: the regime is so repellent that only by an immensely elaborate system of defences – a monstrous array of walls, barbed wire, electrified fences, nets, ditches, tank-traps, mines, fragmentation grenades, guard-dogs, machine-guns, searchlights, watch-towers, electronic devices and many thousand men – can the government prevent its citizens from departing.

One other magnificent irony greets the watcher gazing eastwards on a sunny evening – although this one has nothing to do with Hitler. From the centre of East Berlin rises the slender television tower built by the Russians. Seven hundred feet above the ground is a bulbous, pear-shaped globe which houses a restaurant. By a hideous misfortune, which the architects could not possibly have foreseen, the sun striking this globe from a low angle lights it up in the form of a fiery cross, so that a huge Christian symbol blazes out over the officially Godless city.

For one further treat, the visitor must obtain a visa, go through Checkpoint Charlie in Friedrichstrasse, and walk down Unter den Linden to the handsome neo-classical building which houses the memorial to the victims of Fascism. Inside a bare hall a block of marble covers the ashes of people who died in concentration camps. Although uninspiring, the memorial is at least dignified. Outside, however, there stand guard two soldiers whose uniforms and stance are so idiotic that they look as though they must have staggered out of some fourth-rate repertory production. And when the guard is changed, or a special parade is held, what gait do the troops adopt? Goose-step. It is beyond comprehension, but also a fact, that for their manoeuvres outside the memorial to the victims of Fascism, the East Germans have chosen to emulate the style of locomotion which instantly puts every western observer in mind of one subject only: Hitler and the Nazis.

In the past half-century hundreds if not thousands of people must have shared the feelings of Leslie Jeffers, who wrestled for Britain in Berlin. On 1 August, 1936, as the Führer arrived and was proceeding across the May Field towards the stadium for the offical opening of the Games, he passed within seven or eight yards of where Jeffers stood to attention among his comrades in the ranks of the British team. Fifty years later, the former London policeman is still regretting that he missed such an opportunity. 'If I'd just jumped forward and clobbered him there and then,' he says, 'what an incredible amount of life and trouble I would have saved.'

1936 Olympics: Principal Medal Winners
(German points system)

Nation	Gold	Silver	Bronze	Points
Germany	33	26	30	181
United States	24	20	12	124
Italy	8	9	5	47
Finland	7	6	6	39
France	7	6	6	39
Hungary	10	1	5	37
Sweden	6	5	9	37
Japan	6	4	8	34
Netherlands	6	4	7	33
Great Britain	4	7	3	29
Austria	4	6	3	27
Switzerland	1	9	5	26
Czechoslovakia	3	5	0	19
Canada	1	3	5	14
Argentina	2	2	3	13
Estonia	2	2	3	13

Medal Winners in Track and Field Events
* Olympic Record   † World Record

Gold	Silver	Bronze
	100m	
Owens (USA) 10.3	Metcalfe (USA) 10.4	Osendarp (Holland) 10.5
	200m	
Owens (USA) 20.7*	Robinson (USA) 21.1	Osendarp (Holland) 21.3
	400m	
Williams (USA) 46.5	Brown (GB) 46.7	Lu Valle (USA) 46.8
	800m	
Woodruff (USA) 1 52.9	Lanzi (Italy) 1 53.3	Edwards (Canada) 1 53.6
	1,500m	
Lovelock (NZ) 3 47.8*†	Cunningham (USA) 3 48.4	Beccali (Italy) 3 49.2
	5,000m	
Höckert (Finland) 14 22.2*	Lehtinen (Finland) 14 25.8	Jonsson (Sweden) 14 29.0
	10,000m	
Salminen (Finland) 30 15.4	Askola (Finland) 30 15.6	Iso-Hollo (Finland) 30 20.2
	110m Hurdles	
Towns (USA) 14.2*	Finlay (GB) 14.4	Pollard (USA) 14.4
	400m Hurdles	
Hardin (USA) 52.4	Loaring (Canada) 52.7	White (Philippines) 52.8
	3,000m Steeplechase	
Iso-Hollo (Finland) 9 03.8*	Tuominen (Finland) 9 06.8	Dompert (Germany) 9 07.2

Hitler's Games

50km Walk

Whitlock (GB)
4hr 30 41.1*

Schwab (Switzerland)
4hr 32 09.2

Bubenko (Latvia)
4hr 32 42.2

Marathon

Son (Japan)
2hr 29 19.2*

Harper (GB)
2hr 31 23.2

Nan (Japan)
2hr 31 42.0

4 × 100m Relay

USA
39.8*†

Italy
41.1

Germany
41.2

4 × 400m Relay

GB
3 09.0

USA
3 11.0

Germany
3 11.8

Shot

Wöllke (Germany)
16.20m*

Bärlund (Finland)
16.12m

Stöck (Germany)
15.66m

Hammer

Hein (Germany)
56.49m*

Blask (Germany)
55.04m

Warngard (Sweden)
54.83m

Javelin

Stöck (Germany)
71.84m

Nikkanen (Finland)
70.77m

Toivonen (Finland)
70.72m

Discus

Carpenter (USA)
50.48m*

Dunn (USA)
49.36m

Oberweger (Italy)
49.23m

Long Jump

Owens (USA)
8.06m*†

Long (Germany)
7.87m

Tajima (Japan)
7.74m

High Jump

Johnson (USA)
2.03m*

Albritton (USA)
2.00m

Thurber (USA)
2.00m

Triple Jump

Tajima (Japan)
16.00m*†

Harada (Japan)
15.66m

Metcalfe (Australia)
15.50m

Event by Event Table

Pole Vault

Meadows (USA)	Nishida (Japan)	Oe (Japan)
4.35m*	4.25m	4.25m

Decathlon

Morris (USA)	Clark (USA)	Parker (USA)
7,900 pts	7,601 pts	7,277 pts

Women's Events

100m

Stephens (USA)	Walasiewicz (Poland)	Krauss (Germany)
11.5*†	11.7	11.9

80m Hurdles

Valla (Italy)	Steuer (Germany)	Taylor (Canada)
11.7	11.7	11.7

High Jump

Csak (Hungary)	Odam (GB)	Kaun (Germany)
1.60m	1.60m	1.60m

Javelin

Fleischer (Germany)	Krüger (Germany)	Kwasniewska (Poland)
45.18m*	43.29m	41.80m

Discus

Mauermayer (Germany)	Wajsowna (Poland)	Mollenhauer (Germany)
47.63m	46.22m	39.80m

4 × 100m Relay

USA	GB	Canada
46.9	47.6	47.8

PRINCIPAL SOURCES

Published

Billinger, Karl, *Fatherland*. New York, 1935.

Channon, Sir Henry, *Chips: the Diaries of Sir Henry Channon*. Edited by Robert Rhodes James. London, 1967.

Die Olympische Spiele 1936 Two volumes, various authors. Hamburg, 1937.

Griffiths, Richard, *Fellow Travellers of the Right: British Enthusiasts for Nazi Germany, 1933–39*. London, 1980.

Hitler, Adolf, *Mein Kampf*. English edition, London, 1933.

Holmes, Judith, *Olympiad 1936*. New York, 1971.

Jones, Thomas, *A Diary with Letters, 1931–50*. Oxford, 1954.

Killanin, Lord, and Rodda, John (Editors), *The Olympic Games 1984*. London, 1983.

Kirkpatrick, Ivone, *The Inner Circle*. London, 1959.

Mandell, Richard D., *The Nazi Olympics*. London, 1972.

Miller, Franz, Von le Fort, P., and Harster, H., *So Kämpfte und Siegte die Jugend der Welt*. Munich, 1936.

Mosley, Diana, *A Life of Contrasts*. London, 1977.

Mosley, Leonard, *Lindbergh*. London, 1976.

Nicolson, Harold, *Diaries and Letters 1930–39*. Edited by Nigel Nicolson. London, 1966.

Nowell, Elizabeth, *Thomas Wolfe*. London, 1961.

Price, George Ward, *I Know These Dictators*. London, 1937.

Ribbentrop, Joachim von, *Zwischen London und Moskau*. Druffel Verlag, 1953.

Ruland, Bernd, *Das War Berlin*. Berlin, 1971.

Schirach, Baldur von, *Ich glaubte an Hitler*. Germany, 1967.

Seger, Gerhart, *A Nation Terrorised*. Chicago, 1935.

Shirer, William, *Berlin Diary*. London, 1941. *The Rise and Fall of*

Principal Sources

the Third Reich. London, 1960. *20th-Century Journey, Vol. 2.: The Nightmare Years, 1930–1940*. London, 1985.
Speer, Albert, *Inside the Third Reich*. London, 1970

Reports

The XIth Olympic Games: Berlin, 1936 Two volumes, Berlin 1937. Official report by the Organising Committee.
The Official Report of the XIth Olympiad; Berlin 1936 Edited by Harold M. Abrahams. London, 1937. Official report by the British Olympic Association.
Bulletins of the International Olympic Committee, 1926–1936 Anvers, 1937.

Magazine

Olympic Games, 1936. The official propaganda organ. Sixteen monthly issues, 1935–36.

Pamphlet

Preserve the Olympic Ideal published by the Committee on Fair Play in Sports, New York, 1935.

Unpublished

The Vansittart Papers Churchill College, Cambridge.
Foreign Office Archives Public Record Office, Kew, London. Reports from the British Embassy, Berlin, and Foreign Office memoranda, 1935–36. Reference: FO 371.
U.S. State Department Archives, Washington Reports from the U.S. Ambassador in Berlin, and others, 1933–36. Reference: 862.4063.

INDEX

Index

Index

255